MARGARET THATCHER
A Bibliography

Recent Titles in
Bibliographies of British Statesmen

William Pitt the Younger 1759–1806: A Bibliography
A. D. Harvey

Lord Grenville 1759–1834: A Bibliography
A. D. Harvey

Lord Curzon 1839–1925: A Bibliography
James G. Parker

Lord Nelson 1758–1805: A Bibliography
Leonard W. Cowie

The Duke of Wellington 1769–1852: A Bibliography
Michael Partridge

Charles James Fox 1749–1806: A Bibliography
David Schweitzer

George Grenville 1712–1770: A Bibliography
Rory T. Cornish

William Wilberforce 1759–1833: A Bibliography
Leonard W. Cowie

MARGARET THATCHER

A Bibliography

Faysal Mikdadi

BIBLIOGRAPHIES OF
BRITISH STATESMEN, NO. 18

GREGORY PALMER, SERIES EDITOR

Greenwood Press
Westport, Connecticut • London

Library of Congress Cataloging-in-Publication Data

Mikdadi, F. H.
    Margaret Thatcher : a bibliography / Faysal Mikdadi.
      p. cm.—(Bibliographies of British statesmen, ISSN
1056–5523 ; no. 18)
    Includes bibliographical references and indexes.
    ISBN 0–313–28288–9 (alk. paper)
    1. Thatcher, Margaret—Bibliography. 2. Great Britain—Politics
and government—1979– —Bibliography. I. Title. II. Series.
Z8869.14.M55   1993
[DA591.T47]
016.941085'8—dc20   92–38071

British Library Cataloguing in Publication Data is available.

Library of Congress Catalog Card Number: 92–38071
ISBN: 0–313–28288–9
ISSN: 1056–5523

First published in 1993

Greenwood Press, 88 Post Road West, Westport, CT 06881
An imprint of Greenwood Publishing Group, Inc.

Printed in the United States of America

The paper used in this book complies with the
Permanent Paper Standard issued by the National
Information Standards Organization (Z39.48–1984).

10 9 8 7 6 5 4 3 2 1

Contents

Preface

In discussing the production and distribution of wealth, Victor Hugo talks about England's material power, which he believes will end in bankruptcy. To counteract what may seem like an unwarranted attack on the English, he adds: "England the aristocracy will fall; but England the nation is immortal."

This relationship between wealth and nationhood lies at the heart of Thatcherite doctrines (some would say dogma). Without wealth, a nation is doomed. The creators of a nation's wealth are its people: free to strive, to choose, to accumulate, and to contribute to the public good. This is best achieved by a benign and noninterfering monetarist government that allows the market free reign. Hard work and diligence would do the rest. So believed Thatcher and her supporters.

Did Margaret Thatcher achieve these aims? How did she go about trying to do so? Most importantly, how did she, after "rolling back the frontiers of government," make the people respond—or not respond, as the case may be?

When Thatcher became prime minister in 1979, she believed the British people had abdicated (or causally lost) many of their rights. The famous winter of discontent saw endless strikes, increasing union powers, and rising unemployment coupled with runaway inflation under an interventionist nanny state. Thatcher, however, was going to bring back these abdicated or lost rights. She was going to give power back to the individual, who would then use his or her inalienable commonsense and ambition to revive Britain. Thatcher's government was to be a crusade waging a war for the individual's right to choose. Little wonder that her first public statement in 10 Downing Street was taken from a saint: "Where there is discord, may we bring harmony. Where there is error may we bring truth. Where there is doubt may we bring faith. Where there is despair may we bring hope." There is a terse finality about this statement. It reflects deeply held convictions—almost religious convictions. It was as if Thatcher knew that things would never be the same again. Britain was to be reborn into a brave new world.

Did this happen? Probably. Was it a brave new world?

The biographical essay does not pretend to answer this or the previous questions. It simply and faithfully sets the scene for what came out of the Thatcher era by narrating the facts of that era. It shows how Thatcher, and Thatcher alone, did change the face of Britain finally and unalterably. Her political success or failure is for the researcher to determine, with the help of this bibliography.

This bibliography aims to provide a comprehensive set of references to Thatcher's life, including her writings and major speeches. It is designed for American and British readers, although in a few cases it includes works in languages other than English. Where this is the case, titles are translated in brackets. Where a translation or summary in English is available, reference is made to it. Each entry is followed by a short statement on the work listed except where the title makes it absolutely clear what the work is about. Works that are thought to be most useful have been marked with an asterisk (*). References do not include works of fiction, but interested students may find a subject worthy of research in the plethora of works of fiction where Thatcher or Thatcherism appear in person or in spirit. In addition, this bibliography contains no manuscripts relating to Thatcher's time in office. Cabinet papers are not normally released in the United Kingdom for a period of thirty years after the events. In some cases this period is extended if it is deemed to be in the national interest.

The biographical essay and chronology sections give a comprehensive coverage of Thatcher's life. An attempt has been made in the biography to delineate Thatcher's character where it may be important in understanding her politics. Quotations are attributed within the text; where there is no attribution, the quotation is from Thatcher herself.

A rigorous attempt has been made to exclude the author's personal political views, which have no place in a work of this nature. Where an opinion is voiced, it is attributed to its originator. From the author's point of view, only the bare facts are presented.

Acknowledgments

My wife, Susan, and my children, Catherine and Richard, have, as always, helped and supported me in producing this work. To them I owe a very special debt of gratitude that risks never being duly paid.

I also wish to thank the following for their help in facilitating my researches: Simon Coombs, Member of Parliament for Swindon; Stuart Macwilliam, Assistant Librarian at the University of Exeter Library; Keith Reid of the Conservative Central Office Bookshop; and John Wittingdale, Personal Assistant to The Rt. Hon. Margaret Thatcher, O.M., F.R.S., M.P. and now an M.P. since the April 1992 general elections.

Further thanks are due to the following for their help and encouragement: executive editor Cynthia Harris and production editor Sally Scott for overseeing publication; M. O. Holder, Wiltshire County Council Secretary and Solicitor, for his advice; my colleagues and friends John Palmer, Elaine Long, and Ben Kerwood for keeping me going; my colleague and friend Christine Middleton for her secretarial help; Bibliographies of British Statesmen Series Editor Gregory Palmer for his advice and encouragement; my colleague David Pert; the Executive Vice President of Greenwood Publishing Group, James T. Sabin; my employers—Wiltshire County Council—for permission to produce this work, with special reference to Ivor Slocombe, Chief Education Officer; and Susan Taylor of the Wiltshire Library Services, for her research assistance.

I wish to express my special thanks to Mike Hayes and his economics group at The John Bentley School in Calne, in Wiltshire. The following were kind enough to give me their time to discuss Thatcher and her achievements: James Auld, Michael Baker, Jonathan Bouchta, Joanne Burchell, David Cotton, Sarah Evans, Rosalind Griffin, Darren Hughes, Denise Keen, Rupert Lacey, Krista Lambourne, Andrea Pink, Lisa Rodgers, Mark Tooley, Victoria Uttley, Debbie Wagstaff, Sarah Williams, and Helene Wilson.

MARGARET THATCHER
A Bibliography

The Rt. Hon. Margaret Thatcher, O.M., F.R.S., M.P.

(Produced with the permission of Baroness Margaret Thatcher of Kesteven and provided by her Secretary, Miranda Cracroft.)

Biographical Essay

Childhood and Youth

Margaret Roberts was born on October 13, 1925, in Grantham, in the County of Lincolnshire. She was born into a family that already had one daughter, Muriel, who later became a physical therapist.

Her father, Alfred Roberts, owned a small grocery business in a corner shop. His influence over the young Margaret was enormous: A public-spirited man, he was at one point or another, and sometimes simultaneously, a local councilor, the mayor of Grantham, a secondary school governor of both the local boys' and girls' schools, a justice of the peace, a member of the Rotary Club, a member of the libraries committee, a lay preacher, an alderman, and a regular attendant at the local Methodist church.

Little is known about Margaret's mother, Beatrice Roberts, who was a dressmaker before marrying Alfred. All indications are that she was a hardworking and supportive wife and mother. She spent most of her time looking after the family, helping out in the shop, attending regular church functions, and keeping the house in order with the minimum of financial outlay.

Such thrift was the hallmark of the Roberts family. Alfred Roberts believed in the essentially Victorian values of thrift, duty, hard work, and self-help. For years, the rooms above the shop did not have a bathroom or hot running water, and the family did not buy most modern labor-saving conveniences. Unlike their contemporaries, Muriel and Margaret did not go out to the cinema or the dance hall. For the Roberts, life was a serious business that had to be got on with and had to exclude the fripperies of middle-class entertainment. For a while, Margaret's equally austere maternal grandmother lived with the family. According to Margaret her father and grandmother "would have been horrified if one wanted to go out to a dance."[1] Sundays were spent attending the Methodist church, although Margaret was later to join the Church of England. Even the Sunday newspapers were regarded as an indulgence.

Much has been written to illustrate two factors in Thatcher's life: that her father was a mean killjoy, and that her mother was a weak, downtrodden wife who had little or no influence on Margaret's later life. Alfred was indeed a strict man whose entrenched Victorian values may be anathema to later generations (indeed, they were probably so to his own generation), but his influence on his daughter was supreme and long lasting. Even at the pinnacle of her political career, Thatcher never stopped acknowledging her eternal debt to her father. She clearly had the greatest respect and love for him, and their relationship was obviously a very close one. Alfred was a self-educated man who read avidly. Margaret did likewise, and the two would discuss works they had both read. In his official duty as councilor, mayor, and alderman, Alfred showed that messianic spirit that was to emerge later in the famous Thatcher bluntness and outspoken outpourings. More importantly perhaps was the father's influence over his daughter's spiritual development. From him came her instinct for extreme hard work, her conviction that she was doing right even when everyone around her disagreed, her perception of the need for radical policies needed to change things, and her belief in the inherent greatness of Britain when such radical policies took effect.

Beatrice, however, does seem to have played little part in Margaret's life. In general terms, when interviewed as prime minister, Thatcher seemed reluctant to discuss her mother. The few times that she referred to her, she did so dismissively: "I loved my mother dearly, but after I was fifteen we had nothing more to say to each other. It wasn't her fault. She was weighed down by the home, always being in the home."[2] Muriel Roberts has spoken of the debt that she and her sister owed Beatrice, who "was always there."[3]

Many people have discussed Thatcher's adoption of her father's persona and rejection of her mother in Freudian terms. These discussions make for interesting reading—even funny reading at times. The truth of the matter, however, is that Thatcher grew up very close to her father and somewhat distant from her mother. Modern feminist analysis may find such a state of affairs deleterious for the real development of Margaret the woman. Thatcher clearly did not think so. Her development owed an untold debt to Alfred, whose Victorian view of life was to stalk British politics under Thatcher's powerful and seemingly enduring influence. In later years, during many governmental crises, Thatcher was to return to her origins in winning arguments:

Oh yes, I know, we have recently been told by no less than 364 academic economists that such things cannot be, that British enterprise is doomed. Their confidence in the accuracy of their own predictions leaves me breathless. But having myself been brought up over the shop, I sometimes wonder whether they back their forecasts with their money. For I can't help noticing that those who have to do just that—the investing institutions which have to show performance from their judgement—are giving us a very different message.[4]

One aspect of this Victorian ethic was thrift. Another was hard work. And hard work was what Thatcher lived by. She first attended the Huntingtontower Road Primary School; in 1936 she became a model pupil at the Kesteven and Grantham Girls' Grammar School, where she received a county scholarship. Her school reports reveal a diligent and hard-working pupil who was seen by her teachers as "ambitious" and deserving "to do well."[5] She was also an outstanding contributor to the school's debating club and eventually became head girl. In the sixth form Thatcher studied chemistry, biology, and zoology, excelling in all three. She also continued with her English, Latin, and geography. In 1943 she completed her secondary education.

Alfred Roberts worked hard to help with his daughter's education. When she was eventually accepted to Oxford, he was happy to pay for her, as a scholarship was not available. Her move to Oxford was a last-minute affair, however. A prospective student dropped out, allowing Thatcher to be invited to join Somerville College. Her academic career at the university was fairly successful, since her ethic of hard work continued to operate. She was eventually awarded a second-class honors in chemistry. Her choice of subject was due less to a natural predilection and more to the influence exerted by her brilliant secondary school teacher of chemistry. In fact, Thatcher realized too late that she would have preferred to read law—something she eventually did with her characteristic determination and work ethic. In her fourth year, she became a research assistant contributing to early research into a new antibiotic.

But Thatcher received a more important education while at Oxford. While fully immersed in her studies, she found the time to contribute to the war effort by doing voluntary work at the military canteens, and she found the time to become an active member of the Oxford University

Conservative Association (OUCA). She later became its general agent and eventually its president; during her time, OUCA membership increased dramatically. Thatcher was also the coauthor of a report on the new direction British Conservatism was to take after the disastrous defeat of Winston Churchill's government in 1945. This defeat was attributed, by Lord Beaverbrook, to Neville Chamberlain's weak politics in the 1930s: "The main factor in the political [Labour] landslide lies way back in the years 1938–1940. It was about that time that the great mass of middle class opinion in Britain decided to punish the Conservatives."[6] According to the new Labour prime minister, Clement Attlee, "many people looked upon the Conservatives as a reactionary party which would not carry out a policy answering to peace requirements."[7] Many Conservatives saw the election result as a betrayal of Churchill by an ingrate nation. Only Churchill took things philosophically, as when he remarked to Sir Leslie Rowan: "That's politics, my dear, that's politics."[8]

And politics it certainly was. The Conservatives were divided on issues of peacetime policies. The old guard genuinely believed in the old British consensus politics in which the electoral pendulum simply swung back and forth every few years—a view held by Harold Macmillan, Churchill's close political associate and later prime minister between 1957 and 1963. The old guard believed that all they had to do was to sit tight, and the pendulum would swing back their way the next time. Another faction, with a generally younger membership, believed in the politics of change: A party had to change in order to keep up with the times. Britain needed a new Conservative image with a wider appeal. Such a group included people like Quentin Hogg and his Tory Reform Committee, which led the fight against the Beaverbrook faction by daring to contemplate issues of social security and an interventionist (albeit paternalistic) government.

Thatcher supported the reformers, taking an active part in their affairs. This early involvement in an essentially interventionist government is seemingly difficult to square with Thatcher's later emphasis on noninterference, but it is a clear indication of her belief in action rather than words. She saw the old Conservatives awaiting the inevitable swing of the pendulum. Inactivity was anathema to her, and she found consensus politics an irritant—stale and unproductive. She believed in conviction politics, that is, radical reform in order to institute change rather than the old wishy-washy, no-major-change pendulum shift between the politics of left and right. In 1946 she attended, as a delegate, the Federation of Conservative and Unionist Associations where she proposed a resolution demanding working-class participation in the party.

During her years in Oxford, Thatcher met many budding and actual politicians. Some of the relationships she made were to figure repeatedly throughout her political career. She was also one of many to read Friedrich Hayek's *The Road to Serfdom*, with its trenchantly antisocialist and antiinterventionist arguments that gave a first glimpse of Thatcher's eventual free market economy. But these men (and her associates were largely, if not entirely, men) did not influence Thatcher deeply. She was not a person easy to influence in the conventional sense. The only real influence in shaping her life was her father, and his major advice to his daughter was that she should never allow herself to be swayed or influenced: "You must make your own decisions. You don't do something because your friends are doing it. You do it because you think it's the best thing to do. Don't follow the crowd; don't be afraid of being different. You decide what you ought to do, and if necessary you lead the crowd. But you never just follow."[9] Years later, during her first term of office, Thatcher was to relate her childhood and youth experiences to the business of running Britain: "Deep in their instincts people find what I am saying and doing right. And I know it is, because that is the way I was brought up. I'm eternally grateful for the way I was brought up in a small town. We knew everyone, we knew what people thought. I sort of regard myself as a very normal ordinary person, with all the right, instinctive antennae."[10]

It was this much-repeated lesson taught from her earliest years that was to bring Thatcher success. It gave her the tremendous confidence and reserve to become one of the longest-serving prime ministers with a widespread and unfathomable love–hate relationship with the British people. It was also this strength, turned character flaw, that eventually caused her downfall in 1990.

Early Career

Margaret Thatcher appears to have worked very hard to raise herself above her Grantham origins, although that is not to say that she was ashamed of her origins. Throughout her later political career Thatcher was to make constant references to her father as the guiding light of her life. His was the world of reality, intellect, creed, and spirituality, as opposed to the antonymous qualities that Thatcher was later to despise: perception, instinct, emotion, and physicality. In order to succeed, a nation needed spiritual health, a kind of wholesomeness such as that derived from her relationship to her father. Without these qualities, Britain was bound to immerse itself in what Thatcher refered to as the "fashionable theories and permissive claptrap" of the 1960s.[11] Such theories were associated, in her mind, with the "claptrap" of trendy socialism that she detested. This detestation was deepened in 1952 when her father ceased to be an alderman after being sacked by the Labour party. This event still brought Thatcher to the verge of tears years later when she was prime minister.

Her first job was that of a research chemist at British Xylonite Plastics in Manningtree, Essex. She lived in nearby Colchester and commuted to work. After a while, she was employed by J. Lyons in London in their research department, where she worked for the remainder of her three years as a chemist.

While living in Essex, Thatcher worked hard at the Colchester Conservative Association. Soon she became a Conservative candidate, at only twenty-four, when she contested the Dartford seat in the general elections of 1950. Although she lost what was essentially a safe Labour seat, she fought hard. Her major platform was her attack on the welfare state, which she described as lacking the essential freedom to allow citizens to live their own lives. She joined the new breed of Conservatives who fought for the decontrol of the economy while maintaining a balance with the welfare state's responsibilities toward its citizens. Thus, she had already started what was to become her famous dictum: politics at the household level. Living within one's means and having the freedom to be responsible for one's own decisions were strong personal dogmas.

A year later, when the Conservatives won the next general election, Thatcher again lost the Dartford seat. Meanwhile, with her usual pertinacity, she started studying law, specializing in tax law. She qualified in 1953 and spent the next five years practicing periodically. As a member of the Society of Conservative Lawyers, which she joined in 1953, she met many men who were to play an important part in her life as a politician. Both her speciality and her new fellow members of the society could be seen as important linchpins in her development. Airey Neave would later work hard and brilliantly in helping her get the party leadership. Her knowledge of finance-related law was also instrumental in helping her develop her monetarist policies. It certainly gave her—or rather, increased—her ability to work with figures so effectively. She enjoyed the logical mind derived of a scientific training, the thrift assimilated through natural family frugality, and the knowledge of finance helped along by her education in tax and other laws.

Science, economy, and the law are the three ingredients that produced the Thatcher who led Britain in the 1980s. Later, when she had been prime minister for some time, she related her education to her way of thinking. As a scientist, she said, "You look at the facts and you deduce your conclusions" while as a lawyer "you learn your law, so you learn the structures. You judge the evidence, and then, when the laws are inadequate for present-day society, you create new laws."[12] In 1949, when she became the young Dartford candidate, Thatcher acquired a fourth and crucial ingredient: Denis Thatcher.

Denis Thatcher was an intelligent, hardworking, no-nonsense businessman doing very well with the family business. He was to become a very close and loving partner for years to come. In an essentially sexist society, he was bound to become the butt of tasteless jokes about his wife being "the Boss" and about his dependency. A great deal of this was obviously apocryphal and politically motivated, for the match was clearly one of love and mutual respect. The couple had a great deal in common. Politically, they were of one ilk, with Denis deeply believing in much that his wife stood for as prime minister. He was probably an upholder of Thatcherism even before he met the woman who was to immortalize his family name.

Apart from the moral support that he was to give his wife, he was also able to support her financially. His financial standing meant that she could continue working even after giving birth to their twins, Carol and Mark.

After being turned down by some seats, Thatcher managed to get selected by Finchley in 1958. She then became the Conservative Member of Parliament in the 1959 elections, thus joining Macmillan's party and his "never had it so good" dictum.[13] Finchley was a safe Conservative seat. It also housed a large Jewish vote. As a child, Margaret Roberts had hosted a Jewish pen friend, who had told her stories of Nazi atrocities in Austria, and as a result she became a confirmed supporter of Zionism. The Finchley Jewish vote was hers almost naturally. She was also deeply impressed by the Jewish tradition of self-help and its strong work ethic.

Macmillan's Conservatism seemed to be the very opposite of what Thatcher was later to stand for. His government increased public spending and led the country into an inflationary spiral that would have outraged the Thatcherites of the 1980s. In 1958 Enoch Powell joined Peter Thorneycroft in resigning over an increase in public spending. A great deal of what Powell believed in and fiercely advocated had a strong influence on Thatcher. It is ironic that the scourge of the Conservative party in later years held the very opinions that Thatcher was to articulate during her premiership.

As a new, young M.P., Thatcher made or remade the acquaintance of many men: Lord Hailsham (for whom she had canvased in Oxford), Edward Heath, Enoch Powell, and, most significantly, Sir Keith Joseph. The latter became a strong mentor in a long-lasting political relationship.

Soon after she became an M.P., she won the annual ballot (a type of lottery, which is House of Commons practice, that allows only a limited number of M.P.s to introduce bills in each session), and thus introduced a private member's bill. She gave an excellent performance, showing her unparalleled command of figures and statistics. Her performance drew many compliments from those who heard it. The Public Bodies (Admission to Meetings) Bill, which became an act in 1960, introduced the concept of the public's right to know what their local authorities were spending.

Thatcher was thus beginning to expound some of her monetarist policies—although they were not seen as such. She spoke of her concern over excessive public spending and of the need for stringent accountability—both later to become the heart of her legislative reforms. It was not long before she became a parliamentary secretary at the Ministry of Pensions. Her knowledge of tax laws and her versatility with figures, coupled with her unbelievable hard work, equipped her well for this job. One of the lessons learned at the Ministry of Pensions was her distrust of civil servants. She saw them as a group of people who were unwilling to offer impartial advice but who were, rather, the manipulators later presented so comically on the television programs "Yes Minister" and "Yes Prime Minister." In later years she was to revolutionize the way civil servants worked in Whitehall.

After Macmillan's departure, Lord Alec Douglas-Home led the Conservatives to a defeat against Labour's Harold Wilson. This led to yet another change of party leadership. Thatcher joined those who voted for Edward Heath. His election broke the old Conservative social mold by bringing in a nonestablishment man. Once the mold was broken, it became easy to elect a carpenter's son (Heath), a grocer's daughter (Thatcher), and a circus performer's son (John Major).

Heath quickly used the promising Finchley M.P. by moving her from Pensions to Housing, on to Treasury, and finally to the shadow cabinet where she eventually became Shadow Minister of Education.

While in opposition, Heath started to put in place the groundwork of future Thatcherism: the curbing of union power, the control of social services, the setting up of the economic policy needed by business, the need for tax cuts, and a rigorous approach to law and order. In other words, Heath was creating a seemingly clear philosophy and a solid base from which the party could launch its future governorship. Heath did not succeed in creating an overall coherent philosophy, however. He seemed bogged down with detail and with reactivity to events. The result was a seeming incoherence, although it may be said that what Heath was trying to do failed as a philosophy because the void of the future Callaghan government had not yet appeared. With Wilson—especially when he was clashing with the unions—it seemed as if there was little to choose from between him and Heath. Yet Heath, like Thatcher, believed in market forces, in curbing public spending, and in limiting the money supply. Unlike Thatcher, however, he was unwilling—or possibly he was unable—to go the full distance to achieve these aims. He believed unquestionably in state intervention when things simply needed to be better managed. Thatcher wanted to put the responsibilities for management on those best qualified to handle them, but during this period she largely kept her own counsel.

One example of Heath's inability or unwillingness to be proactive can be seen in his reaction to Enoch Powell's famous Rivers of Blood speech of 1968. Although Powell's language was inflammatory and, to some, highly offensive, his objections to uncontrolled immigration touched an important chord in the British psyche. Heath reacted by torpedoing Powell into political oblivion. It took more than ten years for Powell's Cassandra-like statements to be picked up by Thatcher, not only in the realm of immigration, but also in the areas of public spending and monetarism. Heath had come to office promising "to change the course and history of this nation, nothing less."[14] He left it (in 1974) after making one of the biggest U-turns in recent British political history.

It was during these years, under the Heath government of the early 1970s, that "consensus politics" became a dirty word. Thatcher herself took the opportunity to deliver a lecture that launched an attack on consensus politicians as being ones that seek "to satisfy people holding no particular views about anything."[15] In this statement we see Thatcher's later articulation of the need for radical reforms. Her main philosophy was that of less state intervention and more decision power to the people, for Thatcher saw the individual and his or her freedom as coming first. Once the government controlled the money supply, the individual was free to do what he or she chose with his or her money. This freedom to act was encapsulated in her famous statement on the Good Samaritan, a statement that caused—and still causes—her admirers to applaud their newly found freedom and pragmatism and her detractors to lament what they saw as an image of dark satanic mills concerned only with money to the exclusion of all real human values:

The point is that even the Good Samaritan had to have the money to help, otherwise he too would have had to pass on the other side.[16]

Minister and Leader of the Opposition

Under the Heath government, 1970–74, Thatcher became Minister for Education. This was a department whose business impinged little on the main offices of state. In hindsight, this situation was a blessing in disguise since Thatcher was able to distance herself from Heath's U-turn toward consensus politics, but she continued to take on her share of responsibility for the seeming collective cabinet decisions made under Heath.

Ironically, Thatcher's later obsession with curbing public spending did not show itself during her tenure in Education. Hers was one of the highest-spending departments in the Heath government. She staunchly fought the Treasury for her department's share of public expenditure and successfully fended off proposed large cuts. Those who disliked her in later years saw these as perfect examples of her lack of conviction and of her opportunism. If she believed in curbing public spending, why had she not resigned from the Heath Government as Thorneycroft and Powell had done under Macmillan? There are two possible answers to this seeming inconsistency. Thatcher did her best within her department. She worked tirelessly to make a real success of her years in Education, and therefore she worked within the constraints imposed by the times. Perhaps more importantly, her strong convictions became articulated only in later years. At the time she was a minister with a job to do. In her defense may also be added the fact that she was largely isolated from the real business of government. Heath was determined to keep her in Education rather than have her within the inner cabal. He clearly disliked her style, which he saw as hectoring, strident, and irritating. Only when cabinet papers are released in the next century can this inconsistency be properly clarified.

One of her first acts as minister was to issue the famous 10/70 circular, which ended the pressure on local education authorities to turn all their schools into comprehensive establishments. Selection in education was one of her deeply held convictions. However, she did not—or politically could not—reverse the trend. The ironic result was that during Thatcher's time in Education the vast majority of comprehensivization schemes were approved by her.

There were two major achievements to her credit. The first was her unstinting support for the Open University, which, with its mass media–led learning techniques, was seen by many Conservatives as a typical Labour attempt at dangerous equalization within an essentially unequal society. Her second achievement was her successful defense of the raising of the school leaving age (ROSLA).

In addition, in her famous paper *Framework for Expansion* Thatcher made a commitment to preschool education. This was not merely an opportunistic political move, for Thatcher genuinely believed in affording children a chance in life. She saw nursery education as a valuable tool toward achieving this aim, particularly for children whose background of poverty gave them a disadvantageous beginning in life. This trend of creating chances became her hallmark. The state created the correct environment redolent with chances, and free citizens made what they could of them. It was not the government's business to look after the individual. The responsibility for one's success or failure was the citizen's, not the government's.

During this time, the oil crisis caused much of what the Heath government had planned to go by the board, and be shelved for lack of funds. It can be safely said that the 1973 Middle East war was the first major international affair to give monetarism an almighty shove, because until then the Western world had been living in a fool's paradise. There was an assumption that Keynesian ideals of creating employment through spending would last forever. Lack of public funds, however, made this a clear impossibility. It became clear to men like Sir Keith Joseph that creating full employment through massive public spending caused hyperinflation, which in turn affected demand, causing it to slacken and thus causing rising unemployment. Unemployment needed further public spending and the printing of more money to help eradicate it. So the vicious circle continued, dragging Britain down hill. Sir Keith Joseph began to articulate what was later to lead to the monetarist policies known as Thatcherism.

At the Department of Education and Science (DES), Thatcher was also schooled in the niceties of the civil service. She was a woman of action. Generally speaking, she would listen to advice, but once a decision was taken she expected results—quick results. Her civil servants were not used to this. Whitehall had its own way of doing things. Ministers came and went but civil servants were always there. Their permanence meant that they knew a great deal about the day-to-day business of government, and they believed a part of their job was to curb the excesses of new and naive ministers. Thatcher did not like this way of doing things. She saw her civil servants as obfuscating mandarins who sat uncomfortably in her world of hard work, decisions, and actions. At worst, she saw civil servants as obstructing her in carrying out her duties, and she clashed with them on many issues. As a result, she acquired an intense suspicion of, and dislike for, the civil service—which later subsided into an ability to laugh at it (her favorite television program was "Yes Minister"). In later years she reformed the way Whitehall worked, and as civil servants were reformed, they were therefore no longer seen as a threat.

One area where she did not listen to her advisers was regarding the program that provided free milk to the eight-to-eleven year olds. She saved £8 million by cutting this provision. It was a very unpopular decision that caused a huge furor in the press. Nicknamed "Thatcher the milk snatcher," she was portrayed by the tabloids as "the most unpopular woman in Britain."[17] It was one of many virulent attacks that were inherently sexist and that were to dog her early political life. Being a woman, she was doubly condemned for lacking the maternal compassion that would have ensured that little children received their milk. This form of rampant sexism was something that she had to live with for many years, and it certainly steeled her to prove herself in a man's world. Some critics have seen her seeming harshness and lack of compassion as overcompensation needed to survive sexist strictures. In a prophetic reference to her later sobriquet, "The Iron Lady," she later spoke of this incident by saying: "Iron entered my soul."[18]

Meanwhile, the political scene was being set for her future leadership, although at the time thoughts of leadership—let alone premiership—were very far from her mind. After the Conservatives' defeat in 1974, Thatcher was made Shadow Environment Minister. She put together a package on the rights of tenants to buy their council houses and on the abolition of rates (property taxes). Both became mainstays of Thatcherism. Another facet of Thatcherism had already appeared while she was still in Education. She unsuccessfully proposed that student union funds be controlled by the university and college authorities in order to stop the union executive spending them on political activities.

By 1971 Heath seemed to have dropped most of the policies that brought his party to power. His government began to make one U-turn after another. Their hard-hitting industrial policy collapsed as Heath found mitigating reasons for pumping public money into ailing industries like the Upper Clyde Shipbuilders and Rolls Royce. It was as if Heath lacked the conviction to carry out his promised policies if they were to hurt. His government balked at the prospect of the huge unpopularity attendant upon letting such British institutions go by the wayside. In order to keep men and women employed, the government was using large amounts of public money.

Sir Keith Joseph convinced Heath to set up a new Conservative party research unit. The Centre for Policy Studies' new director was Alfred Sherman, who was reputed to have told Sir Keith Joseph that Keynes was dead. Sherman believed that the real enemy was inflation. He also believed that the money supply must be controlled in a leaner and fitter Britain. He convinced Joseph of the importance of both elements in reestablishing "the philosophy and principles of a free society."[19]

In 1974 Sir Keith Joseph made his famous soul-searching speech at Preston, the first of a series of speeches that articulated his monetarist policies. "The effect of overreacting to temporary recession," he said, "has been to push up inflation to ever higher levels, not to help the unemployed but to increase their numbers."[20] Governments should—indeed, could—no longer print money to keep employment full.

Apart from the deep influence that men like Sir Keith Joseph and Sherman had on Thatcher, something much more powerful was influencing her. For the first time in years, highly placed Conservatives were challenging established practice. A real thought process was going on, and practice was being replaced by radical dogma. The party had lost the general election because Heath had changed his mind on his industrial policies, because he could not stand up to the miners' strike, because he hinged his political career on an incomes policy, and because the party was trying too hard to please everyone. Sir Keith Joseph, Thatcher's mentor, articulated these failures as being the result of consensus policy. For years the government pendulum shifted from Labour to Conservative, and from Conservative to Labour. This resulted in both parties simply doing the same thing. Neither party, on taking office, effected any radical change, and there seemed little to choose between them. More significantly, Joseph came to the conclusion that the further to the left Labour went, the more the Conservatives had to shift ground in order to maintain the historically agreed-upon consensus. The result was a Conservative party steadily moving leftward and seemingly forgetting the principles for which it stood. It was because of this shifting and maneuvering that Heath had failed to maintain himself in office. To put it another way, Heath was not seen to have betrayed anything since, over the years, nothing was left to betray.

Amidst all of this soul searching and far-reaching admissions of guilt, the Conservative party set about the business of electing a new leader. Heath was not willing to step down, which meant that none of his own men was free to stand against him. Sir Keith Joseph was soon out of the race after causing much alarm by condemning working-class women for having too many socially disadvantaged babies. Other men came forward and then retreated, one by one.

Meanwhile, Thatcher, seeing the obvious candidates step down, put herself forward. Her campaign manager was Airey Neave, who ran a meticulously organized and cleverly secretive campaign. Thatcher won the first ballot. By the time Heath had withdrawn his favored candidates did not stand a chance. Thatcher won the second ballot handsomely, beginning her four years as Leader of the Opposition.

Margaret Thatcher's election as Leader of the Conservative Party was not so much an election for her as it was a massive backbench vote of no confidence in Heath. This backbenchers' revolt was an historical accident with far-reaching consequences for Britain's future. She thus had to work very hard to establish her authority over a skeptical party. Furthermore, the Conservatives were generally not sure of her staying power as a woman and as a person with little experience in government. She was seen as a stalking horse candidate and, once the leader, as a stopgap. Personally, she was never particularly liked by the ordinary voter. She was seen as strident and cold. Her voice was irritating. Her mannerisms were hectoring and her attitudes prim, with the quality of a prissy headmistress. Over the next four years she was to undergo a major change of image, although the underlying toughness, reliance on facts, control of those around her, and independence of spirit remained untouched.

In her early days as leader, Thatcher tried hard to reunite the party by keeping several of Heath's men in her Shadow Cabinet. Heath himself chose to ignore her and instead joined the backbenchers. For years he was the eternal dissident within the party. She then surrounded herself with men like Sir Keith Joseph, Geoffrey Howe, John Biffen, Ian Gilmour, William Whitelaw, and David Howell. Her Shadow Cabinet was run as a real cabinet in office, with regular meetings to discuss policies. This was Thatcher's way of training herself and her colleagues for office when it came. The practice was that of compromise, although at her first party conference she did lay the foundation for her later leadership if not policies:

In the next election we shall be fighting with a clear philosophy which asserts and protects the rights of the citizen and his family against ever increasing power and direction by governments. There must be more personal savings, more personal controls of one's own life. Too much is now controlled by the state. In the next election the Conservative Party will go to the country asserting the need to leave more of what is earned in the hands of the taxpayer to spend for himself.[21]

The new leader was beginning to make her mark. More importantly, she was beginning to speak the language of the ordinary voter, a quality that Conservative politicians became increasingly adept in the 1980s and early 1990s. Men like Norman Tebbit began to emerge as Thatcher worked hard to involve her backbenchers in party politics. She also traveled abroad extensively in order to expand her understanding of foreign affairs.

Meanwhile, the Labour government was under economic siege as it continued to borrow frantically to finance the Public Sector Borrowing Requirement (PSBR). Under pressure from the International Monetary Fund (IMF), Labour started adopting policies to combat inflation at the inevitable risk of rising unemployment. Cuts of £1 billion were followed by a further proposed cut of £2.5 billion. Unemployment was set to rise even further.

Ironically, Labour's imposed new policies were the very ones that Thatcher advocated, as they were essentially monetarist. By 1976 Labour broke with Keynes for good. Thatcher moved immediately to set up an Economic Reconstruction Group, which eventually produced *The Right Approach to the Economy*— which can now be seen as mild Thatcherism since it still spoke ambiguously of the Heath-favored incomes policy. That, however, was a political compromise to the times, a compromise that was soon to disappear. A second paper was produced but never published. Its authors, Sir John Hoskyns and Norman Strauss, shifted the fulcrum of the argument from the incomes-policy need and inflation to trade union power. It was the trade unions that were causing the economic problems, they argued, through their excessive wage demands and their pressure to keep employment going at any cost. Therefore, there was a clear need to curb the unions. This would leave the market poised for free collective bargaining with minimum or no government interference. Wage settlements would be dictated by the money supply available and not vice versa. Monetarism would do away with untenable industries, replacing them with new industries and consequently with new jobs.

The message was clear but it was not yet ready to be driven home. The 1978–79 winter of discontent drove the message home—loud and clear. A series of strikes for higher pay brought the country virtually to the three-day week associated with the 1974 miners' strike under Heath. Secondary picketing, a practice whereby goods being delivered were prevented from getting to their port of call, became rife. The gravediggers' strike meant that bodies could not be buried. There were highly charged accusations that patients would be left to die rather than be ambulanced to emergency rooms in hospitals. The strikes created seeming chaos and became an issue of law and order. The government of James Callaghan caved in to the union demands in order to restore peace. He set up the Clegg Commission on pay comparability, thus ending the strikes. Thatcher, by then trenchantly against the concept of unions having undue powers, rode high on a law-and-order ticket. She began to strike a chord in the electors' hearts, if not necessarily in their minds, for they were weary of the long winter of deprivation and misery. What became clear was that Labour could no longer contain the unions. As often happens in moments of national angst, the prime minister's attempt to cool tempers and allay fears backfired. Callaghan, on returning from an international summit in sunny Guadeloupe, was asked about the crisis. He was reported to have replied, "Crisis? What crisis?"[22] He thus projected an image of a prime minister who had completely lost touch with the people rather than the image he wanted to project—a prime minister refusing to be frazzled by events.

The Labour government had been kept in power by the Liberal–Labour pact (the Lib–Lab Pact), but the pact collapsed in 1978 after the Liberals withdrew their support. By May 1979 the Scottish and Welsh members of Parliament also withdrew their support when Thatcher tabled a vote of no confidence in the Labour government.

In the 1979 general elections Thatcher presented herself as an alternative solution to Britain's problems, which she portrayed as being caused by Labour. She began to appear as her own woman when she declared: "I'm not a consensus politician or a pragmatic politician: I'm a conviction politician. And I believe in the politics of persuasion: It's my job to put forward what I believe and try to get people to agree with me."[23] She spoke in tune with the voters, even on matters such as immigration; she conceded that people were "afraid that this country might be rather swamped by people with a different culture."[24] Such a statement might have sat ill at ease with her professed hatred of anti-semitism, but it effectively transferred the extreme right-wing vote to her.

Callaghan projected an image as the urbane, experienced, and kindly elder statesman who would see Britain right, but softly, softly. Thatcher, on the other hand, may have been inexperienced but she knew her mind. No softly-softly approach for her. She offered conviction bordering on a radical revolution. She would curb union powers, control inflation, remove controls and regulations on the economy, restore law and order, control public spending, encourage home ownership, and restore personal incentives to succeed. These policies, along with TV producer Sir Gordon Reece's packaging of her image, ensured her success in winning the election and implementing what she saw as her radical revolution.

With these radical ideas propelling her and her party to government, it is no wonder that she entered 10 Downing Street after reading this extract from St. Francis of Assisi:

Where there is discord may we bring harmony. Where there is error may we bring truth. Where there is doubt may we bring faith. Where there is despair may we bring hope.[25]

Prime Minister

The 1979 general election result can be seen in retrospect as the complete defeat of British socialism. In the following years the British

Labour party was to change beyond recognition as it maneuvered itself toward the center right in order to displace Thatcher. The prime minister herself grew to be admired and respected for what people perceived to be her firmness and strength of character. Although, over the years, public opinion seemed to be sharply divided between those who admired her and those who detested her—with few, if any, in between. It was the nature of the woman to bring out extremes of emotions in the electorate.

Thatcher's premiership started with attempts to hold a divided party together. She put together a cabinet that would be acceptable to all sections of her party, with only Sir Keith Joseph and Norman St. John Stevas of those who had supported her in the leadership elections. In doing this she was largely unable, during her first term of office, to carry out what became known as her radical Conservative revolution.

The essence of Thatcherism was to be "rolling back the frontiers of the state in Britain."[26] Her policies were to concentrate on giving individual citizens as much choice as possible. This was to be done by dismantling the socialist nanny state and replacing it with the free market where workers would retain more of their money to spend as they wished. Some critics argued that such a "free market economy" left the poor and helpless without help or the aid that they deserved. However, such criticism was largely absent during Thatcher's first cautious term of office. She moderated her views largely because of a cautious or, at times, hostile cabinet. This first term of office was remarkable more than anything for the prime minister's pronouncements on the big plans to come once the party had been made to realize the necessity of radical Thatcherism: "We should not expect the state to appear in the guise of an extravagant good fairy at every christening, a loquacious companion at every stage of life's journey, the unknown mourner at every funeral."[27]

Not being able to get rid of the old Heathites, she placed them in the least influential cabinet posts. Geoffrey Howe, a faithful supporter of her policies, was sent to the Treasury, whereas Mark Carlisle, a Heath supporter, was put in charge of Education. Her closest ally, Sir Keith Joseph, took up the Department of Industry. Within the larger cabinet, she created a small economic inner cabinet. This inner cabinet's job was "to do things [and not] waste time having any internal arguments."[28] Whenever such arguments did take place, Thatcher made absolutely certain that she won them.

Before Thatcher and her cabinet could introduce radical policies, there was a clear need to ensure a safe passage for such policies. Thatcher's old ministerial experiences of the civil service convinced her of the need for change; the civil service had to be streamlined, cut down to size, and brought firmly within her political control. This she did in her inimitable way through extreme hard work, an unparalleled attention to detail, and an ability to cut through any gordian knots put before her by Whitehall mandarins. She made a point of visiting Whitehall frequently. Using her combative—and at times aggressive—style, she was soon in control of Whitehall. Such control was assured with a few key appointments such as Sir Robert Armstrong as Cabinet Secretary, Clive Whitmore as her Principal Private Secretary, and the bluff, tough Bernard Ingham as her Press Secretary. Such appointments ensured that her radical policies would be carried through from philosophy into practice without the usual watering-down effected by the civil service in the years before her arrival, that is, during the hated consensus politics years. She also ensured that House of Commons select committees shadowed the relevant Whitehall departments, thus ensuring rigorous vigilance.

Thatcher also had a remarkable ability to compartmentalize affairs of state. Thus, as will become apparent, she was able to tackle each area separately, ensuring its desired culmination or success before moving on to the next. This tactic enabled her electorate to follow developments without obfuscating one with another. It also meant that the prime minister projected a high profile of qualities. For example, when she disputed Britain's role in Europe what emerged was either the negative quality of insularity or the positive quality of knowing what the British wanted in their heart of hearts. Other policies on the economy, education, or taxation did not intrude on the people's perception of her handling of Europe. The spotlight was directed at one issue at a time.

Thatcher was also able to run her inner cabinet with a firm hold on its members. Collective responsibility became a thing of the past. During the steelworkers' strike Thatcher adopted a noninterventionist line, but she worked hard to introduce the legislation necessary to ensure that unions learned once and for all that the free market would rule and that governments would not be swayed by the threats or actualities of strikes. When Jim Prior, Secretary of State for Employment, appeared to be softening his approach to the strikers during the drafting of the 1980 Employment Act, Thatcher delivered one of her many public reproaches disguised as public loyalty when she declared on television that "We all make mistakes. I think it was a mistake, and Jim Prior was very, very sorry indeed."[29] Jim Prior, in other words, was damned with Thatcher's new word for the likes of him: "wets."

These wets included, in addition to Prior, Peter Walker, Ian Gilmour, Lord Carrington, and Norman St. John Stevas. Gilmour expressed the wets' fear that monetarism was little understood and that it would lead to electoral disaster. It did nothing of the sort. On the contrary, it simply led to the disappearance of the wets over the coming years. Even then, for a while the wets seemed to become stronger as Thatcher became increasingly unpopular with the electorate. However, the wets were never quite willing or able to form a group that could really challenge Thatcher's ascendancy. They simply ensured that Thatcherism increased into a virtual messianic message. There Is No Alternative (TINA) became the Thatcherites' war cry. Indeed, the power of Thatcherism may be placed partly in the arena of her public image and partly in that of her opponents' inability to offer any viable alternative to her policies. The public image became increasingly firm, immovable, and resolute. There was never a question of taking a step backward; backward meant changing one's mind. Compromise and adaptation became cardinal sins during the Thatcher years.

When Norman Stevas attacked Thatcherism as theoretically based and as blind to the impending electoral disaster, Thatcher responded with her famous pun and literary allusion rejecting U-turns: "You turn if you want to. The lady's not for turning."[30] Soon after this rare Thatcher joke, Stevas was sent packing. There was no room for wets in her government. Soon the entire cabinet was to be composed of drys.

Two years into her first term of office, things began to look bad for the government. The similarities with the Heath government were uncanny. However, where Heath seemed to give in by compromising, adapting policies, and performing a veritable series of pirouettes, Thatcher remained impassive with a single-mindedness that caused the extremes of adulation and hatred familiar in the British peoples' relationship with her. But even if Thatcher was tempted to waver before the midterm avalanche of criticism, she could not do so because of two factors. First, she had surrounded herself with advisers whose Thatcherism was not subject to electoral vagaries. Second, as she showed in subsequent years, Thatcher veritably blossomed before any opposition. The harder things got, the more messianic she became.

Thatcher initially balked, but was eventually convinced, when Alan Walters advised her that her government needed to take £4 thousand million out of the public sector borrowing requirement (PSBR: the amount of money the government borrows to bridge the difference between what it earns and spends each year). Eventually, a figure of £3.5 thousand million was accepted, producing a stringent budget increasing personal and indirect taxes. She stood by this extremely unpopular budget despite many attempts by the wets, the public, and the experts to tell her that she was wrong. Not only did she believe that the figures made sense, but, more importantly, she saw a clear relation between monetary policy and the whole moral dimension of the nation's way of life. Monetary policies were seen as being not only economically sound but also being agents of change: a leaner, fitter Britain peopled by hard-working citizens whose personal freedoms were generated by an increased awareness of thrift and monetary responsibilities.

After a period of uncertainty during which the wets had their last revolt, Thatcher changed her cabinet. The new ministers became the ones associated with the heyday of Thatcherism: Nigel Lawson, Cecil Parkinson, and Norman Tebbit. This cabinet assured Thatcher an ascendancy she had been working toward for some time. The Heathites or wets were largely gone, some into obscurity and others into impossible posts (like Jim Prior assigned to Northern Ireland). The war on inflation—a firm pillar of monetarism—was started in earnest. Casualties in terms of unemployment and the deindustrialization of Britain were acceptable prices to pay.

A series of union strikes were put down by the Thatcher government as it continued to ensure that its radical monetarist policies were carried out. The government "meant business."[31] The civil service was cut down to size, both metaphorically and in real terms. The Railwaymen, hospital workers, and eventually the miners were also put down. Inner city riots were seen as moral questions of law and order—essentially a question of efficient policing. Human wickedness was countered by rigorous policing and firm laws.

Thatcher's unpopularity increased, reaching rock bottom by the end of 1981. Six months later this situation was dramatically reversed by the start of the Falklands war. Much has been said about Thatcher's so-called good luck in having a little war to boost her government's standing with the electorate. Evidence would seem to indicate, however, that her public image of decisiveness, strength of character, resolution, and firm leadership in winning the war was a reality. The Falklands war showed Thatcher at her very best: positively Churchillian. She thrived on crises of this kind. She gained a second term of office with a dramatically increased majority.

The Falklands war had a powerful psychological effect both on Thatcher and on the British electorate. It convinced her that she had the high moral ground in everything she did. The British, intensely proud of their victory, were yet again presented with the image of an unfaltering leader with a winning streak. The compartmentalization of her achievements reached the point of virtual tunnel vision, where less favorable issues were ignored. More importantly, the war ensured that elusive but deeply felt truth of Western supremacy associated with Thatcher's close ties with the United States.

Meanwhile, the Labour party was busily lacerating itself through a series of internecine wars and through the bumbling, hesitant, and almost comic performances of its leader, Michael Foot. The result was the emergence of the Social Democratic Party (SDP), with its founders being defectors from the fragmenting Labour party. Initially, Thatcher ignored the SDP. Eventually, as the party seemed to gain credence with the electorate, she launched a series of vicious attacks on its policies. Labour, Liberal, and SDP were "all divisions of socialism."[32]

The SDP gained one spectacular by-election after another. Thatcher recognized that Labour was utterly unelectable, but she feared that the SDP might take away much of the center ground in voting patterns. Even then, Thatcher felt confident enough to call a general election in the spring of 1983, which she won handsomely after appointing Cecil Parkinson as party chairman. There were four reasons for Thatcher's overwhelming victory: (1) Her own personal popularity after the Falklands experience; (2) the ridiculous position of a Labour party hell-bent on destroying itself and on refusing to accept the apparent dramatic rejection of its old-fashioned and interfering socialist policies; (3) the British electoral system, which allowed a first-past-the-post result rather than proportional representation; and (4) the general unarticulated sense that the Thatcher government to date had not yet fully carried out its real policies.

Safe with a second mandate and a huge majority in the House, Thatcher proceeded to put some of her radical policies into practice. Her government concentrated its efforts on the fight against inflation, on reducing public spending, and on the privatization of public industries. With Nigel Lawson in the Treasury, all this became effortlessly possible. Parkinson worked to amalgamate the Department of Trade with that of Industry. Whitehall was now fully restructured and trimmed down to suit Thatcher's vision. New blood was brought into the civil service and into Thatcher's own circle— men like Peter Middleton and John Hoskyns. Norman Strauss and, more significantly, Alfred Sherman were on the way out, since they were beginning to have doubts about Thatcherism.

Thatcher's second term in office was also fraught with crises—some with a distinct whiff of scandal. Cecil Parkinson had to resign after Sara Keays publicly announced their affair and her pregnancy. The U.S. invasion of Grenada and the bombing of Libya caused a momentary strain in relations with President Reagan and a strong anti-American feeling among the British. Thatcher's attempts to curb union powers at the Government Communications Headquarters (GCHQ) met with considerable resistance. Her fight with the miners during their strike was seen as a crusade against Arthur Scargill and his Marxist subversion of the workers. Her response to the IRA's attempt to assassinate her by bombing her Brighton hotel was an occasion to show publicly her courage and stamina. Privately, she was understandably shaken. Her handling of the Westland affair (in which a contract for building helicopters for the military was given to an American company) threatened to bring her government down were it not for Kinnock's horrendous incompetence in missing an opportunity of pinning her down in a debate on Westland. He was too busy being verbose and scoring insignificant little points to achieve anything. The government's mishandling of the *Spycatcher* affair (when a book detailing the intelligence-gathering secrets of MI5 and MI6 was initially banned in Britain) was also a missed opportunity by the seemingly endlessly incompetent Labour leadership.

Thatcher's most significant achievements during her second term in office were her government's ability to launch in earnest the creation of a free market, curb union powers, expand Thatcher's foreign affairs experiences, produce the Anglo–Irish agreement against many odds, abolish the Greater London Council (GLC), and—more significantly—continue to present Labour as being eternally unelectable. This last achievement was only partly hers; it was more Labour's own doing, with its electorally misplaced support of the miners' strike, its continued quarrels within its ranks, and its new leader's bombastic verbosity and flagrant immaturity. Furthermore, Thatcher managed to ridicule—either by word or by deeds— the outdated and increasingly perceived as interfering liberalism of the left-wing policies of the 1960s.

As her third term of office approached, Thatcher felt secure enough and sure enough of her policies to raise her political beliefs to the point of lecturing the Anglican church. Wrong-minded egalitarianism, she suggested, came from a mistaken Christian belief in the equality of people. The real values of Christianity lay in freedom of choice—the very essence of professed Thatcherism. Hard work and the creation of wealth were essentially Christian ideals calculated to help the less able and the less fortunate. Thus, once citizens are empowered they cease to turn to the state for everything. "How could we invest for the future," she asked, "or support those wonderful artists and craftsmen whose work also glorifies God, unless we had first worked hard and used our talents to create the necessary wealth?"[33]

In 1985 Norman Tebbit was appointed chairman of the Conservative party; in 1987 he led the party to a third consecutive term in office. Yet again, Thatcher's own charisma, her party's projection of the no-alternative argument, the comic scenario of the two-headed SDP–Liberal Alliance, and the real fact of a lack of any alternative in the new all-image-

and-no-policies Labour party all contributed to her party's victory. Perhaps more important was the working-class vote. The working classes had become owner-occupiers, many with shares in privatized companies and most with the newly acquired middle-class values of acquisitive individualism and enlightened self-interest. After two terms in office the Thatcher generation was ready to graduate into her brave new world.

Thatcher's third term of office saw the speeding up of measures that produced a real free market economy and that attempted to lay the paternalism of the welfare state permanently to rest. Much that the Thatcher government felt unable to do in its first term it tried to do during its second; now, a third term of office meant that one or another form of privatization could go ahead unchallenged—in industry, business, education, the health service, housing, and every other aspect of British life. Power was being transferred from the state to the individual citizen. For example, local education authorities (LEAs) no longer ran their schools; instead, power, that is, financial power, was given to parents and school governors. Thatcherism defined as fiscal rigor, freedom of choice, and individual responsibility became a way of life in Britain.

By 1989, life seemed inconceivable without the ubiquitous populist who had governed Britain for ten years. Critics said that Thatcher out-Thatchered Thatcherism. To a certain extent such alliterative bombast reflected the seemingly moral bankruptcy of any viable opposition outside the party. Within the party, however, opposition was slowly growing. Thatcher, convinced of being absolutely right and sure of her political ground, became oddly indifferent to the opinions of those around her. There had already been internal wranglings within her cabinet, but, like the consummate politician that she was, she repeatedly rode out the storm. When Michael Heseltine dramatically walked out of a cabinet meeting she survived the difficult time ensuing. When Nigel Lawson resigned in high dudgeon over her retention of Alan Walters as economic adviser, again she weathered the storm.

Such triumphs were bound to make her even more combative and more unflinching before arguments against her policies. Even as she continued to fight against what became to be known as European federalism, the British seemed behind her.

It was not so much her government's policies that began to cause her problems in late 1989; it was more her style of government. Her easy rejection of consensus had developed into an overbearing and strident presidential style of leadership. A year later, Geoffrey Howe, her most trusted supporter, had had enough. He resigned over the issue of a united

Europe. His speech in the House announcing his resignation referred not only to Europe, but it also attacked her style, which he perceived as doing harm to Britain's interest.

Soon after Howe's resignation, Thatcher was challenged to a leadership contest within the Conservative party. She failed marginally to secure the votes required. After an undignified assertion that she would stand again, she eventually withdrew her name, opening the way for other contenders. John Major then emerged with a majority of votes, thus becoming Britain's new prime minister.

Economic Affairs

Although monetarism was Thatcher's clearly professed defense against all economic ills, the route that her economic policies would take was not necessarily clear at the outset of her first term of office. The British people had to go through an education process over the next ten years, while the rigors of monetarism were slowly introduced.

Thatcher, as was her style, took a keen personal interest in detail. It was said of her that she was "much more the First Lord of the Treasury than any previous holder of that office."[34] She ensured that the top rate of tax (83 percent) was cut as a symbol of socialism. There was a stated aim of reducing taxes across the board, thus giving citizens the argued incentives and the freedom of choice necessary for a healthy economy. Such cuts could be achieved through a reduction in public spending, which was Thatcher's favorite image of prudent and thrifty housekeeping. Added to this was the necessity of reducing the money supply.

At the beginning of her first term of office, Thatcher realized that these aims could not be easily fulfilled. Labour had left the country with runaway inflation (although they had managed to bring it down to 10 percent), a very high running money supply, and a PSBR racing out of control. Furthermore, the Conservatives had committed themselves to accepting the Clegg Commission's recommendations on the public sector pay, which reached 25 percent in their first year in office. In order to carry out its policies on cuts in direct taxation, the government increased indirect taxation.

Running along these proposed measures were two crucial policies: curbing union powers and denationalizing nationalized industries. The Clegg Commission made a cut in public spending difficult. It was taken as an imperative that union powers had to be curbed in order to ensure reasonable pay settlements.

Monetarism was seen as a clear adjunct of the free market. A free market stabilized itself through its economic performance. Inevitably, inefficient industries were plagued with overmanning and with a lack of a real vision in terms of the profit incentive. The theory was that governments did not intervene. In practice, however, the early Thatcher government did intervene to save British Leyland in order to avoid major social dislocation. This was a rare reversal in the early years. The real result of the free market was eventually to deindustrialize Britain and to turn much of its wealth creation into service industries.

Thatcher felt passionately about her monetarist policies. It was an act of faith with her that Britain was sick: "After almost any major operation, you feel worse before you convalesce. But you do not refuse the operation when you know that, without it, you will not survive."[35] By 1981, however, things were not going according to plan. Despite the rigorous planning through the Medium-Term Financial Strategy (MTFS), the money supply was doubled. Nonetheless, the ground was being prepared for the coming years. For now, unemployment was rising, exports were down because of the high exchange rate, the money supply was up, and borrowing was on the increase. As always, the worse things got, the more adamant Thatcher became that her job was "to let the country begin to exist within sensible and realistic economic disciplines."[36]

By 1982, when Alan Walters was taken on as her economic adviser, the contradictions between policies and practicalities were causing confusion. British business was suffering from high interest rates and a high exchange rate. Walters pushed hard and succeeded in getting public spending reduced by £3.5 thousand million. To counter this, the budget raised personal and indirect taxation. Unemployment was nearing the three million figure, and the economy was contracting fast. Thatcher remained undaunted. She did not believe that the nation could spend its way out of a recession. By the 1982 budget, however, fiscal rigor was relaxed slightly to produce Thatcher's first popular budget.

Thatcher's second term started with promises to cut public spending dramatically through introducing student loans and through curbing the welfare budget. Such promises—leaked to *The Economist*—caused a furor that showed, in hindsight, that the nation was not yet ready for Thatcherism. Eventually, these plans were pushed off the election agenda. They were replaced by promises to reduce taxes, curb public spending, and, most importantly, bring down inflation. Opportunity had to go side by side with the welfare state, for the time being at least. People had to change because, according to Thatcher,

You're going to change the whole of your life, the whole of the nation's life, the whole of the attitude to honesty and integrity, if the pound you put in and save out of your earnings is still there for your retirement. You're going to alter the whole attitude towards investment if a building costs the same when it's finished as when it was started.[37]

Her second term of office saw a series of appointments that were clearly designed to prepare nationalized companies for privatization. John King turned British Airways into a profitable organization by laying off half its workforce. Ian MacGregor did the same for British Steel, which eventually became one of the best-run steel industries in the world after it had previously been losing £8 hundred million per annum at one point. He was moved to the Coal Board, where he presided over the long miners' strike without much success (in Thatcher's eyes).

By the end of 1985 Thatcher's policies were unmistakably monetarist. When Dr. Robert Runcie, archbishop of Canterbury, published his report *Faith in the City*, Thatcherism came under attack for neglecting its obligations to society and for being too concerned with individual greed. Thatcher responded by saying that her policies had a clear Christian basis: "The values of a free society like ours come from religion. They do not come from the state."[38] Since freedom of choice was the anchor of Conservative philosophy, it followed that the Church's report had got it wrong.

By 1986, both British Telecom and British Gas had been sold off into private ownership. Average earnings were steadily rising in real terms, with inflation pegged at an average of 5 percent. By 1987, it was clear that steady economic growth—albeit slow—had been taking place year by year. Eight years into the Thatcher government, it was apparent that her policies were producing the desired results. Personal taxation had gone down to a basic 25 percent. An expanding economy meant that more money could be spent on education and health. Stock market dealings increased, quintupling the Financial Times (FT) index in four years.

When Thatcher was elected for the third time in 1987, everything seemed rosy. Monetarism had led to less public spending, privatization, tax cuts, and a small economic expansion. Wealth creation meant a higher revenue, thus leading to more spending on essential services without an increase in PSBR or taxation. Fiscal rigor implied accountability through choice. In short: Thatcherism had worked, or so it appeared in the midst of a welcome boom. Three million unemployed did not seem to upset the euphoria of success since the benefits outweighed the cost.

During her third term, Thatcher went on to carry out the plans that had caused a furor when leaked to *The Economist* four years earlier. The electorate were ready by now. Water and electricity were privatized. The community charge (or poll tax) was introduced. Housing benefit, a form of welfare, was abolished for anyone with savings of £8,000 or more. Grants for the poor were replaced by loans through the social fund. The top rate of tax was cut to 40 percent. Social security was reviewed, encouraging people to opt out of state earnings–related pension schemes (SERPS). By late 1988, Britain had emerged as a strong economy with low inflation and high productivity. Privatized industries were profitable—when once they were losing hundreds of millions of pounds as nationalized industries—and became better geared to serve their customers.

Such economic and personal strength allowed Thatcher the equally strong position of fighting Britain's role in Europe. This was to eventually bring her down.

Foreign Affairs

When Margaret Thatcher first came to power, her experience of foreign affairs was severely limited to a few trips abroad. Over the next decade she was to acquire considerable expertise in foreign affairs and to become a much admired, respected, feared, and, at times, hated world leader. Her initial relationships with other world leaders were somewhat formal, since she felt that "first name terms can lead to artificial familiarity."[39]

She began her experience of such affairs slowly. Using her customary thoroughness, she prepared herself rigorously for every visit abroad and for every foreign visitor to the United Kingdom. In foreign affairs she was first and foremost a convinced anticommunist. She saw Communism as a moral evil that "never sleeps . . . never changes its objectives."[40] Consequently, she felt that the West needed to remain alert: "Our first duty to freedom is to defend our own."[41] She saw the Soviet Union as a superpower only in the military sense. Prophetically, she spoke of the Soviets as being "a failure in human and economic terms."[42] As a result of her vehement anticommunism, the Soviets dubbed her the Iron Lady, a title of which she became inordinately proud.

When Foreign Secretary Reginald Maudling criticized her anti-Soviet sentiments, he was promptly replaced by Lord Carrington, who helped Thatcher to come to terms with a settlement on Rhodesia. Ian Smith and his white supremacist party were replaced by Robert Mugabe's multiracial state. The transition from Rhodesia to Zimbabwe in April 1980 was seen as a diplomatic triumph for Thatcher, despite her inner misgivings at the apparent left-wing leanings of the newly elected Zimbabwean government.

Thatcher's second foray into foreign affairs was in Europe, where she presided over—and eventually won the day on—the battle over Britain's contribution to the community budget. This became a crusade to get back "our money."[43] There were times when Thatcher's seeming aggressive and strident postures on this subject caused European leaders to despair, but it was not merely questions of money and of equity of distribution that Thatcher was arguing about. She genuinely feared Europe's socialist tendencies: "If we look on Europe as a whole, it is clear that the present fragmentation of the centre and the right gives to the left an advantage which the rest of us cannot afford."[44] Despite an agreement reached in 1980, a year after she became prime minister, Thatcher was to carry on the fight until she got a permanent settlement that favored Britain. This she obtained in Fontainebleau in 1984. Although many saw this as a hollow victory born of stridency, rudeness, and insularity, the British people seemed pleased with her achievement, which reflected their deeper fear of European domination. The result was an upsurge in her reputation as a firm and unconquerable fighter both at home and abroad.

During 1981 Thatcher traveled all over the world for many summits, all of which provided experience that enlarged her understanding of foreign affairs. Meanwhile, she began to establish what became one of the most enduring, powerful, and—to many observers—incomprehensible relationships. The Reagan–Thatcher axis brought Britain firmly within the sphere of the United States and took her away from Europe. Both leaders shared a messianic approach to right and wrong. They were both persons of conviction with strong crusading philosophies. As people they were quite different, with Thatcher the workaholic as a dramatic contrast to one of the most laid back and effectively idle and dilettante U.S. presidents. The two backed each other to the hilt, from Thatcher agreeing to participate in the U.S.-sponsored elections in El Salvador (Britain was the only country to send observers to what was seen essentially as a puppet regime of the United States) to Britain allowing U.S. bombers to use British bases in their Libyan bombing sorties. This special relationship may have been a fool's paradise, considering Britain's connection with Europe, but it was of great use to Thatcher over the next few years. At no time was the United States more helpful than during Thatcher's darkest—and, to many, finest—hour.

In early April 1982, Argentina invaded the Falklands—a small group of islands in the South Atlantic—that, though British territory, were entirely unknown to most British people. Within a few hours of the invasion, Thatcher was busy making preparations to wrest the islands back from Argentina. Lord Carrington resigned after taking responsibility for allowing the "national humiliation" of seeing professional British forces surrendering to the Argentinian conscript forces.[45]

Thatcher created a small war cabinet with representatives from the military. A task force was speedily put together and sent on its way to the South Atlantic. Along with the war preparations, intense diplomatic negotiations were taking place under the aegis of U.S. Secretary of State Alexander Haig. Meanwhile, the Americans were giving Britain invaluable help in gathering intelligence information crucial to the war effort. Once embroiled in its initial Malvinas (the Argentinian name for the Falklands) victory, the Argentinian junta felt unable to compromise. The Argentinian people made a great deal of noise voicing their support for the invasion. President Leopoldo Galtieri, riding high on the temporary euphoria that eclipsed the erstwhile brutality and corruption of his regime, refused to respond adequately to U.S. mediation efforts. War seemed inevitable.

It was at this early stage of the conflict that a Peruvian-sponsored peace plan appeared to offer a bloodless way out. By then, however, the British had sunk the Argentinian cruiser, the *General Belgrano.* This action effectively scuttled the peace initiative.

It will be some time before the controversy over the sinking of the *Belgrano* is cleared up. There was little doubt however, that in subsequent months the Thatcher government did attempt a cover-up of what actually happened. The order to sink the *Belgrano* outside the designated Exclusion Zone certainly came from Mrs. Thatcher, despite the claim that the decision to sink the cruiser was made by the submarine captain in order to avert an immediate threat to the task force. Whether done for political reasons (to scuttle the emerging Peruvian peace plan) or for as-yet-unknown military reasons, the sinking of the *Belgrano* changed the course of the war, leading to eventual British victory after the Argentinian navy withdrew from operations. It also remained a controversial issue that dogged Thatcher for a long time to come.

There were many consequences of the Falklands victory: (1) As mentioned earlier, the Falklands factor ensured Margaret Thatcher a second term of office. (2) Thatcher's own political standing as a world leader increased with a stunning military victory added to her list of qualifications. (3) Her victory saw the end of a much-hated junta, which reinforced her symbolic stand for freedom and democracy. (4) Britain, only recently the sick man of Europe, emerged with enhanced prestige reminiscent of its old battleground glories. (5) The relationship with the United States was strengthened. (6) The supremacy of Western nations' armaments and their armies' professionalism, coupled with the supremacy of democracies over third world militarism, was established yet again, presaging the New World Order that emerged in the early 1990s. (7) The Franks Committee—set up to investigate "the way in which the responsibilities of Government . . . were discharged"—found the government not guilty of "any criticism or blame" for the "act of unprovoked aggression" by Argentina. Yet again, circumstances decreed that Thatcher was not only right but wholly innocent: an image that her imagemakers used intelligently and effectively. (8) Finally, Thatcher's attitude to foreign policy management changed dramatically. Diplomacy was out as an outmoded Foreign Office custom; Thatcherist modalities were in.

The service rendered by the United States to the British war effort was amply repaid in the wake of the American invasion of Grenada. Grenada was a member of the British Commonwealth with Her Majesty the Queen as its titular Head of State. The American invasion, unknown to the British government, was an affront to British dignity and probably a flagrant breach of international law. After an initial fury (of which Reagan was the recipient in the form of the much-talked-about Thatcher tongue lashing), Thatcher reverted to her indestructible friendship both in private and in public.

On another occasion Thatcher repaid the Americans by allowing them to use British soil in launching their bombing raid on Tripoli, in Libya, in 1986. Despite the overwhelming unpopularity of this act, she maintained firm support of the United States. She also stood by Reagan when he proposed to continue research into the Strategic Defense Initiative (SDI), known as Star Wars.

In Europe, Thatcher continued her search for an equitable settlement of the British contribution to the European budget. She was also beginning to talk about British sovereignty and against European federalism. This invariably meant that Europe was seen to be dominated by West Germany and France, clearly an unsatisfactory position considering Britain's newly found claim to be a world—let alone a European—leader. However, she succeeded in settling Britain's contribution by reducing farm prices and by accelerating the common internal market in preparation for European economic unity scheduled to take place in 1992.

In 1983 Thatcher met Alexander Solzhenitsyn, who impressed her with his arguments on the evils of Communism. Despite Reagan's pronouncements on the "evil empire" and Thatcher's avowed hostility to Communism, she made the conscious decision to open the dialogue with the East:

"We've got to do more talking."[46] She assumed a practical position in dealing with détente and the arms talks. Talking became possible at the end of 1984 when she met the hitherto-unknown Mikhail Gorbachev. For the first time, she had met a Communist who impressed her with his practicality, pragmatism, and individual charm: "I like Mr. Gorbachev; we can do business together."[47] A few months later Gorbachev became the new Soviet leader. Thatcher's overtures took on a prophetic turn: "You are much more likely to be able to do business with someone else if you have a realistic assessment of their approach, their strengths, their fears, and you do not go starry-eyed thinking that one day Communism will collapse like a pack of cards, because it will not."[48] Eventually it did collapse, and—although her practical approach never intended this outcome— Thatcher had the pleasurable task of watching Communist nations racing headlong to adopt her policies of the free market coupled with individual freedoms. This collapse she saw as "the culmination of a battle of ideas," a battle where it was apparent who had won.[49] She had, prior to this collapse, visited Hungary, Poland, and the Soviet Union, where she was received with enormous accolade. The Iron Lady became the darling of the Soviet people. She mixed with them, told them a few truths on television, and spent hours chatting to Gorbachev. Her influence on the subsequent events in the East can not be overestimated.

Perhaps more importantly, Thatcher's stature as a world leader increased as she acted as a go-between serving to maintain the dialogue between Reagan and Gorbachev. She managed to moderate Reagan's stand on SDI and to enhance the continuing arms control talks. By the end of 1984 she had scored a diplomatic triumph by helping to draft the Camp David accord. A few months later, in 1985, she addressed a joint session of the U.S. Congress following in the footsteps of Churchill. In Reykjavik, Iceland, Reagan seemingly rejected an offer to abolish all nuclear weapons if such an agreement were to include banning SDI. Thatcher felt that a nuclear deterrent was essential since its abolition would open up Western Europe to conventional warfare in which the Soviets had the upper hand. She managed to consign Reykjavik to the dustbin of history.

Thatcher's foreign policy became intensely personal with considerable isolation when she felt that she was right and the rest of the world was wrong. She refused to go along with the Commonwealth demand for sanctions against South Africa, arguing that sanctions would hurt black workers most of all. With her early experience of Zimbabwe, she also felt that doors must remain open in order to allow for the dialogue necessary to achieve a one-man, one-vote multiracial South Africa. For a long time it was hard for many black leaders to understand her logic—or the lack of it. Things continued to be as bad as ever in South Africa. Thatcher's intransigence got her branded as a racist by many people, both at home and abroad. She was seen as protecting the interests of the business community at the expense of South African blacks. Now and then she would compromise on minor issues, but she seemed to have nothing but contempt for what she saw as the hypocrisy and moral bankruptcy of antiracist and multicultural strategies. In time, as the South African government released Nelson Mandela and began the process of dismantling its racist laws, Thatcher's earlier obduracy seemed partly vindicated.

One area that seemed intractable was the Irish question, which was made more complex by the fact that Americans were contributing money to the coffers of Irish Republicanism. Thatcher seemed utterly disinterested to start with, because to her Northern Ireland was insoluble as a problem. It was a place where the Jim Priors of this world were sent to get them out of the way. However, Thatcher managed what no other recent prime minister had managed before her: the Anglo–Irish agreement. Once she had decided to tackle the Irish problem, she did so with her customary gusto and vigor. The Anglo–Irish agreement was a small step—but a step nonetheless—toward eventually resolving a seemingly impossible issue.

Another seemingly impossible problem was Hong Kong, which was due to be handed back to China in perpetuity by 1997. Thatcher took a great deal of delight in and received even more credit for producing an agreement with China: Hong Kong was to remain a capitalist paradise within the hell of Chinese Communism (if the latter continued to last). This was also seen as making the best of a bad job as China's recent record on human rights did not auger well for the people of Hong Kong. Whatever happened, China was due to extend its sovereignty over Hong Kong by 1997. Thatcher got the best deal she could get out of the inscrutable Communist Chinese. At the end of the day, China may allow Hong Kong to earn its foreign currency, which is much needed by the Chinese. Democracy, however, is another thing. In the early 1990s, China was already setting up structures against democratic reforms through its highly placed Hong Kong China advisers and through its notorious News Agency. But Hong Kong has never known democracy in the real Western sense, but it does know how to make money—and that would no doubt be fine by the Chinese.

In Europe Thatcher continued to harangue fellow European leaders, even after she got her way on the British budgetary contribution. Her opposition to federalism increased in rhetoric, while joining the Exchange Rate Mechanism (ERM) seemed to speak for it. She saw the move toward a common European monetary system (EMS) as being against the sovereignty of the British Parliament. Her famous Bruges speech, which she delivered on September 20, 1988, and in which she attacked the concept of a European super-state, appeared to put the final nail in the European coffin. This stance seemed remarkably impractical since it isolated Britain. And with Ronald Reagan replaced as president by George Bush in 1988, it became apparent that U.S. interests in Britain were directly related to Britain's place in Europe. With Germany emerging as the most powerful country of Europe, Thatcher's seeming insularity became increasingly risky. However, her essential Britishness could not be inveigled into a larger Europeanism. For the first time in her career, her immovable conviction, coupled with her management style, brought her to the brink of political suicide. She departed in 1990, still convinced that she was right.

Union Laws

There were three reasons why Margaret Thatcher wanted to curb union powers: (1) During the 1979 winter of discontent, the country was crippled by a series of public sector strikes over pay. Thatcher's monetarist policies aimed at reducing inflation and public spending, which meant that public pay demands needed to be severely curtailed. (2) In a free market economy, Thatcher felt that managers needed to be allowed to manage their business unhindered by union disputes. (3) British unions had become acutely politicized under Labour, and union barons had easy access to Labour prime ministers. Under Thatcher, there were no longer to be the traditional beer and sandwiches at Number 10 Downing Street. The British people appeared to be largely in accord after the events of 1979, and they did not mind watching the Conservative government giving the unions a thorough drubbing. Added to all of this, many Conservatives had not forgotten Heath's humiliation in the general election in 1974 after the miners' strike. Heath had gone to the country on a "who governs Britain" ticket.[50] Clearly, the electorate did not think that he did.

Therefore, together with her government's monetarist economic policies, Thatcher aimed to reform the trade union law. Any strike and leadership changes were to be subject to a ballot. Closed shops were on the way out, since 80 percent of the workforce had to approve such tactics before they could come into effect. A conscience clause existed for those who dissented. Secondary picketing was easily outlawed, with its violent images from 1979 still reverberating in British minds. Social security benefits became impossible to claim since it was declared that strikers were receiving strike pay from their unions. Soon after these laws were discussed prior to the 1980 Employment Act, British Steel workers went on strike. This soon spread to private steelworkers. Thatcher's government refused to intervene and decided to play a waiting game. When it was settled some three months later, the government had made it clear that it was not going to be moved by strike action. Although hers was a Pyrrhic victory, she had seen her first major strike end in a way that satisfied the antagonistic British public.

Jim Prior's 1980 Employment Act was a considerably watered-down affair compared with what his cabinet colleagues and the prime minister really wanted. For now, however, with the old Heath guard still around, it was only a precursor of things to come.

The next showdown came when the civil servants went on strike after their demand for a 15 percent pay increase was rejected in favor of a counter offer of 7 percent. Five months later, the strike ended with a 7.5 percent settlement and a triumph for Thatcher's government. The government clearly "meant business."[51] Soon thereafter, plans were put into action to trim down the civil service.

In 1982 there was a railway strike, with disruptive action also taken by hospital workers. Again, Thatcher sat firm, refusing to compromise, and saw the strikers back down. She was helped by the recent Falklands victory, which allowed her to represent the strikers as misunderstanding "the spirit of these times." The 1982 Employment Act strengthened antiunion legislation exposing union funds to sequestration following unlawful industrial action. Soon thereafter the government succeeded in outlawing union activities at the Government Communications Headquarters (GCHQ) after a lengthy and acrimonious debate.

Thatcher's major triumph against the unions came in 1984–85 during the miners' strike led by Arthur Scargill. Scargill was a fiery Marxist who, as president of the National Union of Mineworkers (NUM), had vowed to bring Thatcher down: "A fight-back against the government's policies will inevitably take place outside rather than inside Parliament. Extra-parliamentary action will be the only course open to the working class and the Labour movement."[52]

Thatcher took his challenge seriously. She regarded theirs as a fight between good and evil, which she was determined to win. Scargill being a Marxist only added spice to the fight and firmed up her resolution to win. She prepared for the fight by stockpiling coal to ensure that the impending strike would be virtually ineffective since the British had not quite forgotten the three-day week caused by the miners' strike under Heath. She had also ensured that the police were adequately equipped in the event of civil unrest. Armed with these preparations and with the new Employment Acts, the scene was set for a prolonged and ugly fight.

The public were appalled by the scenes of horrific violence enacted on their television screens every night. A great deal of sympathy went to the Nottinghamshire breakaway miners who insisted on continuing to work. The pain experienced by the deprived strikers' families, the strikers at the hands of the police, and the terrified police officers faced by angry mobs seemed to be nothing compared to the projected image of the Scargill evil being crushed by Thatcher's good. Neil Kinnock, as always, presided over a deeply divided opposition worried about its union support. The result was that Thatcher emerged as the champion of wealth creation, law and order, and moral strength. Yet again, she emerged as the victor, while Kinnock emerged as the leader of a party led by unions. Scargill was seen as a destructive, self-centered, publicity-seeking, and extreme wrecker of all that was good in Britain. These images may not have been a true reflection of the realities of the power struggle, but they were strong perceptions and, in politics, seeming is being.

Scargill lost for several reasons: (1) The government was ready for the fight in a clear determination to win it. (2) The new Union of Democratic Mineworkers (UDM) undercut the effectiveness of the strike, psychologically if not practically. Along with this the government was able to avert supportive strikes, such as by Nacods, the pit deputies' union, by allowing members generous settlements. (3) New legislation brought the union to the verge of bankruptcy, with many of its members lacking the stomach for the prolonged fight. (4) Scargill's image became progressively uglier; he was seen as an irresponsible extremist bent on destroying British democracy. (5) The weather, being unduly clement throughout the strike (itself wrongly timed), meant that less coal was needed.

Thatcher had beaten Galtieri in Argentina. She had beaten European bureaucracy. She had won on South Africa and on détente. Now, she had also beaten the evil of Scargill. In doing so, she also opened the way for the very process that prompted Scargill's initial hostility: a massive program of pit closures in an attempt to rationalize the industry, which was destined for privatization.

Most importantly, Scargill's defeat meant the completion of the job of curbing union powers started years before. Further industrial action did take place, although most of it had become largely impotent. The most notorious was the teachers' action, which, through a mixture of incompetence, division, impotence and—at times—crass stupidity, became the most effective professional suicide ever witnessed by a bemused public. Teachers lost their bargaining rights, had a contract imposed upon them, lost any remaining shred of respect that they may have ever had, had a new system of examinations and a new National Curriculum forced upon them, and were consigned firmly back where they belonged: in their classrooms. The British public, never famous for liking what they saw as the dilettante left-wing trendies with long holidays and short working weeks, were delighted.

In 1979 Britain had lost 28,474,000 work days due to strike action. In 1985 the figure was down to 6,402,000. By the time Thatcher had left office the figure was down even further, to the lowest in Britain since 1939.

Education

Thatcher's successive governments had a series of education ministers: Mark Carlisle, Sir Keith Joseph, John MacGregor, Kenneth Baker, and Kenneth Clarke. It is said by practicing teachers that Carlisle smiled and did little, Joseph laughed and introduced the basis of a new contract and a new examination system, MacGregor tittered and did less than Carlisle, Baker grinned and turned education on its side, and Clarke guffawed and turned it on its head!

Thatcher's free market thinking was to change the face of education for good. As was said in the previous section, she was able to curb the nonexistent powers of the teachers' unions and altered the teachers' working conditions, which included the new concept of directed time of 1,265 hours per annum. The real revolution, however, happened in the schools' delivery of education, their relationships with the local education authorities (LEAs), and their management.

Her work started with the universities, which were seen as being less than cost-effective and as demonstrating an uncanny reluctance to come to terms with her radical revolution. Thatcher felt irritated by the intellectual approaches of university departments. Hers was a world of action where people did things rather than just discuss them. The latter was regarded by her as purely pretentious. She cheerfully made enemies out of the intellectual classes; if this meant that she was an antiintellectual, it was probably something that the British public liked. Intellectual snobbery has always been anathema to the ordinary Briton. Thatcher's pragmatic and cynical style made it even more so.

As part of her public spending cuts, most universities had to learn to become largely self-financing institutions with an 18 percent cut in budget. If this meant teaching less Russian or less Sanskrit, then so be it. Student grants were replaced by student loans. Further budgetary cuts took place in the mid-1980s.

Coupled with this onslaught on what the universities perceived to be their intellectual freedom to act, Thatcher set up the school structures necessary for educating the new generation. The new General Certificate of Secondary Education (GCSE) was introduced; its first results, which appeared in August 1988, were hailed as a triumph in raising standards. Many experts felt that standards had not been raised, however, but rather that the examination results were better because standards had been dropped. Nonetheless, the real revolution in education was yet to come, with the introduction of the 1988 Education Reform Act (ERA).

Education in Britain had changed little since the introduction of the 1944 Education Act. During the 1960s, schools and teacher-training institutions went through a massive experimental phase. The result was the introduction of the comprehensive system, experiential learning strategies, and far-reaching pastoral care programs. A great deal of what was happening in schools was based on strong intellectual analyses of the kind that Thatcher despised. Regardless of her dislike for the zany trends of the 1960s, there was much that was valuable in education, especially in terms of pastoral care in schools. However, if education were to be defined as purely a question of rigorous academic learning (which had been, historically, largely what parents were looking for), then the introduction of the comprehensive system was an unmitigated disaster. Children of all social backgrounds and of all abilities were lumped together and given—at best—a mediocre diet of superficial egalitarianism that deprived the most able of any real challenge and ensured that children with special educa tional needs were permanently labeled as failures. Abroad, an education system that had, with all its undoubted faults (particularly in terms of early selection at eleven), been the envy of the world became a source of constant derision. This was the heyday of sociologists and educational psychologists who presided over a plethora of new trends that became old hat before teachers had quite got to grips with them. Several generations of educational failures emerged, and standards dropped dramatically as more and more teacher-training institutions awarded certificates and de grees to any incompetent who could do nothing else. Education was in crisis. The then prime minister, James Callaghan, launched the Great Debate, which was destined to keep discussions going endlessly for years to come.

Thatcher stopped the debate. Her government's controversial 1988 Education Reform Act (ERA) changed the face of education for good. The major effect of this act—and of measures taken regarding higher educa tion—was to centralize education decision-making policy.

There were three major effects of the act: (1) A National Curriculum was introduced, stipulating which subjects were to be taught in schools and to what standard, the manner of the pupils' assessment, the reporting on progress, and the actual content of each subject. In short, the British had adopted the universal system that they had for years derided the French for doing. (2) Parental preference in the choice of their child's school became legally binding. This has had the effect of increasing competitiveness among schools in parents'—and consequently children's—favor. It has also meant a real blossoming of parental power. (3) The local management scheme (LMS) was introduced, whereby money hitherto held by the LEA was to be given to schools to use as they wished. Headteachers and governors held the purse strings. This was probably the most powerful development since it meant a more efficient, cost-effective, and pupil-centered use of money. The more pupils a school attracted, since each pupil brought his or her price (age weighted pupil unit, or AWPU), the more money it got. Pressure on schools to attract parental preference became fierce. This in turn led to a shakeup of the way schools presented themselves to the community. Even the most trenchant anti- Tory would not deny the benefits accrued from LMS. Schools have become leaner, fitter, and more cost-effective units.

In a bid to dismantle the hugely bureaucratic LEA system, schools were given the option of becoming grant maintained (GM). This meant that their money came from central government. Financial inducements were offered to schools that did opt out. By 1992 a flood of opt-outs was expected after the fourth successive Conservative general election victory.

An experiment in excellence was launched in the creation of city technology colleges (CTC), amidst much publicity. As their name implies, they were to produce people with the education relevant to today's world. Eventually all schools were supposed to do so with the introduction of a plethora of alternative qualifications from the academic to the technical to the strictly utilitarian.

National curriculum requirements also meant that teaching and learning strategies had to be changed to adapt to the requirement that assessment be closely assimilated with learning. This in turn meant a different kind of teacher, and hence the introduction of a requirement that teacher trainees spend a considerable percentage of their time in schools rather than in colleges.

Schools have also had to adopt the business ethic of the free market, in the same way that locally managed hospital trusts have had to do. In effect, this has meant that good schools would get better and bad schools would get very much worse. Many saw this as a form of selective education that ignored issues of social deprivation and inner-city problems.

Another effect that has made itself felt has been on the LEA, whose services had to change dramatically to cope with less money—and hence less power—and with new requirements to provide services in a competitive marketplace. At the time of writing it is as yet too early to judge how LEAs will survive this—if they survive at all—since there are plans to return to a system of smaller unitary authorities. There is considerable evidence to show that an LEA required to adapt would become a leaner, fitter, and more cost-effective provider of services within a competitive market. Evidence from privatized industries certainly showed a dramatic increase in profitability as well as in the standards of customer services. LEAs would have to trim down their monstrous bureaucracy, cut down unparalleled waste, and join the queue selling their services. The days of inefficient monopolies were all but over by the early 1990s.

Power was firmly placed in the hands of those directly responsible for the nation's children. Governors, headteachers, and parents had to assume new responsibilities relating to the children's education. A new Children Act emphasized these responsibilities further.

At the time of writing, the Thatcher effect in education is still being felt as more schools enter LMS and as more become grant maintained, as teachers are about to embark on their developmental appraisal schemes, as more national curriculum subjects are coming on stream, as schools become more creative in the use of their budgets, as teachers are trained differently, as school inspections take on a new format, as Her Majesty's Inspectors (HMIs) are being replaced by competitive registered inspectors (RIs), as schools grapple with new reporting requirements and as they come to terms with the legal requirement to hold a broadly Christian act of worship and to teach religious education (RE), as pupils with special educational needs are integrated and offered a differentiated curriculum, as Section 11 funds relate only to teaching English to bilingual minority ethnic pupils. . . . The list is endless.

Teachers would have it that these are the most exciting times of their lives—and the most tiring and stressful. Many would argue that the bureaucracy that is currently being dismantled is being replaced by the even more unmanageable bureaucracy of the Department for Education (DFE). Teachers would also argue that their professional opinions are being completely ignored in favor of political decisions that have little to do with the business of educating the young. Children are being deprived of the much-desired return to basics by unmanageable systems of assessment, time-wasting dogma concerning records of achievement, attempts at offering the same national curriculum diet to all pupils regardless of ability or social background, measures that militate against producing the workers needed for tomorrow's Britain, and so forth. If the act's requirements prove successful—as they appear largely to be—Thatcher's legacy to generations to come will be far reaching. If they fail, the matter does not bear thinking about—but then, Thatcher never worked in terms of anything but perceived determined success. Furthermore, no educational initiative could, in the short term, ever fail in Britain for the simple reason that teachers would always make sure that it worked. Much remains to be seen before any judgments can be made on the ever-changing educational initiatives.

Equal Opportunities

This was the area of Margaret Thatcher's career that provoked most discussion. Feminists regarded her as a woman who had made it and who, once in power, forgot all about being a woman. To ethnic minorities, she was seen as a racist because of her immigration policies, her lack of sympathy for their plight particularly in the inner cities, and her perceived racism over South Africa.

As a woman herself, she succeeded in overcoming the deepest British prejudicial instincts against women. There were remarkably few jibes at her gender. More importantly, very few seemed to doubt her ability to lead. She somehow superseded all obstacles to her sex.

As a young woman, Thatcher believed in equal opportunities. In an article entitled "Wake Up Women," published in the *Sunday Graphic* in February 1952, she wrote: "It is possible to carry on working when families arrive. In this way gifts and talents that would otherwise be wasted are developed to the benefit of the community. The idea that the family suffers is, I believe quite mistaken."[53] By 1982 Thatcher had changed her tune completely when she said:

Look I do believe passionately that many women take the view, and quite rightly, that when their children are young, their first duty is to look after the children and keep the family together. I wasn't a Member of Parliament till after my children were six, at least they went to school, you know I was there with them quite a lot during the early stages.[54]

This was a slight economy with the truth, for the fact of the matter was that Thatcher did not *succeed* in obtaining a seat until the children were six. She had tried when they were one in 1954, when they were three in 1956, and six more times in the next three years.

It would seem that Thatcher's statements on her commitment as a mother were made because they fit the events that had actually taken place rather than because of conviction. In short, she believed in women's rights until such time as it was no longer necessary that she do so. She continued to pay lip service to women's rights without really doing much to help realize them. By the 1970s, when she was Education Minister, she saw no relationship between nurseries and the right of women to work. The change was a gradual one.

In the 1950s, when she was struggling to make it, she asserted women's right to work. In the 1960s, when she had become an M.P., she varied this into something less feminist, saying:

It is possible, in my view, for a woman to run a home and continue with her career, provided two conditions are fulfilled. First, her husband must be in sympathy with her wish to do another job. Secondly, where there is a young family, the joint income of husband and wife must be sufficient to employ a first class nanny-housekeeper to look after things in the wife's absence. The second is the key to the whole plan.[55]

By the 1980s, as prime minister, she was lecturing the nation on the old Victorian values of family life with the woman as keeper of the family hearth. As she rose in her career, she had to change perspectives not least because she needed to survive in a deeply suspicious, condescending, and chauvinistic men's world.

This seeming political opportunism must also be looked at with another quality. Thatcher despised all aspects of antiracism; multiculturalism; and equal opportunities as to race, gender, and ability—all of which she regarded as essentially left-wing trendy claptrap. Such an image was probably enhanced by the worst excesses of certain Labour-run county or borough councils and by the media hype in reporting these excesses. Consequently, institutions such as the Commission for Racial Equality (CRE) and the Equal Opportunities Commission (EOC) were given short shrift. The Swann Report *Education for All* was politely welcomed but its recommendations on the education of black and Asian children as part of the good education of all children were largely ignored.

With this personal background and with her natural antipathy toward many -isms, did Thatcher do anything for equal opportunities?

During the inner-city riots of the early 1980s, Thatcher saw only disorder and chaos that needed to be rigorously policed. She did not see a black community crying out for help. When Lord Scarman, a senior judge, reported on Brixton's blacks, much of what he had to say went largely unnoticed by the government. Thatcher believed that every single citizen could rise by his or her own efforts. She saw her government as setting up the right economic and social atmosphere within which it became possible for the citizen to excel, regardless of his or her gender, race, or physical ability. Clearly, many blacks did not agree that this had happened. Added to this was the perception held by minority ethnic groups of a leader who belonged instinctively in their opponents' camp. They had not forgotten her opportunistic statement of 1978 about the white Britons' legitimate fears of being "swamped" by blacks.[56] Many felt this to be a politically motivated and irresponsible statement, a statement that temporarily destroyed the ugly face of British neofascism by allowing many of its adherents to rejoin mainstream right-wing politics.

Efforts on behalf of minority groups continued during the Thatcher years through Home Office grants, various government commissions, and individual institutional efforts. At government level—and certainly at prime ministerial level—minorities were largely ignored.

By the time she became prime minister, Thatcher felt that "the battle for women's rights [had] largely been won."[57] She added: "The days when they were demanded and discussed in strident tones should be gone for ever. I hate those strident tones we hear from some Women's Libbers."[58] So did most of the people of Britain, who seemed unable to separate women's emotional sexuality from the intellectual integrity of accepting equity of access for women. Women generally did not want a concession to their femininity in a man's world, and Thatcher gave them none.

A great deal of nonsense has been written about Thatcher de-sexing herself in order to survive. The truth of the matter was that the media and her critics saw what they wished to see in her behavior. When she invited television into her private life, it was said that only a woman could do this. When she harangued those around her, it was said that she was denying her inner sexuality in a way that was tantamount to violating the truth. When she fought aggressively, she was strident. When she dressed demurely or aggressively, she was sublimating her femininity beneath a facade of nannyism or mothering domination. In short, she, like all women, could never win. When she did win and survive in a man's world, worse things were said about her. It was said of Neil Kinnock that his lack of success was partly attributable to his inability to be rough with a woman. This statement was probably a reflection on stereotypical male arrogance and inherent stupidity rather than on Thatcher's womanhood. Jim Prior confessed in his diaries that he found it hard "to stomach" Thatcher's challenges because they came from a woman.[59]

Thatcher regarded women as naturally better equipped for leadership. Using her favorite example of housekeeping, she talked about women learning early the art of making instant decisions. She also said, "If you want something said, ask a man. If you want something done, ask a woman."[60] She probably genuinely believed in Sophocles's dictum, "Once a woman is made equal to man, she becomes his superior."[61] To a certain extent, she proved this to be true within her cabinet and within her party.

Perhaps Thatcher's major contribution toward creating an atmosphere in which equity of access for everyone was available was her emphasis on individual freedom, individual choice, and individual responsibility. This atmosphere was successfully created. No structures were set up to aid those in need of help, however. Thatcher's impatience with such artificial structures militated against achieving much equal opportunity under her premiership. The emphasis on wealth creation meant leaving behind a large chunk of unemployed and poor citizens. Dependency became a dirty word, even when some would have it that the helpless did need the necessary social services. The rich became richer with the top 1 percent's earnings growing by 25 percent. The best-off 10 percent earned nine times more than the worst-off 10 percent. However, Thatcher also managed to make such figures acceptable. This was nowhere better illustrated than in the fourth consecutive Conservative victory in 1992, despite high unemployment and a deep recession.

Thatcher's was the age of the individual. Those with guts and stamina could get on. As such, equality of opportunity appeared to have been achieved. By the nature of their disadvantaged position, women, blacks, and the disabled did not benefit much.

Removal from Power

Not long after the tenth anniversary of her accession to power, Thatcher was challenged to a leadership contest by a hitherto little-known member of Parliament. Sir Anthony Meyer's challenge was easily fobbed off, but sixty M.P.s did vote for him—backing his pro-European stance against Thatcher's strident attitude toward Europe. But the year that followed brought more serious problems.

First among these was the community charge, more commonly known as the poll tax. This proved to be an extremely unpopular measure that led to demonstrations all over the country. Thatcher could no longer pretend that such demonstrations—some considerably violent—were to do only with law and order. She refused to budge, nonetheless.

More importantly, there was the question of Europe. In the summer of 1990, one of her ministers, Nicholas Ridley, gave an interview to *The Spectator*, which contained a notorious anti-German statement. In his view, European monetary development was a plot by Germany to take over Europe. He was forced to resign soon afterwards. Then Thatcher's close friend and aide, Ian Gow, was assassinated by the IRA. Despite the expected sympathy vote, the Conservatives lost their Eastbourne seat to the Liberal Democrats. Thatcher was beginning to be seen as an electoral liability by a growing number of Conservatives.

In October 1990 Britain entered the Exchange Rate Mechanism (ERM), despite Thatcher's seeming anti-Europeanism. A schism began to grow between Thatcher and Geoffrey Howe, because the more she appeared to distance herself from Britain's commitments to a single European currency, the more irritated Howe grew. She saw the consequences of ERM as being European federalism with growing state bureaucracy and creeping socialism "by the back door."[62] She rejected such an eventuality vigorously, despite the fact that Britain had joined the ERM.

After one of Thatcher's particularly strident anti-European performances in the House of Commons, Howe resigned. He felt that Thatcher was destroying Britain's chance of influencing developments in Europe. Furthermore, as detailed in his speech to the House, Thatcher's style of management was also in question. He spoke of a conflict between his loyalty to her and his loyalty to the country. The implications of this statement were portentously clear: Thatcher was damaging the country's interests.

Michael Heseltine announced his intention of standing in the forthcoming leadership contest. In order to win at the first ballot, either candidate needed the votes of half the number of M.P.s and a 15 percent lead over the opponent. Both failed to achieve this. Thatcher, in Paris, immediately announced her intention to stand in the second ballot. When she returned to London, she was convinced that she ought to resign, which she promptly did. It was a moment that many remember well—claiming that they recollect exactly where they were when they heard the news, just as they did for President John Kennedy's assassination on the same day twenty-seven years earlier, November 22, 1963.

Thatcher carried on her political career behind the scenes. In August 1991, *The Times* reported her as being the only uncompromising politician to call for the Soviet people "to take to the streets to protest at the coup." She was also the only one to call for allied forces to protect the Kurds from Saddam Hussein after the Persian Gulf War. Her legacy continued, although it was dramatically softened by John Major's approach. In June 1992, Thatcher joined the House of Lords, where she will no doubt continue to lead the fight against European federalism. At the same time, she has continued her work on setting up the Thatcher Foundation, whose influence in diffusing its founder's economic principles will soon be felt in Eastern Europe. In 1991 she was awarded the United States Presidential Medal of Freedom.

Soon after her downfall, I asked a group of young people, who had known no other prime minister, what their perceptions of Thatcher and of her apparent electoral successes were. A sample of their responses was illuminating, despite their apparent simplicity: (1) Her strong personality; (2) a divided opposition; (3) her popularity with the people; (4) her ability to cope; (5) her supporters' value of their vote, more so than the oppositions' supporters; (6) no real alternative; (7) the mess center parties were in; (8) pride in being British; and (9) the fact that she was a real leader.

Perhaps Thatcher's most enduring influence has been the cultural change that she succeeded in effecting throughout Britain. Individual acquisitiveness, thrift, accountability, market forces, competitiveness, and slimline operations have become the norm in British daily life. In 1992, as Labour yet again began to tear itself apart, it appeared that there was still no alternative to Conservatism. It remains to be seen what a fourth successive Conservative term of office, followed by spectacular local election gains, would do with such a legacy.

The image conveyed by Thatcher, both of her leadership qualities and of Britain, can perhaps be best summarized by Mikle Nikitin of Minsk, an ordinary Soviet citizen quoted unaltered and uncorrected in *The Times* after Thatcher's famous visit to the Soviet Union:

I would not like to disturb you, but Margaret Teacher (excuse me, I can't spell correctly) was interviewed on Soviet television today in the evening. That reminded me of you. Even five years ago I could not imagine the possibility of hearing that marvellous interview. We thought all of you were either spies of "capitalist rogues" or "traitors of Soviet people." But nowadays I see a good people well disposed to us. May God bless you. Though our revival remains a very distance dream, let's hope for the best. "Maggi" said good words of support and gave good advice: remedy for us—free business and democracy and get rid of ideological prejudice. We need enterprise and courage, too, said she. Nothing venture nothing have. It would be good for us to obtain this "iron lady" as our leader.[63]

Notes

1. Wendy Webster, *Not a Man to Match Her: The Marketing of a Prime Minister* (London: The Women's Press, 1990), 21.

2. Andrew Thomson, *Margaret Thatcher: The Woman Within* (London: W. H. Allen, 1989), 16.

3. Webster, *Not a Man to Match Her*, 11.

4. Hugo Young, *One of Us: A Biography of Margaret Thatcher* (London: Pan Books, 1990), 217.

5. Ibid., 11.

6. Martin Gilbert, *Never Despair: Winston S. Churchill 1945–1965* (London: Heinemann, 1988), 113.

7. Ibid., 115.

8. Ibid., 119.

9. Kenneth Harris, *Thatcher* (London: Fontana, 1989), 66.

10. Young, *One of Us*, 207.

11. Webster, *Not a Man to Match Her*, 25.

12. Young, *One of Us*, 408.

13. Harris, *Thatcher*, 25.

14. Young, *One of Us*, 66.

15. Ibid., 63.

16. Ibid., 64.

17. Harris, *Thatcher*, 44–45.

18. Young, *One of Us*, 74.

19. Harris, *Thatcher*, 31.

20. Ibid., 35.

21. Ibid., 86.

22. Ibid., 102.

23. Ibid., 109.

24. Ibid., 111.

25. Thomson, *Margaret Thatcher*, 236.

26. Young, *One of Us*, 552.

27. Ibid., 147.

28. Harris, *Thatcher*, 109.

29. Young, *One of Us*, 196.

30. Thomson, *Margaret Thatcher*, 26.

31. Young, *One of Us*, 229.

32. Ibid., 295.

33. Ibid., 425.

34. Ibid., 146.

35. Ibid., 202.

36. Ibid., 207.

37. Ibid., 320.

38. Ibid., 419.

39. Ibid., 174.

40. Ibid., 169.

41. Ibid., 170.

42. Ibid., 174.

43. Ibid., 184.

44. Ibid.

45. Ibid., 265.

46. Ibid., 390.

47. Ibid., 393.

48. Ibid.

49. Ibid., 561.

50. Bernard Ingham, *Kill the Messenger* (London: Harper Collins, 1991), 133.

51. Young, *One of Us*, 229.

52. Ibid., 367.

53. Webster, *Not a Man to Match Her*, 37.

54. Ibid., 38.

55. Ibid., 43.

56. Young, *One of Us*, 111.

57. Ibid., 306.

58. Ibid.

59. Ibid., 139.

60. Thomson, *Margaret Thatcher*, 231.

61. Ibid.

62. Stephen P. Savage and Lynton Robins, eds., *Public Policy under Thatcher* (London: Macmillan, 1990), 20.

63. *The Times*, September 1, 1991, 13.

Chronology

To avoid repetition, "Margaret Thatcher" has been abbreviated to "M.T." in this Chronology.

1925	October	Margaret Thatcher (née Roberts) born in Grantham, Lincolnshire, England
1935	November	M.T. helps as runner between the polling booth and the Conservative party's committee rooms during the general elections
1936	September	M.T. joins Kesteven and Grantham Girls School after completing her primary education at Huntingdontower Road Primary School
1938	March	Hitler invades Austria; an Austrian Jewish pen friend visits the Roberts with stories of Nazi persecution of the Jews
1939	September	World War II breaks out, leaving M.T. with an intense admiration for Winston Churchill's calls to patriotism, self-sacrifice, and courage
1943	July	M.T. completes her sixth form studies, having taken chemistry, biology, and zoology, among other subjects
	October	M.T. goes up to Somerville College (Oxford University) to study chemistry and joins the Oxford University Conservative Association
1945	July	M.T. canvases for the Oxford Conservative candidate, Quintin Hogg, during the general elections;

		canvases against the Grantham Independent candidate, Denis Kendall; first mentioned in the *Grantham Journal*, having been coauthor of the Oxford University Conservative Association subcommittee's report on the association's future organization and aims; Conservatives under Churchill defeated by Labour under Clement Attlee
	August	atom bomb dropped on Hiroshima, Japan
1946		M.T. speaks as delegate to the Federation of Conservative and Unionist Associations; becomes president of the Oxford University Conservative Association; graduates with a second-class degree in chemistry; gets a job as a research chemist at British Xylonite Plastics in Manningtree; joins the Colchester Conservative Association; members of Parliament (M.P.s) have salary raised from £600 to £1,000 per annum; Bank of England nationalized
1948	October	the Conservative Party Conference ends its practice of putting up parliamentary seats to the highest bidder; M.T. attends the party conference as a representative of the Oxford University Graduates Association
	November	Harry Truman reelected President of the United States
1949	February	M.T. nominated and adopted as Conservative parliamentary candidate for Dartford; meets Denis Thatcher
	October	Attlee announces massive cuts in public spending
1950	February	M.T. stands as Conservative candidate for Dartford, losing to the Labour candidate; Labour win general elections by a majority of seventeen; M.T. enrolls at the Council for Legal Education as a part-time law student
	September	wage freeze breaks down as Trade Union Congress (TUC) votes against incomes policy
1951	October	M.T. again loses the Dartford seat; Conservatives win the general elections under Winston Churchill; M.T. reduces the Labour majority by 2,000 over the last elections
	December	M.T. marries Denis Thatcher
1952	January	Alfred Roberts sacked as alderman by the Labour group in Grantham

	February	M.T. publishes an article in the *Sunday Graphic* defending women's right to work and to attain public office; King George VI dies
	November	Dwight D. Eisenhower elected President of the United States
1953	June	coronation of Queen Elizabeth II
	August	M.T. gives birth to twins, Mark and Carol
	December	M.T. passes her bar (law) examinations, eventually joining the Society of Conservative Lawyers; called to the Bar in the next year
1955	April	Winston Churchill retires as prime minister, replaced by Anthony Eden
	May	Conservatives win general elections under Eden
1956	October	Israel attacks Egypt; Anglo–French ultimatum to Egypt and Israel
	November	United Kingdom and France attack Egypt
	December	United Kingdom and France agree to withdraw from Egypt
1957	January	Eden is replaced by Harold Macmillan as prime minister
	July	Macmillan coins his famous "never had it so good" phrase
1958		M.T. becomes Conservative candidate for the safe seat of Finchley
1959	January	Conservative Chancellor of the Exchequer Peter Thorneycroft, along with Nigel Birch and Enoch Powell, resign over excessive public spending
	October	M.T. becomes Conservative Member of Parliament for Finchley with a majority of 16,260; Conservatives win a landslide victory and enter third term of office with a majority of 100; M.T. wins a ballot to introduce a private member's bill (the Public Bodies [Admission to Meetings] Bill), which becomes the 1960 act of the same name
	November	John F. Kennedy elected President of the United States
1961	October	M.T. becomes parliamentary secretary at the Ministry of Pensions
1963	October	Macmillan resigns, replaced by Lord Alec Douglas-Home

	November	President Kennedy assassinated, replaced by Lyndon Johnson
1964	October	Labour wins general elections under Harold Wilson
1965	February	Conservative party introduces new system of electing party leader through M.P.s' votes; appointment of Royal Commission on Reform of Trade Unions and Employers Association chaired by Lord Donovan
	July	Edward Heath elected Conservative Party Leader
	October	M.T. becomes junior minister in Housing and Land
1966	March	Labour wins a large majority under Wilson
	April	M.T. becomes junior minister in the Treasury under Iain Macleod
1967	October	M.T. joins shadow cabinet with portfolio for Fuel and Power, followed by becoming Shadow Minister for Transport
	November	Sterling crisis and devaluation of the pound Sterling
1968	April	Enoch Powell dismissed by Heath after his anti-immigration Rivers of Blood speech
	September	M.T. gives a speech at the party conference (the Conservative Political Centre lecture)
	November	M.T. becomes shadow Minister of Education; Richard Nixon elected President of the United States
1969	January	Wilson's Labour government publishes *In Place of Strife* White Paper on trade unions; later tries and fails to produce law curbing union power
1970	March	Rhodesia declares itself a republic (UDI)
	May	Chronically Sick and Disabled Persons Act; Equal Pay Act
	June	Edward Heath becomes prime minister after the Conservatives win the general elections; M.T. appointed Secretary of State for Education and issues circular 10/70, which stops the pressure on local government schools to go comprehensive
	November	Cecil Parkinson wins a by-election; Industrial Relations Act produced, thus confirming the Heath government reverses on noninterventionist policies and heralding an increase in public spending to prop up lame-duck industries
1972	November	the Heath government agrees on a statutory prices and incomes policy

	December	M.T. brings out the White Paper *Framework for Expansion* on educational developments over the next decade
1973		Britain joins the European Economic Community (EEC); M.T. appointed president of the newly formed Centre for Policy Studies created by Sir Keith Joseph; Sir Alfred Sherman appointed its director
	November	miners take industrial action
	December	three-day week announced to save electricity; big cuts in public spending announced
1974	February	miners decide to strike; Conservatives under Heath lose the general elections by a narrow margin; M.T. given the Shadow Environment post and later moved to shadow responsibility for Treasury affairs
	August	Nixon resigns as President of the United States, replaced by Gerald Ford
	September	Sir Keith Joseph makes his famous Preston speech in which he outlines what became known as "Thatcherism" or "monetarism"
	October	Conservatives lose the second general elections of the year; Sir Keith Joseph, running for the Conservative leadership, makes his speech on eugenics and working-class breeding trends
	November	Sir Keith withdraws from the leadership contest; M.T. puts herself forward
1975	February	M.T. elected leader of the Conservative party in opposition
	September	M.T. makes a highly publicized visit to the United States in answer to critics who deplore her lack of foreign affairs experience; visits to China, the Middle East, and several European nations follow before the general elections of 1979
	October	M.T.'s first party conference as leader
	November	Labour government announces cash limits on public spending
1976	January	M.T. given the famous and much-vaunted sobriquet "The Iron Lady"
	February	public spending White Paper shows massive cuts planned for 1977–78 and 1978–79

	March	Wilson resigns and is replaced by James Callaghan; inflation reaches 26 percent after the Retail Price Index went up 75 percent in 1975; public sector borrowing increases as a result of huge borrowing by the Labour government
	July	Labour government pushes through public expenditure cuts of £1 billion
	September	Callaghan publicly embraces monetarism and breaks with Keynesian methods; M.T. visits India, where she strikes up a close and easy friendship with Indira Gandhi
	October	Labour government agrees to the International Monetary Fund (IMF) imposition of monetary targets as a condition of its loan (a first sign of the move from Keynesianism to monetarism in practical terms); a further £2.5 billion program of cuts is agreed upon
	November	Jimmy Carter elected President of the United States
1977	March	Labour's majority in Parliament secured after a formal pact with the Liberal party
	June	M.T. speaks of Europe not as an economic entity but as a military one against the Soviet Union and a political one against the forces of the left
	October	the Economic Reconstruction Group produces its Conservative economic policy booklet, *The Right Approach to the Economy*
1978	January	M.T. makes her famous declaration about the legitimate fears of white Britons of being "swamped by people with a different culture"
	February	inflation falls below 10 percent
	March	Dennis Healey produces Labour's last budget, reflating the economy by £2.5 billion
	May	the Lib–Lab pact collapses after the Liberals withdraw their support; Labour kept in power by Welsh and Scottish M.P.s
	July	Callaghan and M.T. clash over the government's White Paper on pay policy; M.T. condemns all forms of incomes policies as a waste of time
	September	Amidst strong election fever, Callaghan announces that there is to be no election in 1978—much to the disgust of trade unions

	October	Heath attacks M.T.'s rejection of an incomes policy; M.T. promises a return to free collective bargaining; Labour ahead by 5.5 points in the polls
1979	January	Callaghan returns from the Guadeloupe summit refusing to acknowledge what becomes to be known as "the winter of discontent" in which strikes cripple the United Kingdom; M.T. calls on Callaghan "to re-establish the authority of the Government under the law" (i.e., curb union powers)
	February	the Government cedes to the unions by awarding pay settlements above the pay limit increase of 5 percent; the Trades Union Congress (TUC) agrees to produce a voluntary code of behavior on picketing, strike ballots, closed shop and strikes
	March	The Clegg Commission on pay comparability set up; Thatcher announces that the Conservatives would implement its recommendations in the event of winning the elections; referenda on Welsh and Scottish devolution go against; Scottish and Welsh M.P.s withdraw their support from the Labour Government; Airey Neave, close friend and colleague of M.T., is killed by the Irish National Liberation Army (INLA)
	April	M.T. tables a motion of no confidence in the Labour government; government defeated; general elections called for May 3
	May	the Conservatives win the general elections with a majority of 43 seats; M.T. becomes prime minister and puts together a mixed cabinet of Heathite and monetarists (the latter becoming her inner cabinet); pay raises for the police (20 percent) and the armed forces (32 percent)
	June	Geoffrey Howe's first budget, which embodies Thatcherism, comes out with a 3 percent basic rate tax cut and a 23 percent top rate tax cut; an increase in value-added tax to 15 percent is brought in, as are many other measures such as tighter monetary targets through a reduction in the Public Sector Borrowing Requirement (PSBR), a cut in public expenditure, and an increase of 2 percent on the minimum lending rate
	July	public spending cuts of £3.6 billion agreed in cabinet; M.T. makes a speech in which she commits her

		government to international consultations over Rhodesia
	August	Commonwealth Conference in Lusaka agrees the setting up of a constitutional conference in London to bring Rhodesia to full independence
	September	Bernard Ingham appointed Thatcher's press secretary
	November	M.T. launches her aggressive and initially unsuccessful bid to have Britain's contribution to Europe cut by £1,000 million at the EEC Dublin summit; exchange controls are abolished; M.T. makes parliamentary statement confirming that Anthony Blunt was a Soviet agent; cuts in public spending of £3.5 billion announced for 1980–81
	December	Soviet Union invades Afghanistan
1980	January	steel strike begins at the British Steel Corporation
	February	M.T. undermines Jim Prior's compromise union law by declaring that strikers would be denied social security benefit by being deemed to be receiving strike pay from their union; Sir Ian Gilmour speaks publicly against M.T.'s monetarist policies as being a threat to social order and a threat to political freedom leading to electoral defeat; M.T. survives a no confidence motion
	March	a further monetarist budget is produced
	April	Lord Cockfield tells the House of Lords that monetarism is as logical as a mathematical certainty; Rhodesia becomes the independent Zimbabwe; steel strike over with a much-reduced pay settlement; inflation reaches 21.8 percent
	May	a compromise on a much-increased rebate over three years is made on Britain's contribution to the EEC; M.T. is defeated in cabinet as she backs down over an unpalatable fait accompli, although she eventually gains a permanent deal in June 1984
	July	Employment Act of 1980 restricts picketing and secondary action; inflation reaches 20 percent after having dropped to 10 percent toward the end of the Labour government
	October	cabinet meeting to discuss further public spending cuts is faced with a bleak economic forecast; Agricul-

		ture Minister Peter Walker and leader of the House Norman St. John Stevas make veiled calls for moderation at the Conservative party conference; M.T. utters her famous pun "You turn if you want to. The lady's not for turning"; Callaghan replaced by Michael Foot as leader of the opposition Labour party
	November	Francis Pym threatens to resign and gets most of the money requested by his Defence department; Nicholas Ridley arrives in the Falkland Islands to test his eventually rejected proposed transfer of sovereignty to Argentina, with immediate long-term leaseback to Britain; Ronald Reagan elected President of the United States
	December	M.T. attends her first Anglo-Irish summit in Dublin
1981	January	Norman St. John Stevas removed from his office as leader of the House; Francis Pym moved from Defence to replace him; John Nott becomes Defence Minister and is replaced by John Biffen in Trade, Leon Brittan becomes Chief Secretary at the Treasury; Cecil Parkinson becomes Minister for Trade; Alan Walters becomes Thatcher's economic adviser; the Social Democratic Party created by Labour party dissidents
	February	M.T. is the first foreign leader to visit the new U.S. president; defends the decision to withdraw HMS *Endurance* from the Falklands; inflation down to 13 percent
	March	M.T. awarded honorary doctorate by Georgetown University in the United States; budget cuts PSBR by £3.5 million, increasing personal and indirect taxes; civil servants launch selective strike action in pursuit of a 15 percent pay increase demand
	April	serious inner city riots take place in Brixton, South London
	May	SAS storm Iranian Embassy in London, ending a siege that had lasted several weeks; IRA leader Bobby Sands dies after a sixty-six-day hunger strike in Long Kesh prison
	July	Toxteth riots break out in Liverpool; Howe suggests a further public spending cut of £5,000 million in 1982–83; most ministers in the cabinet go against this proposal with unprecedented vigor; civil servants call

off their industrial action after accepting 7.5 percent pay increase; John Nott withdraws his support for further spending cuts; M.T. and Charles Haughey disagree on Northern Ireland during a European summit in Holland

September   cabinet reshuffle throws out Ian Gilmour, Mark Carlisle, and Christopher Soames; Jim Prior is moved to Northern Ireland; Nigel Lawson, Cecil Parkinson, and Norman Tebbit brought in

October   an opinion poll shows 28 percent of electorate satisfied with Thatcher, as opposed to 65 percent dissatisfied

November   Ian Bancroft retires early as Permanent Secretary at the Civil Service Department, and its responsibilities and duties go to the Treasury; Shirley Williams of the Social Democrats wins a by-election and enters Parliament; Lord Scarman's report on the Brixton riots is published

December   an opinion poll shows that only 23 percent of voters think that Thatcher is doing a good job; Jaruzelski declares martial law in a military take-over in Poland; United States imposes sanctions against the Soviet Union

1982   January   M.T.'s son Mark disappears for six days during a trans-Sahara motor rally

February   Pym gives a speech attacking what he perceives as inappropriate economic optimism; Sir Terence Lewin, chief of the Defence Staff, becomes M.T.'s personal defense adviser

March   a popular tax-cutting budget is produced, remaining essentially monetarist though easing up by revising the money supply target; Argentina occupies the Falklands dependency of South Georgia; M.T. urges Defence Secretary Nott and Foreign Secretary Carrington to prepare adequate response; Roy Jenkins of the Social Democrats wins a by-election and enters Parliament

April   Argentina invades the Falklands; Lord Carrington resigns from the Foreign Office, along with his deputy Richard Luce; Nott's resignation from Defence is rejected; Pym becomes new Foreign Secretary; war cabinet formed with Thatcher, Whitelaw, Pym, Nott,

		Parkinson, and Sir Terence Lewin; White Paper on rolling devolution for Northern Ireland published; South Georgia recaptured
	May	Argentinian cruiser the *General Belgrano* sunk by British submarine with a loss of 368 sailors, HMS *Sheffield* destroyer hit by Argentinian Exocet missile; British troops start landing at San Carlos; *Ardent*, *Antelope*, *Coventry*, and *Atlantic Conveyor* sunk by Argentinians
	June	Galahad and Tristram bombed, with fifty-one persons killed; British forces liberate the Falklands from Argentina; M.T.'s personal rating in the opinion polls rises to 51 percent, Reagan visits Britain and addresses both houses of Parliament
	July	rail strike flounders as some union members ignore the call to strike and report to work; M.T. angered by Archbishop Runcie's prayers for both British and Argentinian soldiers during a victory thanksgiving service; gives a speech castigating feminism and arguing that "the battle for women's rights has largely been won"
	September	a paper proposing stringent cuts in public spending is leaked to *The Economist*
	October	Employment Act of 1982 allows for civil damages against unions taking unlawful industrial action and provides for government funds for union ballots on wage disputes
1983	January	M.T. holds private discussions about the possible date of the next general elections; makes a triumphant visit to the Falklands, where she is awarded the Freedom of the Falklands; Michael Heseltine becomes Minister for Defence, Franks Committee clears government of negligence on Falklands
	February	Social Democrats win another by-election
	March	Reagan announces his Strategic Defence Initiative (SDI), known as Star Wars
	April	M.T.'s popularity increases significantly in the polls
	May	unemployment reaches three million; M.T. meets Alexander Solzhenitsyn and discusses the pernicious power of fashion to impose an intellectual censorship as evil as that of Russia

June	the Conservatives win landslide general elections victory with a 144 seat majority in the new Parliament; Pym is replaced by Howe as Foreign Minister, and Howe is replaced by Nigel Lawson in the Treasury; Leon Brittan becomes Home Secretary, replacing Whitelaw who moves into the House of Lords; Parkinson becomes Minister for Trade, soon to be amalgamated with Industry; Peter Walker appointed Secretary of State for Energy; Stuttgart summit flounders on Britain's contribution to Europe; Central Policy Review Staff (Think Tank) disbanded; inflation down to 3.7 percent
July	Chancellor calls for emergency public spending cuts after an increase of 1.5 percent in interest rate
October	241 U.S. marines killed by a car bomb in Beirut; United States invades Grenada after Maurice Bishop is murdered by extreme Marxists; Neil Kinnock elected Labour party leader; Cecil Parkinson resigns
December	the Athens summit fails to agree on Britain's contribution to Europe
1984 January	trade unions barred from operating in the Government Communications Headquarters (GCHQ); employees are offered £1,000 in compensation
March	National Union of Mineworkers (NUM) go on strike after a period of a ban on overtime in previous months; Brussels summit fails to agree on Britain's contribution to Europe
June	the Fontainebleau summit succeeds in agreeing on a mechanism for Britain's contribution to Europe; in a by-election the Liberal–SDP Alliance wins Portsmouth from the Conservatives
August	Clive Ponting, a senior official at the Ministry of Defence, is charged with leaking *Belgrano* documents
September	Prior is replaced by Douglas Hurd in Northern Ireland
October	in the Brighton Grand Hotel, M.T. survives a bomb explosion that kills five and injures many, including Norman Tebbit and John Wakeham; M.T. climbs down and agrees on a compromise to avert a worsening of the miners' strike through action by pit deputies' unions (Nacods); NUM's assets sequestered

	November	Britain and France agree to build the Channel Tunnel; Reagan quashes the antitrust actions against British Airways before they get to court; M.T. and Fitzgerald hold their second summit on Anglo–Irish relations
	December	Mikhail Gorbachev visits London four months before taking office and has a successful series of meetings with M.T.; M.T. agrees on a treaty with China over the future of Hong Kong; during a visit to the United States, M.T. succeeds in reordering U.S. priorities on arms-control talks, including SDI (Star Wars); M.T. nominated for an honorary doctorate in the Oxford University Gazette; Tory revolt stops Sir Keith Joseph's plan to make parents who can afford it pay more toward student grants; bill to abolish Greater London Council (GLC) passed
1985	January	by 738 votes to 319 the dons of Oxford refuse to grant M.T. an honorary degree; Bernard Ingham (Thatcher's press secretary) infuriates Lawson by briefing the press that her belief in market power means that the prime minister would not object to a one-dollar pound; Michael Heseltine resigns from the cabinet over the Westland affair and over M.T.'s leadership style; Leon Brittan resigns after the Westland debacle; Harold Macmillan, now earl of Stockton, condemns current Conservative economic policies
	February	M.T. addresses a joint session of the U.S. Congress affirming her support for Reagan's SDI decisions; Cabinet Secretary Robert Armstrong appears before the Parliamentary Select Committee on Defence to answer questions on Westland
	March	miners vote to return to work; teachers start their industrial action
	May	Francis Pym unsuccessfully launches his Centre Forward, a pressure group inside the parliamentary Conservative party
	July	in a by-election the Liberal–SDP Alliance wins Brecon and Radnor from the Conservatives
	September	an ex parte injunction is obtained by the attorney general in New South Wales, restraining the publication of Peter Wright's *Spycatcher* in Australia by

		Heinemann; Norman Tebbit appointed chairman of the Conservative party; riots in Brixton
	October	Commonwealth conference in Nassau agrees on a ban on the import of gold Krugerrands and an end to government assistance for trade delegations and exhibitions in South Africa; riots in Tottenham, London
	November	The Irish Taoiseach Garret Fitzgerald and M.T. sign the Anglo–Irish Agreement, which allows for some joint management of security problems in the North
	December	the Archbishop of Canterbury's commission publishes *Faith in the City* attacking Conservative policies and their effect on urban decay; terrorists attack Rome and Vienna airports; White Paper published scaling down the state earnings-related pension scheme (Serps)
1986	January	Libya's Muammar el-Qaddafi threatens retaliation against West European cities if attacked by the United States; plans for the Channel rail tunnel announced
	April	United States bombs Libya after a terrorist attack in Berlin; F-111 bombers based in Britain are used for the attack
	May	at the world economic summit in Tokyo the Reagan–Thatcher declaration on terrorism is accepted; in a by-election the Liberal–SDP Alliance wins Ryedale from the Conservatives; Sir Keith Joseph resigns and is replaced by Kenneth Baker as Education Secretary
	July	plans for the sale of water postponed
	October	Reagan and Gorbachev in Reykjavik, Iceland, stall on their agreement to eliminate all strategic forces after Reagan refuses to stop SDI
	November	M.T. convinces Reagan of the necessity of a European nuclear deterrence as part of NATO's strategy
	December	British Gas privatized
1987	February	court allows the publication of Peter Wright's *Spycatcher*
	March	M.T. arrives in Moscow for a highly publicized and successful visit
	May	general elections called by M.T.
	June	Conservatives win a third successive general election with a majority of 104 seats; Labour's share of the

		vote second worst since 1931, with number of its M.P.s second lowest since 1935
1988	April	the budget includes a cut in the top rate of tax to 40 percent
	May	M.T. delivers her General Assembly of the Church of Scotland speech, relating Christianity with individual responsibility including that of making money
	July	Department of Health and Social Security split into two separate departments; Alan Walters returns as M.T.'s personal economic adviser
	September	M.T. makes her famous Bruges speech in which she attacks the European Community for its bureaucracy and defends Britain's sovereignty
	November	George Bush is elected President of the United States
1989	January	Bush shifts from London to Bonn in Euro–American relations
	June	the Conservatives defeated in the European Parliamentary elections; after Lawson and Howe threaten to resign Britain accepts membership of the European Monetary System (EMS) during the Madrid summit, in principle—promising to do so when United Kingdom inflation is down to French and German levels, thus acceding to stage one of the Delors plan
	July	M.T. upsets the French by declaring, during the celebrations for the bicentennial of the French Revolution, that freedom is a British creation and that the French Revolution only has claim to terror; M.T. reshuffles her cabinet, removing all her opponents (except Lawson), moving Geoffrey Howe to Leader of the House, and conceding deputy premiership to him; John Major is appointed Foreign Minister
	September	M.T. cancels scientific research into the role of heterosexual behavior in the spread of AIDS; Alan Walters takes up his post as M.T.'s personal economic adviser
	October	Nigel Lawson resigns as Chancellor of the Exchequer, claiming lack of trust by M.T. and interference by Alan Walters; John Major appointed Chancellor of the Exchequer and Douglas Hurd moved from the Home Office to the Foreign Office; Sir Anthony Meyer challenges M.T. for the leadership and eventually loses in November

	November	at the Lord Mayor's Banquet, M.T. talks of the collapse of Communism as a result of "a battle of ideas"
1990	May	the Conservatives do better in the local elections than expected, with successes in London despite the unpopularity of the poll tax
	July	Nicholas Ridley resigns after making a trenchantly anti-German and anti-European statement in an interview; Ian Gow, M.T.'s former parliamentary private secretary, is assassinated by the IRA; his seat is won by the Liberal Democrats in a by-election
	October	Britain joins the ERM; interest rate cut by one percent; the principle of a single currency accepted, conditional on eventual ratification by people and government; M.T. declares herself against European federalism
	November	Geoffrey Howe resigns, quoting Thatcher's anti-Europeanism as his reason for doing so; Kenneth Baker, as party chairman, plays down the resignation as about mood and style; Howe delivers a House of Commons speech attacking M.T.'s views on Europe and her management style; Heseltine challenges M.T. in the leadership contest; neither wins the required half of the total votes plus 15 percent more than the losing opponent; M.T. withdraws her nomination; John Major wins, becoming Britain's prime minister after M.T. resigns
1992	March	M.T. is made Chancellor of the University of Buckingham
	April	Conservatives win fourth successive general elections with Major as Prime Minister
	May	Conservatives continue their winning streak in the local elections
	June	M.T. joins the House of Lords as Baroness Thatcher of Kesteven in her native county of Lincolnshire; at the Lisbon European summit Major launches his bid to "curb the EC monster" and to ensure subsidiarity (devolving decision making to member countries); Lady Thatcher describes Maastricht as "a treaty too far"
	July	M.T. calls for a referendum on Maastricht; alleges that governments have lost touch with the people who no longer exercise choice; Prime Minister Major calls

anti-Europeans "little Englanders bereft of hope" and indirectly blames M.T. for keeping Britain on the periphery of Europe; M.T. is paid $1 million to act as an ad hoc consultant to the tobacco company Philip Morris; John Smith replaces Neil Kinnock as leader of the Labour Party; Margaret Beckett is elected deputy leader

I Newspapers and Periodicals

What follows is a very limited selection from newspapers and periodicals. The criteria for compiling these particular entries are twofold: (1) To complement any gaps in the rest of the bibliography; and (2) to provide, coupled with the biography and chronology, a panoramic view of Margaret Thatcher's life, her reactions to events, and her encroachment on every aspect of the British way of life. Readers requiring further information should consult the relevant indices and on-line databases available. Periodical article titles are available from the Public Affairs Information Service, Inc., New York, NY (PAIS International).

A. General Newspapers and Periodicals

1. Barnett, A. "Where there's froth." *New Statesman.* August 26th 1988: 23.

2. Haeger, Robert A. "Britain Learns Thatcher Means Business." *U.S. News.* August 20th 1979: 24+.

   Reports that Thatcher is off to a new quick start in honouring her pledge to turn her country around.

3. Haeger, Robert A. "Britain's Thatcher Swims against the Tide." *U.S. News.* May 12th 1980: 41–42.

   After her first year in office, Thatcher admits that it could take her Government years to achieve prosperity for Britain.

4. Haeger, Robert A. "Is Maggie Losing the New Battle of Britain?" *U.S. News*. December 24th 1979: 27–30.

Argues that although the Thatcher Government began on a note of great optimism; her first months in office have cast a shadow over her future. This article is part of the gloom and doom faced, and eventually overcome, by Thatcher.

5. *Hansard*. See *Parliamentary Debates*, number 44 below.

Hansard is the verbatim record of parliamentary proceedings now officially published as *Parliamentary Debates*.

6. Harris, R. "Prima donna inter pares." *Observer*. January 3rd 1988: 17–18.

7. Harris, Ralph. "Thatcherissima: The Economics of Thatcherism." *Policy Review*. Fall 1983: 30–40.

One of three consecutive articles on Thatcherism.

8. Heath, E. "A State of Secrecy." *New Statesman*. March 10th 1989.

9. Hennessy, Peter. "How to be 'viewy' and survive." *New Statesman*. August 28th 1987: 10.

10. Hoggart, S. "Thatcher: public face private life." *Observer Magazine*. December 2nd 1990: 9.

11. Honor, Tracy. "Don't Listen to Nanny." *Daily Telegraph*. June 30th 1984.

12. Johnson, Christopher. "Britain: The Thatcher Record." *World Today*. May 1987: 77–80.

Discusses economic growth, productivity, unemployment, inflation and fiscal policy under Thatcher.

13. Johnson, Paul. "Margaret Thatcher: the lady's not for turning." *Public Opinion*. February 1981: 15–18.

U-turns bedeviled Heath's Conservative Government. When it was suggested that Thatcher do likewise she responded by declaring that "the lady's not for turning" an obvious pun on "The Lady's Not For Burning," a play by Christopher Fry.

14. Johnson, Paul. "Still the Best Man in the Cabinet." *Daily Mail*. May 1st 1982.

A reference to Thatcher's so-called masculine qualities of strength, single mindedness and assertiveness.

15. Johnson, Paul. "The Strongest Head—but the Softest Heart Too!" *Daily Mail*. October 13th 1984.

16. Kellner, Peter. "For better, for worse." *Independent*. May 2nd 1989: 19.

17. Kellner, Peter. "Hopes and fears of 'Thatcher's children'." *Independent*. May 3rd 1989: 4.

By 1989 many teenagers and young persons knew no other Prime Minister other than Thatcher. They were referred to as Thatcher's children.

18. Kellner, Peter. "Mrs. Thatcher's vision of a fifteen-year Reich." *New Statesman*. May 4th 1984: 7.

Thatcher's Premiership lasted a total of just over eleven and a half years. With their victory in 1992 the Conservatives would have been in power some eighteen years by the next election in 1997 at the latest.

19. Kellner, Peter. " 'Palace': the soap opera where Thatcher plays JR." *New Statesman*. July 25th 1982: 9.

20. Kellner, Peter. "Remember, remember the fifth of November." *New Statesman*. September 12th 1986: 9.

21. Kellner, Peter. "Thatcherism: The Unfinished Jigsaw." *New Statesman*. December 18th 1987.

22. Kellner, Peter. "Thatcherite gospel leaves masses unmoved." *Independent*. May 4th 1989: 4.

23. Kellner, Peter. "Why Tory wets want Thatcher to stay as leader." *New Statesman*. February 21st 1986: 9.

Even Thatcher's most committed opponents within the Conservative Party recognised Thatcher as their electoral ace. This opinion began to be reversed in 1990 when Thatcher first began to be perceived as an electoral liability.

24. Kexiong, Cheng. "Local elections signal Thatcher victory." *Beijing Review*. May 25th 1987: 12–13.

The local elections of May 1987 indicated that the Conservatives were almost certainly heading for victory which they eventually achieved in June.

25. Knight, John. "The Lady's Not for Turning . . . Grey." *Sunday Mirror Magazine.* July 23rd 1989.

See note to Paul Johnson, number 13 above.

26. Lloyd, J. "Fashioned in her own image." *Financial Times.* November 24th 1990: 1.

27. Malcolm, N. "Mrs. Thatcher goes on and on." *Spectator.* July 7th 1990: 9–10.

Written at the height of speculation on Thatcher becoming an electoral liability to her Party.

28. Marrin, M. "Cherchez la femme." *Spectator.* April 15th 1989: 13–14.

29. Matveyev, Vladimir. "The Neo-Conservative Music." *Moscow New Times.* Number 52, December 1981: 26–28.

A critical analysis of Conservative Party policies under Thatcher.

30. NcNeill, P. "The battle for common sense." *New Statesman.* October 21st 1988: 26.

31. New Statesman. "Here be demons." *New Statesman.* March 23rd 1989: 4.

32. New Statesman. "History lessons." *New Statesman.* July 21st 1989: 4.

A facetious look at Thatcher.

33. New Statesman. "Mrs. Thatcher and the Oman contract." *New Statesman.* April 6th 1984: 17.

On her son Mark's and her own involvement in the Oman contract.

34. New Statesman. "The PM's royal wedding week." *New Statesman.* July 25th 1986: 3–4.

35. New Statesman. "Thatcher's fatal flaws." *New Statesman.* October 4th 1985: 10–11.

36. New Statesman. "Vale of cheers? on the tenth anniversary of her regime, Mrs. Thatcher's power may be on the wane." *New Statesman.* May 5th 1989: 4.

37. New Statesman. "Victorian values: historians take issue with Mrs. Thatcher." *New Statesman.* May 27th 1983: i–xvi.

Thatcher was perceived as harping on Victorian values. Where she meant the Samuel Smiles Victorian values of thrift, self-help and hard work, her opponents highlighted the Victorian hypocricies of repression, double standards and social indifference to the less fortunate.

38. O'Sullivan, J. "Britain: under the iron (high) heel?" *Commentary.* September 1989: 47–52.

39. O'Sullivan, J. "Thatcherization." *Commentary.* Summer 1983: 47–54.

40. Otten, Alan L. "The Conservative Mrs. Thatcher." *Wall Street Journal.* June 8th 1979: 18.

41. Otten, Alan L. "Tory Trend." *Wall Street Journal.* January 14th 1981: 1+.

Shows how Thatcher is losing many Britons' support as the recession drags on. Despite all this, there is a strong cadre of loyal Thatcher backers.

42. Owen, G. and Rutherford, M. "A profound change of climate." *Financial Times.* April 9th 1987: 15.

43. Pallister, David. "Finance workaholic's fast lane to riches." *Guardian.* November 23rd 1991: 4.

Son Mark's fortunes built on electronics, leasing and telecommunications.

44. *Parliamentary Debates: House of Commons Official Report.* London: Her Majesty's Stationery Office.

More commonly known as *Hansard*, the regularly published transcript of everything said in Parliament.

45. Pearce, Edward. "The balaclava factor." *Encounter.* April 1984: 34–36.

46. Pearce, Edward. "London commentary: the falling fruits of power." *Encounter.* May 1984: 44–46.

47. Raw, C. "A scoop backfires." *New Statesman.* March 30th 1984: 11.

On the Oman contract and Mark Thatcher.

48. Revzin, Philip. "Toughing It out." *Wall Street Journal.* May 2nd 1980: 1+.

Despite Britain's economic ills, the article shows Thatcher as staying strong politically.

49. Revzin, Philip. "Tough Tory." *Wall Street Journal*. December 17th 1979: 1+.

Thatcher is seen as encountering criticism despite her early successes.

50. Rogers, R. "She-bear in her pride." See P. Wintour, number 925 below.

51. Rook, Jean. "The Best MAN in England? Maggie's a Female Task Force." *Daily Express*. January 12th 1983.

Right wing commentators were unashamedly happy to use sexist language to describe their political idol.

52. Rook, Jean. See Margaret Thatcher, number 455 below.

53. Rook, Jean. See Margaret Thatcher, number 551 below.

54. Rook, Jean. "Tough Cookies Margaret—All the Right Ingredients." *Daily Express*. November 27th 1974.

Another admiring look at Thatcher as tough and uncompromising.

55. Rusbridgen, A. "Funny peculiar." *Guardian*. July 23rd 1988: 19.

Satirical piece.

56. Shepherd, R. "The Court of Queen Margaret." *Guardian*. July 29th 1989.

57. Skidelsky, R. "Britain under Mrs. Thatcher." *Encounter*. January 1985: 55–62.

58. Spectator. "Behind Maggie's stony face." *Spectator*. August 6th 1988: 23.

59. Stein, Herbert. "Britain and the Ordeal of Margaret Thatcher." *Wall Street Journal*. February 25th 1981: 28.

60. Stein, Herbert. "What Margaret Thatcher Knows." *American Enterprise Institute Economist*. August 1979: 1–12.

Analyses the economic policies of the Conservative Government.

61. Stothard, P. "Thatcher's complaint." *New Statesman*. May 18th 1979: 704.

62. Toman, Barbara. "Thatcher's Gamble." *Wall Street Journal.* November 6th 1989: 1+.

Discusses the problems facing Docklands, a property development project on the former site of London's East End docks. One of the major city developments, Canary Wharf, was in serious financial trouble in 1992.

63. Toman, Barbara. "Tory Paradox." *Wall Street Journal.* June 1988: 1+.

Illustrating that in Thatcher's Britain, freer enterprise leads to more state control, despite Conservative Party gospel. Thatcher is seen as centralising power over taxation, schools and the British Broadcasting Corporation (BBC).

64. Trend, M. "The Queen is utterly disgusted." *Spectator.* April 8th 1989: 20–22.

Thatcher's relationship with the Queen was subject to much debate. Anecdotes abounded about the frostiness of their meetings. It became difficult to separate fact from fiction. The relationship was probably strictly proprietorial with Thatcher being as deferential as expected.

65. Truell, Peter and Revzin, Philip. "Mrs. Thatcher's Finance Minister." *Wall Street Journal.* July 22nd 1983: 16.

An analysis of the economic strategy of Nigel Lawson, the then new Chancellor of the Exchequer.

66. U.S. News. "Thatcher's Economic Woes: A Lesson for the U.S.?" *U.S. News.* March 2nd 1981: 29–30.

An interview with the leading British industrialist Sir David Orr.

67. Walden, Brian. See Margaret Thatcher, number 462 below.

68. Wheen, F. "Is Maggie on the slide?" *New Statesman.* October 12th 1979: 537.

Thatcher went through a period of seeming indecision as inflation rose and Britain continued its economic decline in the first year of her administration.

69. Worsthorne, Peregrine. "Can They Forgive Her?" *Sunday Telegraph.* November 27th 1988.

70. Young, Hugo. "The lady's not for turning." *Guardian.* April 4th 1989: 25+.

See note to Paul Johnson, number 13 above.

71. Young, Hugo. "One of us, but different." *Guardian*. April 8th 1989:
     21.

"One of us" is the title of Young's biography of Thatcher. Thatcher was said to have always asked, "Is he one of us?" before appointing anyone. Eventually, Hugo's analysis turns this question on its head by projecting Thatcher herself as "one of us" (i.e., of the people). Young's book *One of Us* is the most definitive biography of Thatcher to date (see number 486 below).

72. Young, Hugo. "Thatcher's airborne debacle." *Guardian*. April 7th
     1989: 25–26.

73. Young, Hugo. "Thatcher V. the intellectuals." *Guardian*. April 6th
     1989: 21–22.

Thatcher's attitude was at best ambivalent and at worst outrightly hostile. She apparently regarded intellectuals as unworldly wise. She regarded only persons of action and deeds as those genuinely contributing to Britain's good. They were seen as wealth creators.

74. Young, Hugo. "The Thatcher years." *Guardian*. 23rd November
     1990: 21–26.

An assessment written immediately after Thatcher's resignation on 22nd November 1990.

B. *The Economist*

The Economist, being a British weekly, obviously covered Thatcher's career regularly and with in-depth analysis. Entries given below are selected on the basis of the criteria given in the general introduction of this chapter.

1979

75. "Britain's proposition." March 24th: 12–13.

76. "Mistress of Downing Street." May 5th: 13–14.

77. "Industrial policy: Mrs. Thatcher's awkward inheritance." May 5th:
     120–21.

78. "Anatomy of Thatcherland." May 12th: 17–18+.

Analysis of major ministrial appointments in Thatcher's first cabinet.

79. "Cabinet-maker." May 12th: 13–14.

Argues that Thatcher has made a virtue of balancing her cabinet, showing that a tough race has started off well.

80. "A cheery wave to Europe." May 19th: 17.

Showing how the Thatcher Government could take the first step towards putting the pound in the European Monetary System which Thatcher eventually did eleven years later in 1990 by joining the Exchange Rate Mechanism (ERM).

81. "Briefcase debutante." June 30th: 40.

82. "Rearrange the molecules before going nuclear." July 7th: 111–12.

Reports on Thatcher's atomic power expansion programme.

83. "Her instinct is wrong." July 14th: 13.

84. "Doing it her way?" September 22nd: 13–16.

85. "Glorious morning again." October 13th: 18.

1980

86. "Two terms into one won't go." February 2nd: 63–65.

Shows that the Treasury's own economic model suggests that Thatcher's economic strategy won't have paid political dividends by the time of the next general elections. This forecast was largely true but the Falklands factor helped Thatcher win the said elections.

87. "Queen of the May?" May 3rd: 20–21.

88. "Britain's two prime ministers." October 4th: 11–13.

1981

89. "Go take a break." April 18th: 13–14.

90. "Anatomy of a leak." July 4th: 62–63.

Discusses how Thatcher can get on better with the press and reduce the scale of cabinet leaks.

91. "Second-stage Thatcherism." August 8th: 11–12.

Suggests that second-stage Thatcherism should mean going back to Tory first principles of cutting inflation and taxation.

92. ["Lady with any lamp?" October 10th: 11–12.

Argues that Thatcher has marked up some dreadful economic statistics and some real achievements. Proposes ways in which she could get interest rates down.

93. "Mrs. Thatcher at mid-term: portrait of a Prime Minister at bay." October 10th: 19–22.

Thatcher's popularity hit rock-bottom by the end of 1981. After the Falklands War of 1982 her popularity rocketed leading her on to an overwhelming victory in 1983.

94. "Thatcher's midnight visitors." October 17th: 13–14.

95. "Seven winter suggestions." November 7th: 15–16.

Gives measures that the Thatcher Government could sensibly introduce, in order to bring unemployment down.

1982

96. "The principle." April 17th: 11–13.

Analyses Thatcher's and Britain's position on the Falklands crisis.

97. "Elizabeth or Boadicea?" May 1st: 11–12.

Discusses Thatcher's handling of the Falklands crisis after the Argentinian invasion.

98. "Thatcher's think-tank takes aim at the welfare state." September 18th: 57–58.

A discussion of the paper prepared by the Government's think-tank of the Central Policy Review Staff proposing major changes in social policy.

99. "Will her luck hold?" October 2nd: 13–14.

Thatcher was dubbed a very "lucky" Prime Minister with events favouring her policies. The title speaks for itself but her luck did hold out—for another eight years.

100. "Mountains out of molehills." October 9th: 58+.

A think-tank report was leaked to *The Economist*, causing a major furor over proposed cuts in welfare public spending. The article argues that the Thatcher Government should publish the report as part of a wider debate on the issues. By 1990 much of what was said in the report had been carried into practice.

101. "Britain's Foreign Office." November 27th: 19–20+.

Relations between Thatcher and the Foreign and Commonwealth Office during the time of Lord Carrington.

1983

102. "Issuc is Thatcher." May 14th: 11.

1984

103. "Mrs. Thatcher starts to plan her third term." January 21st: 47.

104. "She loses by winning." March 3rd: 13.

105. "Silence is leaden." March 10th: 57.

On Mark Thatcher and the Oman contract.

1985

106. "Thatcher under pressure." October 5th: 11–13.

107. "Money for most: the Thatcher Government believes that economic prosperity is founded on business enterprise." October 26th: 72–73.

1986

108. "Thatcher impaired." February 1st: 12–13.

109. "Keep Thatcher." February 15th: 13–14.

110. "She reads him, too." April 19th: 76.

On Thatcher's speech on W. Bagehot.

111. "The Queen and her Prime Minister." July 26th: 51–52.

See note to M. Trend, number 64 above.

112. "Give her a break." August 9th: 37–38.

1987

113. "Thatcher again?" January 3rd: 10–11.

114. "The blue-eyed lady." April 4th: 14–15.

On Thatcher's visit to the Soviet Union.

115. "Mr. Bull's world." May 3rd: 12–13.

116. "Mrs. Thatcher: a profile: a woman with a mission." June 6th: 37+.

Thatcher's political career was certainly seen by her as missionary. Her language was often messianic.

117. "A woman with a mission." June 6th: 61–62.

118. "The warning in her win." June 13th: 11–12.

119. "Election Britain; third term Thatcher." June 13th: 17–18+.

Analyses Thatcher's general election victory of 1987 with a look at the British electoral system.

120. "Conservative economics." October 24th: 23–24+.

The Cambridge University Press published a special issue on economic policy "The Conservative Revolution." The article concentrates on the Thatcher–Reagan claim to have rewritten the rules of economic policy during the 1980s.

121. "Making a European of Mrs. Thatcher." December 12th: 57–58.

Thatcher's crusade against European federalism is well documented. She has a strong suspicion of many things European including issues of culture.

1988

122. "Sterling: hard pounding." May 21st: 62.

123. "Lawson's Pyrrhic victory." May 21st: 97.

In the middle of Thatcher's second term—and up to the months before his resignation in 1989—Lawson was the darling of the Conservative Party.

124. "The most special relationship of all." June 11th: 55–56.

125. "Thatcher's touch." July 23rd: 13–14.

126. "Mrs. Thatcher's flight of fancy." August 13th: 47–48.

127. "Society lady." October 8th: 13–14.

128. "My Government is still radical." November 26th: 61.

1989

129. "A cosy date in Oggersheim." February 25th: 47.

On Thatcher's visit to West Germany.

130. "The greening of Margaret Thatcher." March 11th: 55–56.

Late in her Premiership and under intense lobbying pressure, Thatcher picked up issues of the environment.

131. "Cabinet gossip." March 25th: 59–60.

132. "Margaret Thatcher's ten years: a singular Prime Minister." April 29th: 19–22.

An article celebrating Thatcher's tenth anniversary as Prime Minister. It concludes that whatever her failures, she has been Britain's most outstanding peacetime leader of the twentieth century.

133. "Turning on the northern lights." June 3rd: 57–60.

An analysis of Thatcher's attempt to relate the new entrepreneurial spirit and efforts to bridge the North–South divide. The Conservatives saw wealth creation as the way to reverse urban decay.

134. "Unsovereign lady." June 3rd: 62.

135. "Margaret Thatcher's wartime memories." June 24th: 60.

136. "Better service, more smiles." July 29th: 45–46.

On Thatcher's cabinet reshuffle.

1990

137. "Privatising Britain's housing: an Englishman's council home." February 24th: 17–18+.

Elements of the Thatcher Government plan to sell state-owned housing and factors in its slow implementation.

138. "Britain's economy: whatever became of the Thatcher miracle?" June 23rd: 17–18+.

Effects of economic reforms on inflation, the current account deficit, output growth and unemployment.

139. "The Thatcher record: to the victor these spoils." November 24th: 17–20.

Overview of privatisation, welfare policies and labour relations and the methods underlying Thatcher's economic experiment.

140. "Pulled down." November 24th: 29–30.

On the fall of Thatcher after the leadership contest that brought John Major to power.

C. *The London Times*

Publication of *The London Times* was suspended from January 1, 1979 to November 12, 1979. There were further stoppages in subsequent years. References covering this period are to other newspapers clearly named in the citations. References to a Sunday date are to *The Sunday Times*. References between quotation marks are verbatim titles of articles with a few explanatory words added where necessary. When entries are followed by page numbers after a letter of the alphabet, the letter refers to the relevant section of *The Sunday Times* or any other Sunday paper used instead. All these entries cover Thatcher's premiership, with a few entries relevant to the periods just before and just after her tenure of 10 Downing Street.

1979

141. *Daily Telegraph.* Outlines and some details of Conservative proposals to curb union powers. January 8th: 1.

142. *Daily Telegraph.* Comments on public's reaction to the first woman Prime Minister. May 1st: 1.

143. *Daily Telegraph.* "Woman of decision." May 4th: 12.

144. *Daily Telegraph.* United States reaction to her election victory. May 5th: 5.

145. *Daily Telegraph.* Swedish women politicians criticise radio reporter's coverage of campaign as sexist. May 10th: 2.

146. *Daily Telegraph.* "No job for a woman indeed?" May 12th: 14.

147. *Sunday Telegraph.* "Can she strike a deal with the unions?" June 24th: 17.

148. *Daily Telegraph.* Meeting with the Trade Union Congress (TUC) discussed in leading article. June 27th: 18.

149. *Daily Telegraph.* "The Iron Lady's 'metal fatigue' fails to discourage Salisbury." August 10th: 12.

150. *Daily Telegraph.* "Mrs. Thatcher speaks for Britain." October 15th: 20.

151. "Can Thatcher invoke the Dunkirk spirit?" November 18th: 16.

152. Election campaign used as a model by the United States Republican Party. December 9th: 10.

153. "Patriotism must be the policy now." December 20th: 12.

154. "Mrs. Thatcher could almost run for the White House." December 23rd: 5.

1980

155. Stresses Government will continue policy of cuts until the nation is living within its means. February 13th: 2.

156. "How Thatcher can beat crisis of authority." February 17th: 16.

157. "Has Thatcher's strategy been upset?" February 23rd: 12.

158. "The young men that Mrs. Thatcher must convince of her strategy." March 21st: 14.

159. "The striking style of being right." April 27th: 35.

160. Expected to announce cutting of further seventy thousand jobs in the civil service. May 10th: 2.

161. Announces a further cut of seventy-five thousand jobs in the civil service. May 15th: 5.

162. Details of proposals to streamline Whitehall. May 23rd: 1.

163. "President and Prime Minister: the contrast in leadership." July 4th: 16.

164. "Mrs. Thatcher: the best Prime Minister at last." July 6th: 16.

165. Labour Members of Parliament (MP) deplores sexist slogans applied to Thatcher. October 4th: 3.

166. "The critics who wish the lady would turn a little." October 16th: 12.

167. "How Mrs. Thatcher could make her policies work." July 27th: 16.

168. Thatcher's antipathy towards open government examined. September 11th: 4.

169. "Why Mrs. Thatcher's days could be numbered." October 3rd: 12.

170. Sends warm message of congratulations to Reagan on his presidential election victory. November 6th: 10.

1981

171. "The lady's not for cutting and running." February 7th: 14.

172. "Wrong, Mrs. Thatcher, wrong, wrong, wrong." February 8th: 16.

173. Reagan reveals that Thatcher admitted to mistake over her economic policies. March 5th: 7.

174. "Mrs. Thatcher: the first two years." Interview. May 3rd: 33.

175. Accused of petty vindictiveness for removing some civil servants from Queen's Birthday Honours List. June 14th: 1.

176. Greater London Council (GLC) leader accuses Thatcher of dragging nation into a mire of racism. July 11th: 2.

177. "Is the iron lady showing signs of metal fatigue?" July 17th: 14.

178. "Mrs. Thatcher at half time." August 2nd: 12.

179. Prior to Northern Ireland in what is seen as last attempt to build a Cabinet in tune with her economic aims. September 15th: 1.

180. "Why Mrs. Thatcher didn't sack the lot and start again." September 16th: 10.

1982

181. Relations with the United States and President Reagan discussed. March 14th: 32.

182. "Is Reagan worth waiting for?" August 4th: 10.

183. "Mrs. Thatcher to change now would be mad." November 21st: 16.

1983

184. "Can Maggie save the pound?" January 16th: 61.

185. "Is Mrs. Thatcher really such a bossy lady?" January 19th: 12.

186. "Election: trust a woman's intuition." February 17th: 10.

187. Fights Cabinet battle to pledge future Conservative Government to big spending cuts. March 25th: 32.

188. "The birth of the Thatcher factor." March 31st: 14b.

189. "The dangers of a Churchill posture." October 7th: 14.

1984

190. "Europe's odd woman out." March 22nd: 12.

191. Accused by European Commission President of being anti-European. April 14th: 1.

192. "Mrs. Thatcher's modern Europe." July 5th: 12.

193. Draws parallel between miners' strike and the Falklands War attacking tactics of miners' leaders and praising courage of those going to work. July 20th: 1.

194. "Blocks on EEC rebate wrecks Thatcher's plan." July 29th: 11.

195. "Cuts: why their promises have foundered." August 13th: 8.

196. The Clive Ponting case and exchanges on it. September 17th: 1. September 30: 2. October 9th: 1.

1985

197. Article describes attitude of imaginary character "Martha Scarthatch" who is a cross between Thatcher and NUM leader Scargill. January 8th: 10.

198. Says there are a lot of heavily loss-making pits which must be shut down if coal industry is to prosper. January 25th: 1.

199. Oxford dons vote against award of honorary degree by 738 votes to 315. January 30th: 1.

200. "Does Oxford speaks for the nation?" On Oxford dons' voting not to award Thatcher honorary doctorate. February 1st: 12.

201. "Fellows who are anti-female." On Oxford's refusal to award Thatcher honorary degree. February 2nd: 6.

202. "It's the dons who need scrutiny." On Oxford dons' refusal to award Thatcher an honorary degree. February 6th: 12.

203. Public opinion poll shows majority of voters believe she is doing a bad job in managing the economy. February 10th: 1.

204. "Ten years on, time for a returning." That is ten years since becoming leader of the Conservative Party. February 14: 12.

205. Labour leader accuses her of fostering policies like those which gave rise to fascism in the 1930s. May 7th: 1.

206. Says Government would welcome take over of individual pits by miners' cooperatives. May 22nd: 2.

207. Calls on those spreading gloom about unemployment to stop being "moaning minnies." September 12th: 1.

208. "The Thatcher factor: which way does it work now?" October 7th: 12.

1986

209. "Crusader who went too far." January 11th: 8.

210. "Where Thatcher went wrong." January 29th: 10.

211. "Change of style at No. 10?" January 30th: 12.

212. "Fall of the Wizard of Oz." February 2nd: 12.

213. Belief in the American way not shared by majority of Britons according to poll with implications discussed. March 2nd: 21.

214. Enthuses about "popular capitalism" in interview. March 28th: 4.

215. Comments on unemployment prospects in interview. March 28: 4.

216. Labour leader comments on popular image. August 29th: 2.

217. Her performance compared with Labour leader's. September 7th: 27.

218. "The price of survival." October 19th: 27.

1987

219. Backs U.S. statement that husband of U.S. diplomat who escaped prosecution was allegedly involved in indecent assault and not rape. January 21st: 3.

220. "Thatcher faces EEC fight as funds sink." January 25th: 16.

221. "Thatcher may bite the Alliance bullet." February 8th: 29.

222. "Gorbachev: the Tory gamble that could fail." March 28th: 20.

223. "How Thatcher changed her Gorbachev line." April 2nd: 14.

224. "Riding high with her enemies divided." May 17th: 11.

225. Complimentary remarks made by United States President. May 27th: 4.

226. Questioned about religious beliefs; equates Conservative values with Christianity and says it hurt when churchmen describe Government policy as immoral. June 6th: 8.

227. "Abrasiveness abroad." June 6th: 10.

228. "Thatcher factor—the facts." June 8th: 16.

229. "Maggie's magical hat-trick." June 12th: 10.

230. "How Thatcher broke the mould . . . and Kinnock failed to come a good second." June 14th: 11.

231. "Thatcher must move quickly for change." June 21st: 26.

232. "In search of immortality." June 22nd: 12.

233. "The courtiers at No. 10." June 26th: 16.

234. Note on United States media comments on election. June 27th: 8.

235. "How Thatcher avoided being bounced." July 2nd: 6.

236. "Thatcher was not so tough after all." July 5th: 13.

237. "The secret campaign: how Mrs. Thatcher really won the election." July 5: 43.

238. "Soft spots in Iron Lady's tough summit stand." July 6th: 6.

239. "Wobbly Thursday: Mrs. Thatcher's secret path to victory." July 12th: 43.

240. Praises United States President as great leader and warns United States not to be deflected from exercising leadership on world stage. July 18th: 1.

241. Wins high praise from United States for courage and experience. July 20th: 7.

242. "Remarketing Margaret." July 30th: 12.

243. "Knives out for the abrasive housewife." December 4th: 12.

244. "Thatcher: the reality." October 10th: 10.

245. "Triumph of the lady with a will of iron." October 11th: 34.

1988

246. Leading women comment on Thatcher as she is about to become century's longest serving Prime Minister. January 1st: 13.

247. "Tory rivals line up for a mid-term exit." April 10th: B3.

248. "Leading lady leaves Kinnock in the wings." April 17th: B3.

249. "Looking for Mr. Right—but not just yet." May 8th: B3.

250. "Kinnock penetrates Thatcher's armour." May 15th: B3.

251. Edited text of speech to the General Assembly of the Church of Scotland spelling out what she sees as the spiritual underpinning of the Thatcher revolution. May 22nd: A13.

252. "The lady was for learning." May 22nd: C7.

253. "Making mountains of financial molehills." July 24th: B2.

254. "Hidden dynamite in that sermon." A reference to Thatcher's speech to the General Assembly of the Church of Scotland relating Christian morality to Conservatism. May 27th: 16.

255. "Flawed theory of Thatcher's guru." July 24th: D6.

256. "Maggie: the artful dodger." July 31st: B1.

257. "Saleswoman supreme." August 2nd: 10.

258. "Housekeeper-in-chief holds all the strings." November 6th: B3.

1989

259. "Where is the iron fist?" January 13th: 12.

260. "Thatcher's empty crusades." January 31st: 12.

261. Authoritarian style of government attacked by Social Liberal Democratic Party (SLDP) leader and Labour deputy leader. February 5th: A4.

262. "The Thatcher decade." April 17th: 16.

263. "Judging the Thatcher decade." April 30th: 22.

264. "Doing well . . . and not so well." April 30th: 46.

265. "Thatcher's nemesis?" April 30th: 59.

266. "She who must be hated." May 5th: 12.

267. "How Kinnock could ruin the lady's waltz." May 7th: B3.

268. Insists she is "European idealist." May 16th: 16.

269. Criticises idealistic view of French Revolution on eve of Paris summit. July 12th: 9.

270. Article discusses attitude towards French Revolution. July 14th: 16.

271. "Carving a presidential role." July 27th: 16.

272. "Pass the vitriol, it's that lady on the menu again." August 27th: B2.

273. "50 years on: is Thatcher Churchill's true heir?" September 3rd: B3.

274. "Thatcherwasm glee should be tempered." September 10th: A13.

275. Chancellor Lawson's resignation speech following disagreement over European Monetary System (EMS). November 1st: 1.

276. "Ten years at home." December 3rd: 36.

277. "Thatcher softens on EMS as early entry recedes." December 7th: 14.

278. "Thatcher rules the waverers on Europe." December 17th: A13.

1990

279. Meets representatives of 1922 Committee to discuss complaints about high-handed attitude of formulating policy. February 8th: 2.

280. Article discusses whether the time is ripe for the Prime Minister to resign leadership. February 3rd: 10.

281. Unease about Prime Minister's leadership continues. March 17th: 1.

282. Thatcher declares personal commitment to lead Party into next general election. March 13th: 24.

283. "How long can she last?" March 25th: A14.

284. "Time for the Iron Lady to soften her mettle." March 25th: C3.

285. Prime Minister reiterates determination to lead Party into next election. March 31st: 1.

286. Further speculation about leadership contest. March 31st: 4.

287. "Can Thatcher be ousted?" April 7th: 10.

288. "Why she must have another term." May 7th: 10.

289. "Lessons on how to make a mess of things at No. 10." June 24th: 3.

290. Popularity discussed. June 29th: 10.

291. "Radicalism in retreat." August 1st: 10.

D. *The New York Times*

By its national nature, *The New York Times* has fewer references to Thatcher than its sister paper in London. Added to the selection criteria given in this chapter's introduction, another criterion used here is that of choosing references common to both papers. A great deal can be learned about Thatcher from reading non-British articles, because, apart from anything, such reading gives a deeper understanding of Anglo-American relations. Some entries below do not provide page numbers.

1979

292. Is elected first woman Prime Minister of a European nation. May 4th: 1.

293. Some comments on domestic, international and social issues since taking British Conservative Party leadership in 1975. May 4th: 1.

1980

294. Abortion. February 9th.

295. Communist-Western international relations. May 22nd.

296. Agriculture in European Economic Community (EEC). June 3rd.

297. Middle East Israeli–Arab conflict. June 13th.

298. Presidential elections. July 6th.

299. Royal family in Great Britain. July 9th.

300. Women. December 17th: 25.

1981

301. To become first woman to receive William J. Donovan Award. January 12th: II.

302. International monetary system. February 27th.

303. Receives honorary doctor of law from Georgetown University, Washington, D.C. February 28th: 4.

304. Economic conditions in the United States of America. February 28th. March 6th.

305. Northern Ireland. March 6th.

306. Prince of Wales. March 13th.

307. Internal security. March 24th.

308. Reagan attempted assassination. March 31st.

309. Armament and the United States of America. April 16th.

310. West Germany. May 12th.

311. European Economic Community (EEC). May 13th.

312. The Pope and the Roman Catholic Church. May 14th.

313. Middle East: Israeli–Arab conflict. June 10th.

314. Government employees. September 16th.

315. International Monetary System. October 23rd.

316. Republic of Ireland. November 7th.

317. European Economic Community. November 27th.

1982

318. Mark Thatcher returns home. Mother repeatedly disapproves of sport. January 16th: 15.

319. Labour Party in Great Britain. February 14th.

320. Follow-up article on Prime Minister's promise to foot any unpaid bills that might otherwise fall on British taxpayers as a result of the rescue of her son. February 19th: II.

321. Comment on article on Prime Minister in the London magazine *Woman*. Article was written by her daughter Carol Thatcher. March 4th: III.

322. Budget: United States of America. March 30th.

323. · Economic conditions in the United States of America. March 30th.

324. Credit in the United States of America. March 30th.

325. Falkland Islands occupied by Argentina. April 3rd.

326. European Economic Community. May 19th. May 21st. And agriculture. May 21st.

327. Anglican churches. May 22nd.

328. Middle East: Israeli–Arab conflict. June 5th. June 7th.

329. Agriculture in the European Economic Community. June 12th.

330. Arms control. June 16th. June 23rd.

331. International trade. July 2nd.

332. Northern Ireland. July 21st.

333. The Labour Party in Great Britain. July 22nd.

334. International trade. September 19th.

335. Northern Ireland. December 8th.

336. Bank of England. December 24th.

1983

337. Citizenship. January 2nd.

338. Middle East. January 5th.

339. Arms control. January 20th.

340. Europe. February 16th.

341. International trade in oil. February 24th.

342. Northern Ireland. March 17th.

343. Middle East. March 19th.

344. Fourteen-year-old unidentified London boy accused of mailing letter bomb to Prime Minister is released in parents' custody by court. Is ordered to appear in court for another hearing in May. Device was intercepted at postal sorting office and defused. March 25th: I.

345. Europe. April 14th.

346. British Leyland Ltd. May 12th.

347. Arms control. May 18th.

348. Woman in the news articles on Prime Minister. June 10th: I.

349. Europe. June 13th.

350. Arms control. June 13th.

351. Drug traffic. June 18th.

352. European Economic Community. June 20th.

353. Capital punishment. July 8th.

354. Slight tear in Thatcher's right eye is surgically repaired. August 4th: I.

355. Northern Ireland. August 13th.

356. Arms control. September 6th.

357. Revolutionary war. September 30th.

358. Europe. September 30th.

359. Grenada. October 26th.

360. Europe. October 29th.

361. Grenada. November 3rd.

362. Northern Ireland. November 7th.

363. Middle East. November 8th.

364. Europe. November 16th.

365. Grenada. December 4th.

366. European Economic Community. December 7th.

367. Middle East. December 7th.

368. Economic conditions in the United States of America. December 9th. December 10th.

369. Fourteen-year-old boy pleads guilty to sending letter bomb to Prime Minister. December 17th: I.

370. Northern Ireland. December 18th.

1984

371. Arms control. January 16th. January 22nd. November 7th. December 21st.

372. Middle East. January 21st. February 8th.

373. European Economic Community. January 24th. March 18th. March 20th. March 26th. April 10th. June 27th. July 28th. December 3rd.

374. World War Two. April 5th.

375. Grenada. April 6th.

376. Northern Ireland. May 17th. September 11th. October 13th. October 14th. October 15th. October 16th. November 20th. November 23rd. November 24th. November 25th. December 5th.

377. Terrorism. June 6th.

378. Labour. July 15th.

379. Grantham. July 25th.

1985

380. Former Scotland Solicitor General Nicholas Fairbairn tells House of Commons that Prime Minister rejected sexual advances from unidentified drunken dignitary. He said that the incident took place at Holyrood Palace in Edinburgh. January 26th: I.

381. Oxford University refuses, by 738–319 votes, to grant Prime Minister honorary degree because British Government has cut funds for education and research. January 30th: I.

382. Congress in the United States of America. February 21st.

383. Northern Ireland. February 21st. February 22nd. February 25th. March 9th. May 19th. June 30th. August 29th. September 6th. October 6th. November 14th. November 16th. November 17th. November 24th. December 5th.

384. European Economic Community. March 31st.

385. Europe. April 9th.

386. Nazi era. April 28th.

387. Terrorism. July 18th.

388. International democratic union. July 27th.

389. British newspaper report that Prime Minister was nearly killed last month when airliner had to take emergency action to avoid colliding with her helicopter at London's Heathrow Airport. August 18th: I.

390. United Nations. October 24th. October 25th.

1986

391. Terrorism. January 16th.

392. Crime and criminals. January 27th.

393. Europe. March 12th.

394. Education and schools. May 7th.

395. State of Israel. May 25th.

396. Arms control and limitation and disarmament. June 18th. July 15th. October 17th. November 9th. November 14th. November 16th.

397. Enters London hospital for operation on her hand. She has condition known as Dupuytren's Contracture, which causes little fingers to withdraw into palm. If untreated, could cause loss of use of hand. August 6th: I.

398. European Economic Community (EEC). December 6th.

399. European Parliament. December 10th.

1987

400. Arms control and limitation and disarmament. March 3rd. March 29th. July 4th. December 8th.

401. Europe. March 8th. March 29th. March 31st. July 4th. December 8th.

402. Taxation. March 18th. October 29th.

403. Union of Soviet Socialist Republics. March 31st.

404. Space weapons (Star Wars). March 31st.

405. Books and literature. May 14th.

406. Republic of South Africa. October 17th. October 18th.

1988

407. Labour. February 3rd. September 11th.

408. Presidential elections. February 15th.

409. United States politics and government. April 15th.

410. Oxford University. April 24th. October 5th.

411. European Economic Community (EEC). July 31st. September 22nd. September 28th.

412. Anglican churches. August 2nd.

413. Europe. October 30th.

414. Colleges and universities. November 22nd.

415. Middle East. December 11th. December 16th.

416. Food contamination and poisoning. December 17th.

1989

417. Legal profession. January 30th.

418. Nicaragua. May 9th.

419. Luxembourg. April 19th.

420. People's Republic of China. June 7th. June 9th. June 24th.

421. Hong Kong. June 7th. June 9th.

422. Poland. June 11th. December 3rd.

423. Republic of South Africa. June 24th. October 19th. October 23rd.

424. Labour. June 25th.

425. International trade and world market. September 21st.

426. Vietnam. December 12th. December 13th. December 19th.

427. Panama. December 21st.

1990

428. Vietnam. January 5th.

429. East Germany. March 10th. March 20th.

430. South Africa. April 17th. May 20th. June 27th. July 4th. July 5th.

431. France. May 5th.

432. Air pollution. June 19th. June 28th.

433. Aspen Institute. July 17th.

434. Women. September 7th.

435. Children and youth. September 7th.

436. Czechoslovakia. September 17th.

437. Prime Minister to celebrate her 65th birthday at Conservative Party conference in Bournemouth. Says she hopes to be in office on her 70th birthday. October 12th.

438. Says she will resign as Prime Minister of Britain after eleven and a half years, as soon as a new Conservative Party leader is chosen. November 23rd.

439. John Major succeeds Margaret Thatcher as British Prime Minister. November 29th.

See also: *New York Times Magazine.* "Thatcher puts a lid on: censorship in Britain." (no. 558).

II Personal Writings

Apart from her speeches and other Conservative Party Central Office publications, Thatcher wrote no major works reflecting her policies. Her few writings comprise newspaper and periodical articles. References below include a few representative interviews; other interviews are included in Chapter I, Newspapers and Periodicals.

440. *Cooke, Alistair. *Revival of Britain.* See Margaret Thatcher, number 447 below.

441. Gale, George. See Margaret Thatcher, number 448 below.

442. Hall, Unity. See Margaret Thatcher, number 449 below.

443. Oakley, Robin. See Margaret Thatcher, number 453 below.

444. Oakley, Robin. See Margaret Thatcher, number 454 below.

445. Thatcher, Margaret. *Britain and Europe.* London: Conservative Policy Centre, 1988. 9.

Thatcher's most contentious views are those on Europe. After her resignation, she has consistently adopted an anti-European stance calling for a referendum on the Maastricht European treaty. During her premiership, a referendum was considered wrong in principle.

446. Thatcher, Margaret. *Chat.* March 18th 1989.

Interview with Thatcher.

447.   *Thatcher, Margaret and Cooke, Alistair (editors). *The Revival of Britain*. London: Aurum Press, 1989. 280.

Thatcher's speeches compiled by Alistair Cooke, covering home and European affairs from 1975 to 1988. Includes her famous anti-European speech of Bruges in September 1988.

448.   Thatcher, Margaret and Gale, George. *Daily Express*. July 26th 1982.

449.   Thatcher, Margaret and Hall, Unity. *News of the World*. February 20th 1983.

Interview with Thatcher.

450.   Thatcher, Margaret. *Illustrated London News*. Number 7018, volume 271, May 1983.

Interview with Thatcher.

451.   *Thatcher, Margaret. *In Defence of Freedom*. London: Aurum Press, 1986. 150.

Thatcher's speeches on Britain's relations with other countries covering 1976 to 1986. Includes the House of Commons debate on the United States bombing of Libya.

452.   Thatcher, Margaret and Macintyre, Donald. *Sunday Correspondent*. November 5th 1989.

Interview with Thatcher.

453.   Thatcher, Margaret and Oakley, Robin. "Now It's up to the People." *The Times*. October 26th 1988.

Interview with Robin Oakley.

454.   Thatcher, Margaret and Oakley, Robin. *The Times*. November 24th 1989.

Interview with Thatcher.

455.   Thatcher, Margaret and Rook, Jean. *Daily Express*. November 1st 1989.

Interview with Thatcher.

456.   Thatcher, Margaret. *She*. February 1989.

Interview with Thatcher.

457. *Thatcher, Margaret. *Small Today—Bigger Tomorrow: Three Speeches from the Small Business Bureau Conference, 1984*. London: Conservative Policy Centre, 1984. 32.

Small business received a massive boost from Thatcher's economic policies. However, by the time that she left office small business bankruptcies hit record proportions.

458. Thatcher, Margaret and Turner, Graham. *Sunday Telegraph*. July 27th 1986.

Interview with Thatcher.

459. Thatcher, Margaret. "Visit of Prime Minister Margaret Thatcher of the United Kingdom." *World Comp. Press Documents*. December 24th 1979: 2264–68.

Exchanges between Carter and Thatcher during the latter's visit of December 17th 1979. Also includes text of a White House statement dated December 18th 1979.

460. Thatcher, Margaret. "Visit of Prime Minister Margaret Thatcher of the United Kingdom." *World Comp. Press Documents*. March 2nd 1981: 194–202.

Exchanges between Reagan and Thatcher during the latter's visit of February 26th and February 27th 1981.

461. Thatcher, Margaret. "We Have to Keep on with Tough Policies." *U.S. News*. August 25th 1980: 35–36.

An interview with Margaret Thatcher.

462. Thatcher, Margaret. "Why I Can Never, Never Let up." *Sunday Times*. May 8th 1988.

Interview with Brian Walden.

463. Thatcher, Margaret. "Why I Want a Third Term." *Illustrated London News*. June 1987.

Interview with James Bishop.

464. Thatcher, Margaret. *Woman*. September 11th 1982.

Interview with Thatcher.

465. Thatcher, Margaret. *Woman*. June 4th 1988.

Interview with Thatcher.

466. Thatcher, Margaret. *Woman's Own*. October 17th 1981.

Interview with Margaret Thatcher.

467. Thatcher, Margaret. *Woman's Own*. August 28th 1982.

Interview with Thatcher.

468. Thatcher, Margaret. *Woman's Own*. October 31st 1987.

Interview with Thatcher.

469. Thatcher, Margaret. *Woman's Own*. April 17th 1989.

Interview with Thatcher.

470. Thatcher, Margaret. *World Comp. Press Documents*. November 21st 1988: 1505–12.

Exchanges between Thatcher and Reagan.

See also: Thatcher, Margaret. "How to fight and survive." (no. 549); Thatcher, Margaret. "Wake up women." (no. 521).

III   General Biographies

There are several biographies of Thatcher that were written during her premiership. It is notoriously difficult to write definitive biographies of serving politicians since proper analysis is precluded by ongoing events. A few biographies are purely narrative and hastily produced. Other biographers, such as Kenneth Harris and Andrew Thomson, have written unashamedly hagiographic works. Many appear to have a hefty ax to grind. To date, the most comprehensive work with probably the best analysis of Thatcher's policies is Hugo Young's long biography.

471.   Brock, George. *Thatcher*. See Nicholas Wapshott, number 484 below.

472.   Foster, Leila M. *Margaret Thatcher: First Woman Prime Minister of Great London*. London: Children's Press, 1990.

Aimed at a younger audience and for use at schools.

473.   Garfinkel, Bernard. *Margaret Thatcher*. Burke's World Leaders Past and Present Series, 1986. 112.

474.   *Harris, Kenneth. *Thatcher*. London: Fontana, 1989. 339.

A readable and flowing life of Thatcher by the associate editor of *The Observer* and an admirer of Thatcher. The book also has a useful biographical section of Thatcher's major contemporaries.

475.   Hughes, Libby. *Madam Prime Minister: A Biography of Margaret Thatcher*. London: Dillon Publications, 1989.

476. Junor, Penny. *Margaret Thatcher: Wife, Mother, Politician.* London: Sidgwick and Jackson, 1983. 208.

Seen as the richest account in terms of human interest.

477. Kieser, Egbert. *Margaret Thatcher: eine Frau veraendert ihre Nation: eine Biographie* (Margaret Thatcher: a woman changes her nation: a biography). Bechtle, 1989. 422.

Political career of Thatcher with economic, social and defence policy orientations and emphasising the privatisation programme and law and order agenda.

478. Lewis, Russell. *Margaret Thatcher: A Personal and Political Biography.* London: Chapman and Hall, 1984.

A revised edition of the 1975 publication.

479. Moskin, Marietta D. *Margaret Thatcher of Great Britain.* London: Julian Messner in Focus Biographies, 1990.

480. *Murray, Patricia. *Margaret Thatcher.* London: Star Books, 1980.

A biography of Thatcher with specific emphasis on the human interest aspects of her life.

481. Nallon, Steve. *I, Margaret: Unofficial Autobiography of Mrs. Thatcher.* London: Papermac, 1989. 224.

482. Smith, Ronald A. *Margaret Thatcher: The Premier Years.* London: Taylor and Francis, 1990. 228.

483. *Thomson, Andrew. *Margaret Thatcher: The Woman Within.* London: W. H. Allen, 1989. 247.

Andrew Thomson was Thatcher's Conservative Party Agent looking after Thatcher from 1982 to 1987 when he retired. Although interesting as an insider's view of Thatcher, it lacks any political analysis. It simply gives anecdotal glimpses of Thatcher.

484. Wapshott, Nicholas and Brock, George. *Thatcher.* London: Futura, 1983.

A political narrative by two *Times* journalists.

485. Young, Hugo. *The Iron Lady: A Biography of Margaret Thatcher.* New York: Farrar, Straus and Giroux, 1990. 570.

Another readable piece by probably the best Thatcher author.

486. *Young, Hugo. *One of Us: Life of Margaret Thatcher.* London: Macmillan, 1989. 302. Also published in paperback by London: Pan, 1989. 589.

Updated to cover Thatcher's final few months, the book is also published by Macmillan, 1991, in its final version. Arguably the most comprehensive and possibly the best work on Thatcher to date. Although at times uncomplimentary, Young is able to assess Thatcher's achievements impartially. The book covers Thatcher's entire life until November 1990 when she resigned. The title "One of Us" is a reference to Thatcher's alleged preference for offering jobs only to those who agree with her. Young extends this to Thatcher being "one of us" (i.e., the whole nation). He also succeeds in making the work readable through creating an atmosphere of the times and through a neat compartmentalization of Thatcher's achievements. A definitive life of Thatcher.

See also: Abse, Leo. *Margaret, Daughter of Beatrice: Politician's Psychobiography of Margaret Thatcher.* (no. 514); Boycott, Rosie and Leitch, David. *Young Margaret Thatcher.* (no. 515); Gardiner, George. *Margaret Thatcher, from Childhood to Leadership.* (no. 518); Jones, Christopher. *No. 10 Downing Street: The Story of a House.* (no. 502); Lewis, Russell. *Margaret Thatcher: A Personal and Political Biography.* (no. 520); Longford, Frank. *Eleven at No. 10 A Personal View of Prime Ministers 1931–1984.* (no. 510).

IV Background Readings

Thatcher is the product of—or rather, the reaction to—interwar Conservatism. In order to better understand her life, her thinking, and her policies, it is necessary to understand the recent history of twentieth-century Conservatism. Among the works listed are a few by her contemporaries and opponents.

487. Adams, Jad. *Tony Benn: A Biography.* London: Macmillan, 1992. 536.

Benn was very much a lone voice for the extreme left. He spoke against much—if not everything—that Thatcher stood for. He also made Kinnock's life difficult. The last seventy pages are useful in understanding the strength of feelings of anti-Thatcherites.

488. Behrens, Robert. *Conservative Party from Heath to Thatcher: Policies and Politics, 1974–1979.* Saxon House, 1980. 180.

Assesses, amongst other things, the leadership contest which brought Thatcher to the leadership of the Conservative Party. Also charts the changes made after Heath resigned to give way to Thatcher.

489. Bellairs, Charles E. *Conservative Social and Industrial Reform.* London: Conservative Policy Centre, number 600, 1977. 128.

A record of the Conservative Party legislation between 1800 and 1974. Foreword is written by Margaret Thatcher.

490. *The Bible.* The Authorised King James Version of 1611 A.D.

The Bible had a most profound effect on Thatcher. As a strict Methodist, her father took his family to Chapel twice every Sunday. Thatcher's own views of the world as being propelled by good and evil, her insistence on self-help, thrift and hard work and her views on family/community values derive entirely from her Christian background. Her speech style and its content constantly exerted by her reading of the *Bible.* A similar influence on her language/attitudes was her favourite poet Rudyard Kipling.

491. Cockerell, Michael. *Live from Number 10.* London: Faber and Faber, 1987. 352.

The inside story of Prime Ministers and television.

492. Cosgrave, Patrick. *Carrington: A Life and a Policy.* London: Dent, 1985.

A life of Lord Carrington who resigned as Defence Secretary, taking responsibility for the Argentinian invasion of the Falklands.

493. *Cosgrave, Patrick. *The Lives of Enoch Powell.* London: The Bodley Head, 1989. London: Pan, 1990. 518.

Thatcher was heavily influenced by Enoch Powell, especially in the development of her monetarist policies. This is a most readable book despite Cosgrave's failure to see any fault at all in anything that Powell—a great Parliamentarian—ever did or said. Powell's views on Thatcherism make interesting reading.

494. Fair, John D. and Hutcheson, John A. "British Conservatism in the Twentieth Century: an Emerging ideological Tradition." *Albion.* 1987: 549–78.

As a result of the challenges of fascism in the 1930s and of left-wing politics since the turn of the century Conservatism has undergone some dramatic reactive changes. Edmund Burke's influence became more apparent in the 1930s with Chamberlain's programme of policies. This reached a peak of ideological dogma under Margaret Thatcher.

495. Gilmour, Ian. *Britian Can Work.* Oxford: M. Robertson, 1983.

Ian Gilmour was sacked by Thatcher for being a 'wet'.

496. Gilmour, Ian. *Inside Right: A Study of Conservatism.* London: Quartet Books, 1978. 294.

A readable work by a Conservative so-called wet.

497. *Hayek, Freidrich August von. *The Road to Serfdom.* London: Routledge, 1991. 194.

A work which has had a most profound effect on Thatcher's development. Hayek's work is trenchantly antisocialist and antiinterventionist, arguments which led on to Thatcher's free market economy. Another relevant work by Hayek is *A Time for Greatness.*

498. *Hennessy, Peter. *Cabinet.* Oxford: Blackwell, 1986. 230.

Analysis of the cabinet system, the capability of postwar governments in dealing with economic, social and foreign policy problems and assesses Thatcher's changes to cabinet government.

499. Hennessy, Peter. *Ministerial Responsibility.* Oxford: Oxford University Press, 1989.

Includes Marshall's "The Westland Affair" on the issue that caused two ministerial resignations.

500. *Hennessy, Peter. *Whitehall.* London: Martin Sacker and Warburg, 1989. Fontana Press, 1990. 857.

The most comprehensive and readable history of the civil service to date. It contains an insightful analysis of the Thatcher effect on Whitehall (pages 589 to 687).

501. *Heseltine, Michael. *Where There's a Will.* London: Hutchinson, 1987. Arrow Books, 1990. 323.

A number one best-seller arguing for radical political reform in pursuit of British industrial strategy. Includes very readable sections on inner city crises and their solutions. It also includes arguably a Conservative politician's most enduring testament on equal opportunities and race (pages 177 to 194).

502. Jones, Christopher. *No. 10 Downing Street: The Story of a House.* London: British Broadcasting Corporation (BBC), 1985. 192.

A glossy work with attractive photographs and prefaced by Margaret Thatcher. Pages 158 to 182 concern Thatcher as 10 Downing Street's first woman principal occupant.

503. *Joseph, Keith. *Monetarism Is Not Enough.* The Stockton Lecture, 1976.

Another one of Joseph's honest, open and—at times—self-destructive soul-searching sessions.

504. *Joseph, Keith. *Reversing the Trend*. London: Barry Rose, 1975.

Keith Joseph had a profound influence on Thatcher's political thought and development.

505. *Joseph, Keith. *Stranded on the Middle Ground: Reflections on Circumstances and Policies*. London: Centre for Policy Studies, 1976. 80.

506. Khudolei, K. K. Izbranie E. khita liderom konservativnoi partii velikobritanii v 1965 (The election of Edward Heath as leader of the Conservative Party of Great Britain in 1965). g. Vestnik Leningradskogo Universiteta: Seriia Istoriia, *Iazyka i Literatury*. 1985. 21–28.

Discusses the changes made by the Conservative Party in order to enable its leader to be elected. The result of these reforms was that all leaders elected since then have been from outside the conventional Conservative upper classes: Edward Heath as a carpenter's son, Margaret Thatcher as a shopkeeper's daughter and John Major as a circus performer's son. The article argues that this process has actually led the Conservative Party more towards the right than ever before, culminating in Thatcher's extreme dogma.

507. Khudolei, K. K. Vybory lidera konservatorskoi partii velikobritanii v fevrale 1975 (The elections for the leader of the British Conservative Party in February 1975). g. Vestnik Leningradskogo Universiteta, Seriia 2: Istoriia, Iazykoznanie, *Literaturovedenie*. 1987: 15–22.

Shows how the Conservatives under Heath suffered two election defeats and eventually turned to Thatcher and her conviction politics. Examines the leadership pre-election moves within the Party alleging that Thatcher's success was a victory for the lower ranks of the Party.

508. Lawson, Nigel. "Riddled with errors, reeking of bile." *Spectator*. July 13th 1991: 8–9.

A criticism of Nicholas Ridley's account of the Thatcher years as being more fiction than fact. See number 512 below.

509. Letwin, Oliver. *Privatising the World: A Study of International Privatisation in Theory and Practice*. London: Cassell, 1988. 176.

Thatcher's strongest impact, both in Britain and abroad, has been on privatisation. As this policy spread to the welfare service sector it wrought a dramatic and seemingly permanent enterprise cultural change.

510. Longford, Frank. *Eleven at No. 10: A Personal View of Prime Ministers 1931–1984.* London: Harrap, 1984. 189.

A short analysis of Thatcher's populism, motivation and leadership. Longford argues that her statements and dogmas were somewhat crude and simplistic. Pages 155 to 168.

511. Overbeek, Henk. *Global Capitalism and National Decline.* London: Unwin Hyman: International Thomson Publishing Services, 1989. 276.

512. *Ridley, Nicholas. *'My Style of Government': The Thatcher Years.* London: Hutchinson, 1991. 275. London: Fontana, 1992. 288.

Ridley occupied a series of key Government Cabinet posts until his resignation in the summer of 1990 over his attack on German hegemony in Europe. The work gives an insight into Thatcher's management style, her policies with specific reference to Europe and the economy. Ridley was a great admirer of Thatcher and of Thatcherism.

513. Tuxill, A. C. *Liberal Ideology and Public Sector Policy from Bentham to Thatcher.* See Chandler, J. A. number 565 below.

See also: Blake, Lord Robert. *Conservative Party from Peel to Thatcher.* (no. 630); Hall, Stuart. *The Hard Road to Renewal: Thatcherism and the Crisis of the Left.* (no. 794); King, Anthony. *The British Prime Minister.* (no. 815); Thomson, Andrew. *Margaret Thatcher: The Woman Within.* (no. 483); Walters, Alan. *Britain's Economic Renaissance: Margaret Thatcher's Reforms, 1979–1984.* (no. 1019); Young, Hugo. *One of Us: Life of Margaret Thatcher.* (no. 486).

V Childhood and Youth

Little has been written on this period of Thatcher's life. Newspaper articles and general biographies plug this gap, so reference should therefore be made to the relevant chapters.

514. *Abse, Leo. *Margaret, Daughter of Beatrice: Politician's Psychobiography of Margaret Thatcher*. London: Jonathan Cape, 1989. 336.

A Freudian analysis of Thatcher alleging that she turned away from her mother as every girl has to in order to take her father as her new love object (necessarily, love for a man). In this work Leo Abse refers to Beatrice Roberts (Thatcher's mother) and her mother Phoebe Stevenson (Thatcher's grandmother) as ruling Britain from their graves! Abse also refers to a novel entitled *Rotten Borough* which was written by a local journalist in 1936. It depicts a local councillor and corner shop owner who was a humbug "with wandering eyes and hands." The novel was hastily withdrawn under threat of libel action. Although eminently readable, Abse's work must be approached with tongue slightly in cheek.

515. Boycott, Rosie and Leitch, David. *Young Margaret Thatcher*. Century Publications Co., 1990. 256.

516. Himmelfarb, G. "Victorian values/Jewish values." *Commentary*. February 1989: 23–31.

There was a strong Jewish influence on Thatcher partly through her friendship with a Jewish girl who had told her stories of Nazi atrocities and partly through the strong Jewish vote in Finchley.

517.   Leitch, David. *Young Margaret Thatcher*. See Rosie Boycott, number 515 above.

See also: Webster, Wendy. *Not a Man to Match Her: The Marketing of a Prime Minister*. (no. 1309); Young, Hugo. *One of Us: Life of Margaret Thatcher*. (no. 486).

VI   Early Career

This section should be used in conjunction with chapters I (Newspapers and Periodicals), III (General Biographies), and IV (Background Readings).

518.   Gardiner, George. *Margaret Thatcher, from Childhood to Leadership*. London: William Kimber, 1975.

Written by a leading Conservative backbench supporter.

519.   Haddon, Celia. "Portrait of a Brainy Lady in a Tory Hat." *The Sun*. November 25th 1971.

The Sun, that quintessentially most English of papers, remained a staunch Thatcher supporter for years. The British tabloid press comes in for a great deal of criticism for simplicity, crudeness, racism, sexism and every ism that mushrooms out of fertile liberalism, but their influence on the formation or reflection of public opinion can not be overestimated. Labour's loss of the 1992 general elections was blamed by Kinnock on the right wing tabloids. It is proverbially difficult to decide whether papers such as *The Sun* actually affect public perception or simply reflect it. Either way, to ignore *The Sun* or *The Mirror* or other tabloids as irrelevant is to observe Britain's political progress with blindfolds on!

520.   Lewis, Russell. *Margaret Thatcher: A Personal and Political Biography*. London: Routledge and Kegan Paul, 1975.

A readable and well-informed biography of Thatcher.

521. *Thatcher, Margaret. "Wake up Women." *Sunday Graphic.* February 17th 1952.

Thatcher's article on women's right to work as well as being mothers and wives.

VII   Minister and Leader of the Opposition

522. Ball, Robert and Melville, Frank. "What Britons Will Get If the Tories Win." *Fortune.* May 7th 1979: 226–28+.

Argues that Thatcher is an unapologetic Conservative, far to the right by present-day standards, but if she comes to power the heart will be tempered by the head. The authors got this all wrong since Thatcher, the conviction politician, went all the way.

523. Brompton, Sally and Tyler, Rodney. "Everything Ted Heath Ought to Know about Margaret Thatcher." *Daily Mail.* January 24th 1975.

The British press was predominantly pro-Heath during the 1975 Conservative leadership election.

524. *Cosgrave, Patrick. *Margaret Thatcher: A Tory and Her Party.* London: Hutchinson, 1978. 224.

Centres on the leadership contest. A revised version of this work came out as *Margaret Thatcher: Prime Minister* in 1979 (Bodley Head).

525. *Daily Telegraph.* "A woman at the helm." March 30th 1979: 18.

526. *Daily Telegraph.* Leading article discusses emphasis on individual liberty in general election campaign. March 31st 1979: 18.

527. *Daily Telegraph.* Thatcher issues pamphlet discussing six essential steps to Britain's recovery with details from text. April 16th 1979: 1.

528. *Daily Telegraph. Washington Post* columnist reports initial impressions of Thatcher. April 26th 1979: 10.

529. *Daily Telegraph.* Thatcher opposes introduction of immigrants' mother tongues as compulsory element of school curriculum and calls for continued religious education in state schools. April 27th 1979: 12.

530. Economist. "The Fall and Rise of Margaret Thatcher." *The Economist.* April 21st 1979: 39–42.

531. Economist. "Issue is Thatcher." *The Economist.* March 31st 1979: 9–10.

532. Economist. "It all depends on what you call the middle ground." *The Economist.* April 21st 1979: 21–22.

533. Economist. "It's getting close." *The Economist.* March 24th 1979: 11–12.

534. Economist. "It's not because she's a woman." *The Economist.* April 28th 1979: 23.

535. Economist. "Not Quite Disraeli." *The Economist.* July 23rd 1977: 13–14.

Comments on Thatcher's political views.

536. Economist. "Only one prime minister." *The Economist.* April 28th 1979: 13–17.

537. Economist. "Plans for power." *The Economist.* February 17th 1979: 21+.

538. Economist. "The Thatcher Years." *The Economist.* June 9th 1979: 120–21.

539. *Mayer, Allan J. *Madam Prime Minister: Margaret Thatcher and Her Rise to Power.* New York: Newsweek Books, 1983. 224.

540. Melville, Frank. "What Britons Will Get If the Tories Win." See Robert Ball, number 522 above.

541. Money, Ernle. *Margaret Thatcher: First Lady of the House.* London: Taylor and Francis, 1975.

542. Revzin, Philip. "Could Thatcher Change Things?" *Wall Street Journal*. April 11th 1979: 22.

In 1992 such a question seems almost odd, because Britons suffer from collective amnesia as to what things were like in April 1979. Thatcher did change things—dramatically.

543. Revzin, Philip. "Tory Challenger." *Wall Street Journal*. October 10th 1978: 1+.

On Thatcher trying to spur prospects of the Opposition Conservative Party.

544. Russell, T. *The Tory Party*. London: Penguin, 1978.

545. Shrimsley, Anthony. "Heaven Help Anyone Who Tries to Stand in Her Way." *Daily Mail*. February 12th 1975.

546. *Sunday Telegraph*. "Can Tories make Britain work?" January 21st 1979: 16.

547. *Sunday Telegraph*. "Can Mrs. Thatcher win the Women's vote?" April 8th 1979: 17.

It was argued that women's votes gave Thatcher her victory in 1979.

548. *Sunday Telegraph*. Thatcher's views on socialism discussed. April 8th 1979: 16.

549. Thatcher, Margaret. "How to Fight and Survive." *Sunday Express*. February 9th 1975.

550. *Thatcher, Margaret. *Let Our Children Grow Tall: Selected Speeches, 1975–1977*. London: Centre for Policy Studies, 1977. 114 (available in hardback and paperback).

551. Thatcher, Margaret and Rook, Jean. *Daily Express*. April 30th 1979.

Interview with Thatcher.

552. *The Times*. "Thatcher's debt to Powell." June 15th 1987: 10.

Enoch Powell, the pariah of the Conservative Party, had a profound influence on Thatcher's political development.

553. Tyler, Rodney. "Everything Ted Heath Ought to Know about Margaret Thatcher." See Sally Brompton, number 523 above.

554. U.S. News. "How the Conservatives Would Deal with Britain's Troubles." *U.S. News*. September 12th 1977: 69–71.

An interview with Margaret Thatcher as Leader of Her Majesty's Opposition.

555. Waldegrave, William. *The Building of Leviathan*. London: Hamish Hamilton, 1978.

William Waldegrave was a member of Thatcher's Cabinet. He is currently Secretary of State in Major's Cabinet.

556. Woods, Roger. "Margaret Thatcher and Secondary Reorganisation, 1970–74." *Journal of Educational Administration and History*. 1981: 51–61.

During 1970–74 Thatcher was Secretary of State for Education. She oversaw the reorganisation of secondary education allowing the comprehensivisation of schools to go ahead although she did allow authorities wishing to retain selection at eleven to continue to do so. Although her impact on education was considerable, there was no clear indication at the time of the radical reforms that were to take place under her premiership.

VIII   Prime Minister

By the nature of its subject this chapter is the longest in this volume. An attempt has been made to divide it into relevant sections for ease of reference, but there is considerable overlap in some cases. At the end of each section, essential cross referencing has been made.

A. Analysis and Criticism of Thatcher's Policies

557.   *Archbishop of Canterbury's Commission on Urban Priority Areas. *Faith in the City*. CIO Publishing, 1985. 398.

A report by the Church which is heavily critical of Thatcher's policies as being too oriented towards individual acquisitiveness. It argues that her Government is not doing enough to improve inner-city poverty, housing, education and unemployment. The report received short shrift from most Conservatives who saw it as advocating a return to the inefficiencies and to the impoverishing practices of the "nanny" state.

558.   Atlas, J. "Thatcher Puts a Lid on: Censorship in Britain." *The New York Times Magazine*. March 5th 1989.

Thatcher's Government had many confrontations with media over reporting events such as the Falklands, the United States bombing of Libya and election coverage. The BBC was constantly accused of being anti-Conservative.

559. Barry, Norman P. and Plant, Raymond. *Citizenship and Rights in Thatcher's Britain: Two Views*. Institute of Economic Affairs, 1990. 77.

Personal liberties were perceived to suffer under Thatcher. There is evidence to support both the for and against views.

560. Bown, William. "Thatcher's x-ray vision leaves astronomers out in the cold." *New Scientist*. Volume 131, number 1780, August 3rd 1991: 7.

On the agreement signed by Thatcher in 1988 which committed Britain to spending millions on a satellite. The author alleges that the satellite was unwanted.

561. Brendon, Piers. "Amendment envy." *Columbia Journalism Review*. Volume 30, number 4, November 1991: 68.

Argues that the lack of a written constitution in Britain clouds the issue of freedom of the press. Also alleges that the British press often acts as an arm of Government giving the official position. Under Thatcher, the author argues, freedom of the press has been challenged in a dangerous and unacceptable way which goes far beyond the traditional censorship that had always existed.

562. Campbell, D. "Big Buzby is watching you." *New Statesman*. February 1st 1980.

On telephone tapping in Britain.

563. Campbell, D. "British teletap inc." *New Statesman*. April 3rd 1981.

On telephone tapping in Britain.

564. Campbell, John. "Symposium: The Thatcher years." *Contemporary Record*. Volume 1, number 3, 1987: 2–31.

An analysis of Thatcher's record since 1979 by eight British historians.

565. Chandler, J. A. and Tuxill, A. C. *Liberal Ideology and Public Sector Policy from Bentham to Thatcher*. London: Pavic Publications, 1989.

Jeremy Bentham (1748–1832) was a Tory philosopher, economist and theoretical jurist. His theory of Utilitarianism led to the liberal concept of legislation being the "greatest happiness of the greatest number." He believed in the extreme logical application of Adam Smith's principles with every person being the best judge of his/her advantage. He produced a list of what the state must and should not do—the latter being much longer than the first. Amongst other principles he advocated regular elections, equal electoral districts, a wide suffrage and secret ballots. Bentham's *An Introduction to the Principles of Morals and Legislation* is essentially Thatcherite in nature.

566. Cohen, Jeff. "Off with their heads: Maggie Thatcher wants to abolish the London City Council, and she may just get her way; what has the GLC done to so irritate the PM? You name it." *Mother Jones*. June 1985: 13–14.

It is not too difficult to assess what the GLC had done to irritate Thatcher. The popular press projected an image of loony wishy-washy liberalism with its antiracism, feminism, overt sexuality, Marxism and all things hateful to the Prime Minister.

567. Comfort, N. "Is the state becoming too powerful?" *Daily Telegraph*. October 27th 1988.

568. Cosgrave, Patrick. *Thatcher: The First Term*. London: Bodley Head, 1985.

Cosgrave was a special adviser to Thatcher in the 1970s. His inside knowledge is of value up to 1981.

569. *Dalyell, Tam. *Misrule: How Mrs. Thatcher Has Misled Parliament, from the Sinking of the Belgrano to the Wright Affair*. Sevenoaks: New English Library, 1988. 214.

Tam Dalyell was Thatcher's scourge with his constant criticism of her policies and his endless fight to expose her over the *Belgrano* incident.

570. Durham, Martin. "The Thatcher Government and the moral right." *Parliamentary Affairs*. January 1989: 58–71.

Amidst much criticism Thatcher withdrew financial support for research into the transmission of AIDS through heterosexual behaviour. This article looks at the Government's record on issues of sexual morality arguing that despite the rhetoric on moral issues Thatcher has not launched a new moral offensive.

571. *Ewing, K. D. and Gearty, Conor A. *Freedom under Thatcher: Civil Liberties in Modern Britain*. Oxford: Oxford University Press, 1980. 305.

Argues that since the early 1970s there has been a serious decline in the levels of political freedom in Britain. It argues that Thatcher's freedoms (consumer choice) detract from his/her freedoms of expression and association. These are exacerbated by the increase of police powers and the legal responses to terrorism. Britain, it is alleged, has become a "national security state." Since the book is well documented and cites authentic cases, it makes for somewhat frightening reading.

572.   Forgan, L. "A gag that hurts us all." *The Times*. November 5th 1988.

On censorship and civil liberties in Britain.

573.   Gallop, Geoff. "The future of Thatcherism." *Australian Outlook*. August 1986: 75–83.

Thatcher's achievements up to 1985 are discussed.

574.   Gamble, Andrew. "The decline of Britain." *Contemporary Record*. Volume 2, number 5, 1989: 18–23.

Political debates over issues of efficiency, modernisation and social domocracy are reviewed. Argues that political and socioeconomic decline have been arrested by the Thatcher Government.

575.   Gamble, Andrew. "The politics of Thatcherism." *Parliamentary Affairs*. Volume 42, number 3, 1989: 350–61.

Examines the development of Thatcher's ideology, political style and social and economic policies showing how these became to be collectively known as Thatcherism.

576.   Gardyne, Jock Bruce. *Mrs. Thatcher's First Administration*. London: Macmillan, 1984. 216.

A survey of Thatcher's first term written in a narrative form by a Treasury minister.

577.   Gearty, Conor A. *Freedom under Thatcher: Civil Liberties in Modern Britain*. See K. D. Ewing, number 571 above.

578.   Gelb, Norman. "Mrs. Thatcher's dog days: the Tories are restless." *New Leader*. July 9th 1984: 7–8.

In hindsight, this is an interesting insight into the periodic unpopularity suffered by Thatcher. She always managed to ride above it.

579. Gorodetskaia, I. "Padenie populiarnosti pravitel'stva tori"(A fall in the popularity of the Tory government). *Mirovaia Ekonomika i Mezhdunarodnye Otnosheniia.* Number 6, 1986: 105–12.

Examines the Conservative Party's problems in the light of the Westland affair with their impact on Thatcher's popularity during 1985–86.

580. Graham, Cosmo and Prosser, Tony. "The constitution and the new Conservatives." *Parliamentary Affairs.* Volume 42, number 3, 1989: 330–49.

Assesses the impact of Thatcherism since 1979 with emphasis on legislation, political leadership and domestic policies.

581. Graham, Cosmo and Prosser, Tony (editors). *Waiving the Rules: The Constitution under Thatcherism.* Milton Keynes: Open University Press, 1988. 212.

582. Green, David G. *The New Right: The Counter-Revolution in Political, Economic and Social Thought.* Brighton: Harvester Press, 1987. 238.

Examines the so-called gap between liberal thought and the Thatcher and Reagan practical politics.

583. Hale, David. "Thatcherism." *Across the Board.* December 1981: 48 57.

Argues that "Thatcherism" is a word being used almost as an expletive in comparing Thatcher's economic policy with Reagan's. Asks the question, "How valid are the comparisons?"

584. Hartley, Anthony. "After the Thatcher decade." *Foreign Affairs.* Volume 68, number 5, 1989: 102–18.

Argues that although Neil Kinnock's new Labour Party image has threatened Thatcher's Government, it would be impossible for any new Government to reverse the march of Thatcherism if it came to power. Shows that the Conservative Party has vastly expanded its electoral base to include most of the middle class. Thatcher's powerful ethos of enterprising individualism would be unlikely to disappear if she were to be removed from power.

585. Holmes, Martin. *First Thatcher Government, 1979–1983: Contemporary Conservatism and Economic Change.* Brighton: Wheatsheaf Books, 1985. 256.

586. International Currency Review. "Thatcherism: The policy contradictions continue." *International Currency Review.* November 1981: 41–47.

Problems facing Thatcher are seen as resulting from "monopoly legacies of socialism in the public sector and labour markets."

587. Jackson, P. *Implementing Government Policy Initiatives: The Thatcher Administration.* London: RIPA, 1985.

Includes a section on Thatcher's industrial policy up till 1983.

588. Jacobs, Michael. "Thatcher and the increase of state power in Britian." *Canadian Dimension.* Volume 20, number 2, 1986: 32– 35.

Thatcher's extension of the use of the British Intelligence Agency MI5 in her attempts to control the media and to investigate private citizens.

589. Jessop, B., Bonnett, K., Bromley, S. and Ling. T. *Thatcherism: A Tale of Two Nations.* Oxford: Basil Blackwell.

Thatcher is said to have produced two nations in more than one way: the haves and the have nots, North and South, Scotland and England, and so forth.

590. Kirtley, Jane E. "A walk down a dangerous road." *Government Information Quarterly.* Number 2, 1988: 117–35.

An analysis of the British press and censorship with special emphasis on Thatcher's actions on Peter Wright's *Spycatcher.*

591. Lee, J. M. "The machinary of Government." *Parliamentary Affairs.* Autumn 1980: 434–47.

Discusses the prospect of redefining the issues under Thatcher's new one-year-old administration.

592. Lloyd, John. "Mrs. Thatcher and disestablishment: Thatcher's challenge to the establishment." *Contemporary Record.* 2(6), 1989: 18–26.

Argues that Thatcher has an aversion to Britain's conventional Conservatism. This is seen through her challenge of the establishment and through her impact on the production of a new middle class that is seen as materialist, hedonist and internationalist.

593. Loney, Martin. *The Politics of Greed: The New Right and the Welfare State.* London: Pluto Press, 1986. 200.

Critical of Thatcher's economic policies and their effect on the welfare state.

594. *Raban, Jonathan. *God, Man and Mrs. Thatcher.* London: Chatto and Windus Counterblasts Series, 1989. 72.

Critical of Thatcher's speech to the General Assembly of the Church of Scotland in which she relates Christian morality to Conservative policies.

595. Thompson, Kenneth. "Transgressing the boundary between the sacred and the secular/profane: a Durkheimian perspective on a public controversy." *Sociological Analysis.* Volume 52, number 3, Autumn 1991: 277+.

Criticisms made by the bishops of the Church of England against Thatcher's policies.

596. Thornton, P. *Decade of Decline: Civil Liberties in the Thatcher Years.* London: National Council for Civil Liberties (NCCL), 1989. 104.

597. Walters, Peter. "The crisis of 'responsible' broadcasting: Mrs. Thatcher and the BBC." *Parliamentary Affairs.* July 1989: 380–98.

On conflicts between the British Broadcasting Corporation (BBC) and Thatcher's Government on the coverage of the Falklands War, Northern Ireland and political accountability.

See also: Jenkins, Peter. *Mrs. Thatcher's Revolution: Ending of the Socialist Era.* (no. 795); Webster, Wendy. *Not a Man to Match Her: The Marketing of a Prime Minister.* (no. 1309).

B. The Civil Service

598. Fortin, Yvonne. "Madame Thatcher et la politisation des échelons supérieurs de l'administration centrale en Grande-Bretagne, 1979–1984: mythe ou realité?"(Mrs. Thatcher and the politicisation of the civil service in Great Britain 1979–1984: myth or reality?). *International Revue of Administration Sciences.* Number 4, 1984: 337–54.

599. Fry, Geoffrey K. "The attack on the civil service and the response of the insiders." *Parliamentary Affairs.* 37(4), 1984: 353–63.

Analyses Thatcher's alleged failure in implementing her economic policies as reflected in the public disapproval of her handling of the press criticism of the civil service.

600. Fry, Geoffrey K. "The British career civil service under challenge."
      Political Studies. December 1986: 533–55.

Thatcher worked hard to trim down the civil service and cut down its
pervasive influence in policy decision making.

601. Fry, Geoffrey K. "The development of the Thatcher Government's
      'Grand Strategy' for the civil service: a public policy perspective."
      Public Administration. Autumn 1984: 322–55.

602. Fry, Geoffrey K. "The Thatcher Government: the financial manage-
      ment initiative, and the new civil service."*Public Administration*.
      Spring 1988, 1–20.

On Thatcher's reforming of the civil service, the impact of the financial
management initiative and concludes that the old civil service has not
really changed much under Thatcher.

603. Hennessy, Peter. "Mrs. Thatcher's poodle? The civil service since
      1979." *Contemporary Record*. 2(2), 1988: 2–15.

Assesses how Thatcher's long tenure of office has affected the character
of the British civil service since 1979.

604. Peters, B. Guy. "Burning the village: the civil service under Reagan
      and Thatcher." *Parliamentary Affairs*. January 1986: 79–97.

On Thatcher and Reagan's civil service reforms. Alleges that though
intended to increase efficiency, the reforms have led to low morale and a
deterioration in working conditions.

605. Ponting, Clive. *Whitehall: Changing the Old Guard*. London:
      Unwin Hyman, 1989.

Ponting was tried under the Official Secrets Act for leaking information
on the *Belgrano* affair. He was acquitted.

606. Ponting, Clive. *Whitehall: Tragedy and Farce*. London: Sphere,
      1986. 272.

Exposes the civil service of which Ponting was a member before being
tried over the leaking of information on the *Belgrano*. He was acquitted.

607. Ridley, F. F. "The British civil service and politics: principles in ques-
      tion and traditions in flux." *Parliamentary Affairs*. 36(1), 1983: 28–48.

Discusses the neutrality of the civil service with its recent politicisation
under Thatcher. Assesses the future of the service.

608. Rose, Richard. *Loyalty, Voice or Exit?* Glasgow: University of Strathclyde Centre for the Study of Public Policy, 1988. 28.

Margaret Thatcher posed the biggest challenge ever faced by the civil servants. The old conflict between serving elected ministers and the Crown intensified as Thatcher trimmed down the service reshaping it into her own image.

609. Thomas, Rosamund M. "The politics of efficiency and effectiveness in the British civil service." *International Review of Administrative Sciences.* Number 3, 1984: 239–51.

See also: Hennessy, Peter, *Whitehall.* (no. 500); *The London Times.* "Accused of petty vindictiveness for removing some civil servants from Queen's Birthday Honours List." (no. 175); *The London Times.* "Expected to announce cutting of further 70,000 jobs in the civil service." (no. 160).

C. Consensus

610. Bosanquet, Nick. *After the New Right.* Oxford: Heinemann, 1983.

611. Bradley, Ian. *The Strange Rebirth of Liberal Britain.* London: Chatto Windus, 1985.

612. *Hennessy, Peter and Seldon, Anthony (editors). *Ruling Performance: British Governments from Attlee to Thatcher.* Oxford: Basil Blackwell, 1987. 344.

Covers each administration and its Prime Minister's style in the light of Britain's changing role in the world. Each section is followed by a useful chronology. The sections on the Heath, Wilson and Callaghan Governments set the scene for a better understanding of Thatcher's policies within a progressive context.

613. *Kavanagh, Dennis and Morris, Peter. *Consensus Politics from Attlee to Thatcher.* Oxford: Basil Blackwell, 1989. 152 (hardback and paperback available).

British consensus was epitomised by the quinquennial shift in Party politics. Thatcher made a radical move away from consensus politics replacing it with conviction politics.

614. *Kavanagh, Dennis. *Thatcherism and British Politics: The End of Consensus?* Oxford: Oxford University Press, 1990. 339.

A revised reprint of the 1987 work. Places Thatcherism in the context of post-war Britain arguing the breakdown of political consensus.

615. Kavanagh, Dennis. "Whatever happened to consensus politics?" *Political Studies.* 33(4), 1985: 529–46.

Examines the nature of British consensus politics, its emergence and its decline under Thatcher with the extremes of conviction politics being represented by her on the right and by Wedgewood Benn on the left.

616. Middlemas, K. "Will she have to listen this time?" *New Statesman.* July 3rd 1987: 12–14.

617. Morris, Peter. *Consensus Politics from Attlee to Thatcher.* See Dennis Kavanagh, number 613 above.

618. Rich, Paul B. "British imperial decline and the forging of English patriotic memory, c1918–1968." *History of European Ideas.* 9(6), 1988: 659–80.

Shows how patriotic ideology has changed since 1918 with the rejection of imperialism as morally repugnant in the mid-1920s. Baldwin, the Conservative Prime Minister, helped this process along replacing it with English rusticity and homogeneity. After the Second World War a new welfare state ideology came into being. Enoch Powell eventually replaced all this with the concept of British patriotism, the free market economy and an independent foreign policy all of which were picked up by Thatcher in the 1980s.

619. Rose, Richard. *Politics in England: Change and Persistence.* London: Macmillan, 1989. 381.

Impact of the Thatcher Government with emphasis on party government, political culture and socialisation, mass media, pressure groups, political programmes and political leaders.

620. Scanlon, Joan (editor). *Surviving the Blues: Growing up in the Thatcher Decade.* London: Virago, 1990. 240.

621. Schwarz, Walter. *New Dissenters: The Non-conformist Conscience in the Age of Thatcher.* London: Bedford Square Press, 1989. 96.

622. Smith, Geoffrey. "The British scene." *Foreign Affairs.* Summer 1986: 923–38.

Examines the consequences of Thatcherism, its effect on the Labour Party and the birth of the Social Democratic Party (SDP), the Falklands War, the miners' strike and Westland.

623. Wallace, W. "What price independence? Sovereignty and interdependence in British politics." *International Affairs.* Volume 62, number 3, 1986.

624. Wheatcraft, Geoffrey. "That woman versus the chattering classes."*Atlantic.* Volume 268, number 6, December 1991: 26.

Discusses Thatcher and her attitude toward British intellectuals for whom she had a feeling little short of contempt.

625. Williams, Walter. "Central government capacity and the British disease." *Parliamentary Affairs.* 42(2), 1989: 250–64.

Argues that the main British disease (i.e., economic decline) has not been cured by Thatcher. Offers the reason as being the structure of central government which opposes political modernisation.

626. Young, Wayland (editor). *The Rebirth of Britain.* London: Weidenfeld and Nicolson. 1982.

See also: Crewe, Ivor. "What's left for Labour." (no. 674); Douglas, James. "The Conservative Party, from pragmatism to ideology and back?" (no. 634); King, Anthony. *The British Prime Minister.* (no. 815); Revzin, Philip. "Tory challenger." (no. 543).

D. The Conservative Party

627. Alderman, Geoffrey. *Britain: A One Party State?* Christopher Helm, 1989. 165.

How economic and social change have contributed to the dominance of the Conservative Party.

628. Aughey, Arthur. "Mrs. Thatcher's philosophy." *Parliamentary Affairs.* 36(4), 1983: 389–98.

Shows that Thatcher's philosophy is based on a distinctive reading of Conservative Party history leading to her policies of limited government, private enterprise, tax cuts and personal advancement.

629. *Bell, David S. (editor). *The Conservative Government 1979–1984: An Interim Report.* London: Croom Helm, 1985. 217.

A collection of essays covering the policy aspects of Thatcher's first five years.

630. *Blake, Lord Robert. *Conservative Party from Peel to Thatcher*. London: Fontana, 1985. 402.

A revised edition of Blake's original *Conservative Party from Peel to Churchill.*

631. Cassidy, John. "The Tory family at war." See Andrew Grice, number 1356 below.

632. Crewe, Ivor and Searing, Donald D. *Thatcherism: Its Origins, Electoral Impact and Implication for Down's Theory of Party Strategy*. Colchester: University of Essex Department of Government, number 37, 1986. 45.

Origins of Thatcher's rise to the Conservative Party leadership, the ideological structure of the parliamentary Conservative Party at the time of Thatcher's election as Leader, the relationship between Thatcherite policies and trends in public opinion among the British electorate.

633. Deedes, William. "What will the Conservatives do?" *Political Quarterly*. October 1977: 400–409.

634. Douglas, James. "The Conservative Party: from pragmatism to ideology—and back?" *West European Politics*. 6(4), 1983: 56–74.

Argues that the Conservative Party has kept a sense of unity which prevents any divisions affecting other parties. Under Thatcher, ideology has become more important than unity as shown by the 1983 general elections manifesto produced by the Conservatives.

635. Farr, Diana. *Five at 10—Prime Ministers' Consorts Since 1957*. London: Andre Deutsch, 1985. 232.

An interesting insight into Denis Thatcher as a supporter, admirer and moderator of his wife's work. 170–216.

636. Harris, Robin. *The Conservative Community*. London: Centre for Policy Studies, 1989.

The roots and future of Thatcherism.

637. Hartley, Anthony. "From Disraeli to Thatcher: the avatars of English Conservatism."*Encounter*. April 1986: 43–44.

Compares Disraeli's ideology between 1868 and 1874 with Thatcher's modern Conservatism.

638. Hughes, David. "The Tory family at war." See Andrew Grice, number 1356 below.

639. Hutcheson, John A. "British Conservatism in the Twentieth Century: an emerging ideological tradition." See John D. Fair, number 494 above.

640. Norton, Philip. "Choosing a leader: Margaret Thatcher and the Parliamentary Conservative Party 1989–1990." *Parliamentary Affairs*. 43(3), 1990: 249–59.

Argues that, contrary to popular belief, Thatcher's hold on her Party has been a hard job. Identifies her inherent political vulnerability and potential difficulties.

641. Norton, Philip. "The lady's not for turning: but what about the rest? Margaret Thatcher and the Conservative Party: 1979–1989." *Parliamentary Affairs*. January 1990: 41–53.

Analyses the political stance of the Conservative Members of Parliament (MPs) through their voting behaviour and membership of particular groups and Thatcher's influence on the Party.

642. *O'Gorman, Frank. *British Conservatism: Conservative Thought—Burke to Thatcher*. London: Longman Documents in Political Ideas Series, 1986. 256.

Edmund Burke (1729–1797) was a British statesman whose work *Reflections on the Revolution in France* made him a champion of Conservatism and in opposition of Jacobinism. He was a Member of Parliament who expounded the principle of MPs being representatives and not delegates. He preached that the state should make possible the full realisation of human potential whilst representing agreements on norms and ends. The stable and habitual life of society should be allowed to develop without extensive state interference. Thatcher's Conservative philosophy owes some debt to Burke.

643. Painter, Chris. "Thatcherite radicalism and institutional Conservatism." *Parliamentary Affairs*. 42(4), 1989: 463–84.

Suggests that Thatcher did not really have much effect on the political institutions associated with central government.

644. *Patten, Chris. *The Tory Case*. Harlow: Longman, 1983.

Chris Patten was the Conservative Party Chairman responsible for the 1992 election victory. However, he lost his own Bath seat. He is currently Governor of Hong Kong.

645.   Peele, Gillian. "Political parties in the 1980s." *Contemporary Record.* 1(4), 1988: 2–4.

Assesses the revival of British political parties with special reference to the Social Democratic and Liberal Alliance and the Conservatives.

646.   Prosser, Tony. "The constitution and the new Conservatives." See Cosmo Graham, number 580 above.

647.   *Pym, Francis. *The Politics of Consent.* London: Hamish Hamilton, 1984. Revised second edition, Sphere, 1985.

Francis Pym was eventually sacked for being critical of Thatcher's policy. His attempt to create a Conservative opposition to her failed miserably.

648.   Rose, Richard. "The British Conservative party." In Morgan, R. and Silvester, S. (editors). *Moderates and Conservatives in Western Europe.* Oxford: Heinemann, 1982.

649.   Ross, John. *Thatcher and Friends: The Anatomy of the Tory Party.* London: Pluto Press, 1983. 122.

A socialist analysis of Thatcherism produced at the height of the Falklands factor.

650.   *Schoen, Douglas E. *Enoch Powell and the Powellites.* London: Macmillan Press Ltd., 1977. 317.

An understanding of Powell is important to the understanding of Thatcherism, especially aspects of public spending cuts.

651.   Studentsov, V. B. "Dva techeniia v sotsial'noi filosofii britanskogo konservatizma" (Two currents in the social philosophy of British Conservatism). *Voprosy Filosofii.* 1985: 103–13.

Discusses the two currents that exist in the Conservative Party. Thatcher is seen as paternalistic whilst the wets of the Party represent the less openly ideological.

652.   *Tebbit, Norman. *Upwardly Mobile.* London: Futura, 1989. 359.

Norman Tebbit was Thatcher's Secretary of State for Employment and later Trade and Industry. In 1987 he was credited with Thatcher's third electoral victory as Conservative Party Chairman. He was outspoken and at times provocative. This is his very readable autobiography. It includes two very readable chapters, one on Heath's disasterous Premiership and the second on Tebbit's horrifying experiences at Brighton where both he and his wife were seriously injured.

653. *Whitelaw, William. *The Whitelaw Memoirs*. London: Headline Book Publishing, 1990. 370.

A readable narrative which throws light on both the Heath and Thatcher Governments. More importantly, it gives an interesting insight into internal Conservative Party politics.

654. Willetts, David. *Modern Conservatism*. Harmondsworth: Penguin Books, 1992. 216.

A history of Conservatism as a movement towards economic and political belief sustained by a shared culture. Gives a readable analysis of monetarism and Thatcherism, ending with an assessment of Britain in Europe.

655. Williamson, Nigel. *New Right: Men behind Mrs. Thatcher*. Nottingham: Spokesman Books, 1984. 24.

656. Zieba, Andrzej. "Wspolczesna doktryna brytyjskiej partii konserwatywnej" (Contemporary doctrine of the British Conservative Party). *Studia Nauk Politycznych*. (6), 1984: 89–112.

Assesses Conservatism with Thatcher's brand of it seen as concentrating on property and free market monetarist economics along with limited government. It argues that, although Thatcher moved away from the concept of the strong state, she adopted strong measures in legal and police issues.

See also: Carter, Neil. "A very Tory coup: the ousting of Mrs. Thatcher." (no. 1380); Gilmour, Ian. *Inside Right: A Study of Conservatism*. (no. 496); Grice, Andrew. "The Tory family at war." (no. 1356); Jenkins, Roy. "Challenging patterns of leadership: from Asquith via Baldwin and Attlee to Mrs. Thatcher." (no. 813); Matveyev, Vladimir. "The neo-Conservative music." (no. 29); Russell, T. *The Tory Party*. (no. 544); Toman, Barbara. "Tory paradox." (no. 63).

E. Defense

657. Benton, S. "The triumph of the spirit of war." *New Statesman*. May 29th 1987: 12–14.

658. Carver, Michael. *Tightrope Walking: British Defence Policy since 1945*. London: Hutchinson, 1992. 191.

Assesses, after a contextual history, Britain's defence needs. Advocates radical changes if Britain is to survive. Chapters 8 to 10 cover the Thatcher years and associated defence cuts.

659. *Harris, Robert. *Gotcha! The Media, the Government and the Falklands Crisis*. London: Faber and Faber, 1983.

The media coverage of the Falklands War and the Government's handling of news coverage caused a controversy in 1982. "Gotcha!" was a rather tasteless headline accompanying a photograph of an exploding Argentinian ship.

660. McIntoch, Malcolm. *Managing Britain's Defence*. London: Macmillan, 1990. 272.

Covers the administrations of three Conservative Defence Secretaries: Francis Pym, John Nott and Michael Heseltine.

661. Norpoth, Helmut. "Guns and butter and government popularity in Britain."*American Political Science Review*. 81(3), 1987: 949–59.

Shows how the Falklands War increased Thatcher's popularity, giving it an increase of 5 percent in the 1983 election. It shows that unemployment but not inflation also had an effect on the election results.

662. *Ponting, Clive. *The Right to Know: Inside Story of the* Belgrano. London: Sphere, 1985.

Ponting was a civil servant who was prosecuted and acquitted under the infamous Official Secrets Act. He tells his story and argues for the public's right to know.

663. Sanders, D. "Government popularity and the Falklands War: a reassessment." *British Journal of Political Science*. Volume 17, number 3, 1987.

664. Smith, Dan. "Nostalgia for empire." *Monthly Review*. 33(6), 1981: 52–58.

Shows how Britain's military planning and spending seek to reassert Britain's strong political position in the world. This trend coincides with U.S. interests.

665. Strong, Robert A. "Nuclear protest in Britain and America." *Arms Control*. 4(2), 1983: 97–110.

Discusses the British Campaign for Nuclear Disarmament and the American nuclear freeze movement and their re-emergence under Thatcher and Reagan.

See also: Cosgrave, Patrick. *Carrington: A Life and a Policy*. (no. 492); *The London Times*. "Cuddling up to the bear." (no. 1110); Chapter X, Section C, on the Falklands.

F. Elections

666. Berrington, Hugh. "The British general election of June 1987: Have we been here before?" *West European Politics*. 11(1), 1988: 116–21.

Considers how the general election result was a reflection of the permanent social change caused by Thatcher. Also assesses the status of the losing Labour Party.

667. Bondy, François. "Margaret Thatcher's overkill." *Schweizer Monatshefte*. 63(7–8), 1983: 541–43.

Analyses Thatcher's overwhelming election victory of 1983.

668. Brennan, W. "The right weapon against an elective dictatorship in Britain." *Independent*. May 26th 1989.

669. *Butler, D. and Kavanagh, D. *The British General Election of 1979*. London: Holmes and Meier, 1980. 443.

The Conservatives won with a majority of 43 seats.

670. *Butler, D. and Kavanagh, D. *The British General Election of 1983*. London: St. Martin, 1984.

The Conservatives won by a majority of 144 seats.

671. *Butler, D. and Kavanagh, D. *The British General Election of 1987*. London: St. Martin, 1988. 392.

The Conservatives won by a majority of 102 seats.

672. Cozens, Peter and Swaddle, Kevin. "The British general election of 1987." *Electoral Studies*. 6(3), 1987: 263–66.

673. *Crewe, Ivor. *How to Win a Landslide without Really Trying: Why the Conservatives Won in 1983*. Colchester: University of Essex Papers in Politics and Government, number 1, 1984.

674. Crewe, Ivor. "What's left for Labour." *Public Opinion*. July 1987: 52–56.

Examines the role of gender, age and class in the 1987 general election results. Also analyses the reasons for Labour's dismal performance. This is an abridged version of the original article published in *The Guardian* of June 15th and 16th 1987.

675. Curtice, John. *How Britain Votes*. See Anthony Heath, number 676 below.

676. Heath, Anthony, Jowell, Roger and Curtice, John. *How Britain Votes*. Oxford: Pergamon Press, 1985. 264.

Thatcher's presence changed voting patterns quite dramatically.

677. Heath, Anthony and others. *Understanding Political Change: The British Voter 1964–1987*. Oxford: Pergamon Press, 1991. 348.

Traditional voting patterns have changed dramatically since the 1960s. This work shows how this has happened because of an electorate becoming more sophisticated, shifts in social class and Thatcher's influence in reshaping social and political structures.

678. Jowell, Roger. *How Britain Votes*. See Anthony Heath, number 676 above.

679. Kavanagh, D. *The British General Election of 1979*. See D. Butler, number 669 above.

680. Kavanagh, D. *The British General Election of 1983*. See D. Butler, number 670 above.

681. Kavanagh, D. *The British General Election of 1987*. See D. Butler, number 671 above.

682. McAllister, Ian. *The Nationwide Competition for Votes: 1983 British Election*. See Richard Rose, number 686 below.

683. McAllister, Ian. *Voters Begin to Choose: from Closed Class to Open Elections in Britain*. See Richard Rose, number 687 below.

684. Roberts, Geoffrey K. "El parlamento Britanico en 1983." (The British Parliament in 1983). *Revista de Estudios Politicos*. 1984: 237–54.

Shows how the general elections of 1983 dominated activities in the House of Commons where parties were too busy electioneering to work on long-term planning.

685. Roberts, G. K. "El parlamento Britanico en 1984." (The British Parliament in 1984). *Revista de Estudios Politicos*. 1985: 235–51.

Shows how, during the 1984 session, the House of Lords allegedly took more progressive stands on issues than did the House of Commons.

686. Rose, Richard and McAllister, Ian. *The Nationwide Competition for Votes: 1983 British Election*. London: Pinter, 1984.

687. Rose, Richard and McAllister, Ian. *Voters Begin to Choose: From Closed Class to Open Elections in Britain*. London: Sage, 1986. 192.

688. Searing, Donald D. *Thatcherism: Its Origins, Electoral Impact and Implications for Down's Theory of Party Strategy*. See Ivor Crewe, number 632 above.

689. Shell, Donald R. "The House of Lords and the Thatcher Government." *Parliamentary Affairs*. 38(1), 1985: 16–32.

Outlines the conflicts between Thatcher and Members of the House of Lords for five years because of the strong political opposition and unreliable support from some of the Lords. Thatcher believed that the use of the Whip was all that was required.

690. Swaddle, Kevin. "The British general election of 1987." See Peter Cozens, number 672 above.

691. *Thatcher, Carol. *Diary of an Election*. London: Sidgwick and Jackson, 1983. 192 (available in hardback and paperback).

Carol Thatcher followed her mother during the 1983 general elections. This is a record of these events.

692. Worcester, Robert M. "The polls: Britain at the polls 1945– 1983." *Public Opinion Quarterly*. 48(4), 1984: 824–33.

Discusses voting patterns in the United Kingdom from 1945 to Thatcher's second victory.

See also: *Economist.* "Election Britain: third-term Thatcher." (no. 119);
Kellner, Peter. "Mrs. Thatcher's vision of a fifteen-year Reich." (no. 18);
Kexiong, Cheng. "Local elections signal Thatcher victory." (no. 24);
Mooney, Bel. "Votes and seats for women." (no. 1302); Webster, Wendy.
Not a Man to Match Her: The Marketing of a Prime Minister. (no. 1309).

G. Environmental Issues

693.   Blowers, Andrew. "Transition or transformation? Environmental
       policy under Thatcher." *Public Administration.* 65(3), 1987: 277–
       94.

Describes environmental policy since 1979 after which, mediated by
both ideology and pragmatism, it became fairly significant in national
politics.

694.   Cairncross, Frances. "Thatcher's Environmental Politics." *Finan-
       cier.* May 1989: 12–17.

An article showing the change in Thatcher's thinking as pressure
mounted on the threats of global warming and climatic change.

695.   Darke, Roy. *Environmental Planning and the Thatcher Govern-
       ment.* Sheffield: University of Sheffield Department of Town and
       Regional Planning, 1985. 12.

696.   Dawkins, L. A. "The politics of energy conservation and industrial
       interests in Britian." *Parliamentary Affairs.* 40(2), 1987: 250–64.

Among other things, it discusses the Association for the Conservation
of Energy which was established in 1981 by major companies to promote
public awareness of energy issues. Also examines Thatcher's energy
policy.

See also: *Economist.* "The greening of Margaret Thatcher." (no. 130).

H. Health Service

697.   Cairncross, Frances. "For better UK health service, management,
       competition needed." *Financier.* December 1987: 11–15.

Analyses the Thatcher Government's efforts to improve National Health
Service (NHS) efficiency.

698. Cairncross, Frances. "Hard Thatcher scrutiny finding UK Health Service is doing fine." *Financier.* December 1988: 12–16.

699. Judge, Ken. *Health Policy in the Thatcher Era, 1990.* Southampton: Spiral University Southampton, 1990. 48.

700. Klein, Rudolph. "Why Britain's Conservatives support a socialist health care system." *Health Affairs.* Spring 1985: 41– 58.

With trusts set up and private insurance encouraged, Thatcher has introduced a mixed economy into the health service.

See also: Daykin, Norma. *Unhealthy Transitions: Young Women, Health and Work in the 1980s.* (no. 1444); Higgs, Paul. *Privatisation and the Politics of Hegemony: A Study of the Attitudes of Striking NHS Ancillary Workers Towards Privatisation, 1984–1985.* (no. 1447); Pardey, Kenneth. *The Welfare of the Visually Handicapped in the United Kindom.* (no. 1453).

I. Image

701. *Atkinson, Max. *Our Masters' Voices: Language and Body Language of Politics.* London: Methuen, 1984. 224.

Study on the change in Thatcher's voice over the years. Her original somewhat squeaky and strident tones were replaced by image-makers with a quieter and softer tone.

702. Cockerell, Michael. "The marketing of Margaret." *The Listener.* June 16th 1983.

Over the years the Thatcher image was modified with changes made to her voice, her appearance and the presentation of her policy.

703. Tyler, Rodney. *Campaign! The Selling of the Prime Minister.* London: Grafton Books, 1987.

See also: Greig, Gordon. "The Prime Minister's punishing programme." (no. 1347); Johnson, Paul. "Still the best man in the cabinet." (no. 14); Johnson, Paul. "The strongest head—but the softest heart too!" (no. 15); Malcolm, N. "Margaret Thatcher, housewife superstar." (no. 1349); Warden, John. "Maggie, a Churchill in carmen rollers." (no. 1352).

J. The Law and Civil Liberties

704. Bindman, G. "Spycatcher: Judging the judges." *New Law Journal.* January 20th 1989.

Peter Wright's memoirs as a senior intelligence officer were subject to a prolonged legal battle in an unsuccessful attempt by the Thatcher Government to stop them.

705. Carr, Josephine. "The UK lawyers' big bang." *International Financial Law Review.* March 1989: 7–11.

Examines the implications of the Government's radical proposals to restructure the UK legal profession for commercial law firms. Carr concludes that the restructuring opens the door to Europe for United States law firms.

706. Chesshyre, Robert. *The Force: Inside the Police.* London: Sidgwick and Jackson, 1989. 227.

Thatcher increased both the salary and status of the police in a bid to affirm her belief in law and order. This work is based on the author's research on the Metropolitan Police in the London Streatham division.

707. Gamble, Andrew and Wells, Celia (editors). *Thatcher's Law.* GPC Books, 1989. 160.

708. James, Michael. "Thatcher unveils police-state bill." See Janet Miller, number 885 below.

709. Jenkins, Roy. "The encroaching power of government." *Index on Censorship.* Spring 1988: 24–28.

Showing that academic freedom and other pluralist values are under threat as Thatcher's personal power increases its influence over government, independent institutions, and dissenting opinions.

710. Johnson, F. and Verity, C. "Liberty and the pursuit of Thatcher." *Sunday Telegraph.* March 12th 1989.

On civil liberties under Thatcher.

711. Loughlin, Martin. "Law, ideologies and the political–administrative system." *Journal of Law and Society.* 16(1), 1988: 21–41.

Considers intergovernmental relations and legislation under Thatcher.

712. Levin, Bernard. "Who will defend us against the bullies in blue?" *The Times.* December 17th 1985.

Policing, law and order were a high priority under Thatcher. The police were given increases of 25 percent during Thatcher's first term. Cynics had it that she was preparing for a possible confrontation with trade unionists and with socially disaffected members of an acquisitive society.

713. Norrie, Alan and Adelman, Sammy. "Consensual authoritarianism and criminal justice in Thatcher's Britain." *Journal of Law and Society.* 16(1), 1988: 112–28.

Suggests that the relationship between Thatcher's Government and the legal system is based on a form of authoritarian populism.

714. Terrill, Richard J. "Margaret Thatcher's law and order agenda." *American Journal of Comparative Law.* Summer 1989: 429–56.

Margaret Thatcher fought all three elections on a strong law and order ticket. This article focuses on legislation illustrating her policy with a discussion on the issue of police discretion.

715. Wells, Celia (editor). *Thatcher's Law.* See Andrew Gamble, number 707 above.

716. Verity, C. "Liberty and the pursuit of Thatcher." See F. Johnson, number 710 above.

See also: Field, Frank. *Losing out: The Emergence of Britain's Underclass.* (no. 1319); Gordon, P. *Citizenship for Some: Race and Government Policy 1979–1989.* (no. 1331); Gorz, Andre. *Farewell to the Working Class.* (no. 1291); Chapter XIII, Section C, The Law.

K. Local Government

717. Brooke, Rodney. "A look at English local government." *Public Meeting.* March 1989: 16–19.

The abolition of the Greater London Council (GLC) was but a start in a massive move towards centralisation. Local government is still reeling from the impact of Thatcher's policies.

718. *Butcher, Hugh and others. *Local Government and Thatcherism.* London: Routledge, 1990. 171.

Impact of the Conservative Government on local housing, education, social services, economic development initiatives, racial inequality and decentralisation.

719. Chandler, J. A. *Local Government under the Thatcher Governments*. London: Pavic Publications, 1988. 23.

Local government was dramatically reorganised under Thatcher. The Greater London Authority was abolished.

720. Davies, Howard J. "Local government under siege." *Public Administration*. Spring 1988: 91–101.

Discusses the impact of Thatcherism on local government with emphasis on the Audit Commission.

721. Hambleton, Robin. "Urban government under Thatcher and Reagan." *Urban Affairs Quarterly*. March 1989: 359–88.

Centralisation under Thatcher meant a dramatic decline in urban regeneration as central Government lost touch with the urban masses.

See also: Heseltine, Michael. *Where There's A Will*. (no. 501); Jones, Bernard M. *Local Government Finance: Change in the Thatcher Years*. (no. 954).

L. The Media

722. *Ingham, Bernard. *Kill the Messenger*. London: HarperCollins, 1991. 408.

Bernard Ingham was Thatcher's at times controversial Press Secretary for most of her Premiership. Apart from its insights into many events in Thatcher's time, it is also a very interesting analysis of the relations between Government and the mass media.

723. Newton, Ken. *Liberal Neutrality and the News Media*. Colchester: University of Essex Department of Government, number 53, 1988. 31.

Compares the policies of market and content regulation in the United States and Great Britain.

724. Tant, Tony. *Constitutional Aspects of Official Secrecy and Freedom of Information: An Overview*. Colchester: University of Essex Papers in Politics and Government, number 52, 1988. 33.

See also: Baxter, Sarah. "Thatcher and the media." (no. 1314); *Economist*. "Anatomy of a leak." (no. 90); Harris, Robert. *Gotcha! The Media, the Government and the Falklands Crisis*. (no. 659); Heath. E. "A state of secrecy." (no. 8); *The London Times.* "The Clive Ponting case." (no. 196); Murray, Nancy. *Racism and the Press in Thatcher's Britain.* (no. 1315); Atlas, J. "Thatcher puts a lid on: censorship in Britain." (no. 558).

M. Miscellaneous

725. Campbell, Beatrix. *Wigan Pier Revisited.* London: Virago. 1984.

726. Fernand, Deidre. "Mother's little helper." *Sunday Times.* Section 3. April 21st 1991:1.

Criticism of Mark Thatcher on taking over the management of his mother's financial affairs.

727. Fenwick, John and others. *The Public Domain in an English Region: Aspects of Adaptation and Change in Public Authorities.* Glasgow: Studies in Public Policy, number 175, 1989. 43.

728. Foot, P. "Larry the lion or Larry the lamb?" *New Statesman.* April 13th 1979: 511.

729. Fortune. "There aren't any brand-new formulas." *Fortune.* May 16th 1983: 158–60.

Interview with Thatcher on economic, political and foreign policy.

730. Garrison, Terry. *Mrs. Thatcher's Casebook. Tutor's Pack.* Huntingdon, U.K.: Elm Publications, 1987. 400 (also available in loose-leaf folder).

731. Hennessy, Peter and Walker, David. *Sources Close to the Prime Minister.* London: Macmillan, 1984.

732. James, C. E. "Pauline conversions and inversions." *New Statesman.* June 3rd 1988: 15.

733. Jeremy, David J. "The emigrants to a new world gallery at the Merseyside Maritime Museum, Liverpool." *Technology and Culture.* 31(2), 1990: 278–83.

The Merseyside Maritime Museum was restored with funding from the Thatcher Government and the European Economic Community and opened in 1986. The article praises the opening of the museum whilst criticising it for not addressing issues of racism in today's Britain and Europe.

734. Johnson, Paul. "Margaret Thatcher and morality." *Svensk Tidskrift.* 75(6), 1988: 289–93.

Shǫws how Thatcher took the moral initiative away from the Labour Party and turned her crusade against the unions into a moral question. Argues that her economic policy is working and that her refusal to spend more money without the wealth creation necessary goes hand in hand with achieving capitalist effectiveness.

735. Kellner, Peter. "Exclusive: the script of No. 10's Christmas pantomime." *New Statesman.* December 19th 1986: 5.

736. Kendrick, Stephen and McCrone, David. "Politics in a cold climate: the Conservative decline in Scotland." *Political Studies.* 37(4), 1989: 589–603.

In the 1950s the Conservatives did quite well in Scotland. This article argues that Thatcher's rhetoric has alienated Scotland both economically and in real terms.

737. Lawson, M. "The history woman." *Independent.* December 1st 1990: 28.

738. Lee, Anthony. "Queen of Comedy." *New Statesman.* Volume 4, number 179, November 29th 1991: 21.

On Thatcher's way of life.

739. Lee, M. "Tread softly Iron Lady." See P. Bowring, number 1092 below.

740. Macintyre, Donald. "Interview with Thatcher." See Margaret Thatcher, number 452 above.

741. McCrone, David. "Politics in a cold climate: the Conservative decline in Scotland." See Stephen Kendrick, number 736 above.

742. McGlone, Francis. "Away from the dependency culture? Social security policy." In *Public Policy under Thatcher* (see number 907 below) 159–71.

743. Middleton, P. "For 'Victorian' read 'Georgian.' " *Encounter.* July 1986: 73–76.

Alleges that Thatcher's values of hard work, cleanliness and patriotism belong more to the post–World War I era.

744. Moncur, Andrew (editor). *Margaret Thatcher's History of the World.* London: Fourth Estate, 1989. 128.

745. Oakley, Robin. "A lot more to life than slickness." *The Times*. June 11th 1987: 8.

746. Oakley, Robin. "That Iron Lady's mask slips more often than you think." *Daily Mail*. January 15th 1982.

747. Observer. "10 years at number 10." *Observer*. April 30th 1989: 9+.

748. Rutherford, M. "A profound change of climate." See G. Owen, number 42 above.

749. Stanyer, Jeffrey. "Administrative developments in 1979: a survey." See David R. Steele, number 818 below.

750. Turner, Graham. "Interview with Thatcher." See Margaret Thatcher, number 458 above.

751. Turner, John. *Ungovernability Revisited*. See Peter Madgwick, number 879 below.

752. Villiers, Charles. *Start Again Britain*. London: Quartet Books, 1984. 288.

753. Vinen, Richard. "Pierre Poujade and Margaret Thatcher." *History Today*. Volume 41, August 1991: 5.

Poujade started a movement for the protection and help of businessmen and artisans (l'union de defence des commerçants et artisans). The movement, started in 1954, became known in France as "poujadisme."

754. Walker, David. *Sources Close to the Prime Minister*. See Peter Hennessy, number 731 above.

755. Wilks, Stephen and Cini, Michelle. "The redirection of science and technology policy under the Thatcher Government." *Public Money and Meeting*. Summer 1991: 49–56.

Analyses research and developments during the 1980s.

756. Winkler, Matthew. "U.K. comeback." See Gary Putka, number 996 below.

757. Wright, Peter. *Spycatcher: The Candid Autobiography of a Senior Intelligence Officer*. New York: Viking, 1987.

The book that Thatcher tried to stop without success. The whole case had serious implications for secrecy and open government.

N. Satire and Humor

758.   Ingrams, Richard and Wells, John. *Bottoms up!: Further Letters of Denis Thatcher.* London: Andre Deutsch and Private Eye, 1984. 80.

See entry for number 762 below.

759.   Ingrams, Richard and Wells, John. *Down the Hatch: Further Letters of Denis Thatcher.* London: Andre Deutsch, 1985. 80.

See entry for number 762 below.

760.   Ingrams, Richard and Wells, John. *Just the One: Further Letters of Denis Thatcher.* London: Andre Deutsch, 1986. 80.

See entry for number 762 below.

761.   Ingrams, Richard and Wells, John. *One for the Road: Further Letters of Denis Thatcher.* London: Andre Deutsch, 1982. 80.

See entry for number 762 below.

762.   Ingrams, Richard and Wells, John. *Other Half: Further Letters of Denis Thatcher.* London: Andre Deutsch and Private Eye, 1981. 80.

The "Dear Bill" letters published in *Private Eye* offer a satirical view of Thatcher and her husband. These letters became extremely popular in the eighties. They provide the best example of crass sexism in their portrayal of a Prime Minister and her spouse.

763.   Ingrams, Richard and Wells, John. *Still Going Strong: Further Letters of Denis Thatcher.* London: Andre Deutsch and Private Eye, 1988. 80.

See entry for number 762 above.

764.   Machale, Des. *World's Best Maggie Thatcher Jokes.* London: Angus and Robertson, 1989. 96.

Thatcher was said to have a somewhat feeble sense of humour. Since her resignation, she has, nonetheless, managed a rare Thatcher joke in her House of Lords maiden speech. There is, however, no shortage of jokes about her.

765.   Rushton, William. *Spy Thatcher: The Collected Ravings of a Senior MI5 Officer.* Sevenoaks: New English Library, 1988. 128.

766.   Wells, John. *Bottoms up! Further Letters of Denis Thatcher.* See Richard Ingrams, number 758 above.

767. Wells, John. *Down the Hatch: Further Letters of Denis Thatcher.* See Richard Ingrams, number 759 above.

768. Wells, John. *Just the One: Further Letters of Denis Thatcher.* See Richard Ingrams, number 760 above.

769. Wells, John. *One for the Road: Further Letters of Denis Thatcher.* See Richard Ingrams, number 761 above.

770. Wells, John. *Other Half: Further Letters of Denis Thatcher.* See Richard Ingrams, number 762 above.

771. Wells, John. *Still Going Strong: Further Letters from Denis Thatcher.* See Richard Ingrams, number 763 above.

772. Woddis, Roger. "Spectacula!" *New Statesman.* Volume 4, number 182, December 20th 1991: 24.

Satire on British politics and politicians including Thatcher, Major, and Kinnock.

See also: Abse, Leo. *Margaret, Daughter of Beatrice: Politician's Psychobiography of Margaret Thatcher.* (no. 514); Rusbridgen, A. "Funny peculiar." (no. 55).

O. Social Welfare

773. Burridge, Roger. "Housing tales of law and space." See Ann Stewart, number 786 below.

774. Johnson, Norman. *Reconstructing the Welfare State: A Decade of Change 1980–1990.* Brighton: Harvester Wheatsheaf, 1990. 251.

Critical of Conservative social policy including social security, the National Health Service (NHS), education, housing and inner-city policies.

775. Judge, Ken and others. "Public opinion and the privatisation of welfare."*Journal of Social Policy.* October 1983: 469–89.

Subtitled "some theoretical implications," the article examines the extent to which the social policy of the Thatcher Government reflects what people want.

776. Lait, J. *Breaking the Spell of the Welfare State.* See D. Anderson, number 1022 below.

777. Lewis, Jane. "It all really starts in the family: community care in the 1980s." *Journal of Law and Society.* 16(1), 1988: 83–96.

Suggests that Thatcher's idea of family care for the elderly really means family care by women.

778. Marsland, D. *Breaking the Spell of the Welfare State.* See D. Anderson, number 1022 below.

779. Malpasse, Peter. *Reshaping Housing Policy: Subsidies, Rents and Residualisation.* London: Routledge, 1990. 196.

Examines the impact of Thatcherism on housing policy with special emphasis on council housing.

780. Metcalfe, Les and Richards, Sue. *Improving Public Management.* London: Sage Publications, 1987. 243.

The Thatcher Government set out to improve efficiency across the board. This work, published for the European Institute of Public Administration examines this "efficiency strategy."

781. Richards, Sue. *Improving Public Management.* See Les Metcalfe, number 780 above.

782. Roistacher, Elizabeth A. "A tale of two Conservatives: housing under Reagan and Thatcher." *Journal of the American Planning Association.* 50(4), 1984: 485–92.

Argues that any gains in efficiency in Thatcher's and Reagan's housing policies are paid for in terms of the loss experienced by the low-income renters and other households.

783. Savage, Stephen P. "A war on crime? Law and order policies in the 1980s." In *Public Policy under Thatcher* (see number 907 below). 89–102.

784. Smith, Geoffrey. "Post-Falklands: Full-scale Thatcher social cuts now politically possible." *Institute of Socioeconomic Studies Journal.* Autumn 1982: 15–24.

Whereas Thatcher's radical economic policies were initially more apparent in what she said rather than in what she did, her Falklands victory gave her the popularity, personal confidence and the ability to start public spending cuts in a major way.

785. Squires, Peter. *Anti-Social Policy: Welfare, Ideology and the Disciplinary State.* Brighton: Harvester Wheatsheaf, 1990. 229.

Examines state intervention into poverty and deviance to assert social control. Critical analysis of Thatcher's policies.

786. Stewart, Ann and Burridge, Roger. "Housing tales of law and space."*Journal of Law and Society*. 16(1), 1988: 65–82.

Examines the legal framework and social impact of national efforts in the housing sector.

787. Stewart, Murray. *Urban Policy in Thatcher's England*. Bristol: Univerity of Bristol School for Advanced Urban Studies, 1990. 48.

788. Thompson, R. J. "Reagan, Thatcher and social welfare: typical and non-typical behaviour for Presidents and Prime Ministers." See D. H. Clayton, number 948 below.

789. Waine, Barbara. *Rhetoric of Independence: Myth and Reality of Social Policy in Thatcher's Britain*. Berg Publishers, 1991. 192

790. Woodburn, Jack. "Housing: a burning question." *Labour Movement*. January 1981: 17–20.

Critical of Thatcher's housing policies.

See also: Archbishop of Canterbury. *Faith in the City*. (no. 557); Bellairs, Charles E. *Conservative Social and Industrial Reform*. (no. 489); *Economist*. "Thatcher's think-tank takes aim at the welfare state." (no. 98).

P. Socialism

791. Ali, Tariq. *Who's Afraid of Margaret Thatcher?: In Praise of Socialism*. See Ken Livingstone, number 801 below.

792. Barry, Brian. *Does Society Exist?: Case for Socialism after Thatcher*. London: Fabian Society, 1989. 24.

Thatcher is reputed to have said that there is no such thing as society. Her emphasis is on individualism and individual acquisitiveness.

793. Gelb, Norman. "Undoing Britain's socialism: Mrs. Thatcher's rollback." *New Leader*. November 29th 1982: 11–12.

794. Hall, Stuart. *The Hard Road to Renewal: Thatcherism and the Crisis of the Left*. New York: Verso, 1988. 283.

The Labour party was in a mess when Thatcher came to power in 1979. During her years in power the Labour Left was virtually annihilated partly by her policies' populism and partly by the Labour Party jockeying for the more acceptable centre road.

795. *Jenkins, Peter. *Mrs. Thatcher's Revolution: Ending of the Socialist Era*. London: Jonathan Cape, 1987. 224.

Also published in paperback by Pan Books, 1989. 432. Jenkins, associate editor for *The Independent*, used to be political columnist for *The Guardian*. In this very readable work he argues that the failure of consensus politics allowed Thatcher to employ her radical solution to Britain's economic and social problems. Her conviction politics also allowed her to place Britain in the forefront of nations and above her political opponents at home. His analysis of the 1987 general elections is exciting to say the least. He shows how the centrist Alliance Party willfully destroyed itself thus allowing Thatcher her triumph. Jenkins shows Thatcher as, more than anyone else, articulating the aspirations and moral doubts of her age. Although he foresees her end, he clearly sees her as having set the agenda for the future.

796. Jessop, Bob; Bonnett, Kevin; Bromley, Simon; and Ling, Tom. "Authoritarian populism, two nations and Thatcherism." *New Left Review*. Number 147, 1984: 32–61.

Assesses attempts by the Left to interpret Thatcherism in terms of political successes and economic disasters as authoritarian populism.

797. Jessop, Bob; Bonnett, Kevin; Bromley, Simon; and Ling, Tom. "Thatcherism and the politics of hegemony: a reply to Stuart Hall." *New Left Review*. 1985: 87–101.

Examines the writings of Stuart Hall and discusses the implications to the left of hegemonic politics.

798. Keys, David and others. *Thatcher's Britain: A Guide to the Ruins*. London: Pluto Press, 1983. 120.

A socialist critique of Thatcherism.

799. Kurzer, Paulette. "A decade of Thatcherism: the debate on the left." *Comparative Political Studies*. 23(2), 1990: 257–77.

A socialist critique of Thatcherism with emphasis on the analyses of leftist authors such as Bob Jessop, Stuart Hall, Henk Overbeek and Andrew Gamble.

800. Labour Research. "Holding public service staff to ransom." *Labour Research*. September 1989: 7–9.

Argues that the transport and council workers' strikes scared Thatcher into threatening to ban them. Compares current British legislation with that of other European Community countries.

801. *Livingstone, Ken and Ali, Tariq. *Who's Afraid of Margaret Thatcher?: In Praise of Socialism.* New York: Verso Editions, 1984. 128.

Ken Livingstone is currently a Labour Member of Parliament. He used to be the Leader of the Labour group in the new defunct Greater London Council (GLC). Tariq Ali is best known for his extreme left views associated with the student revolt of the 1960s.

802. *Livingstone, Ken. *If Voting Changed Anything They'd Abolish It.* London: Collins, 1987. 367.

Thatcher's Government abolished the Greater London Council (GLC) which it saw as too expensive and as too left wing. During the years of upheaval that preceded this abolition, Ken Livingstone was the controversial Leader of the GLC. He fought hard, though unsuccessfully, against Thatcher's attempts to end local government.

803. Mitchell, Austin. *Can Labour Win Again?* London: Fabian Society, 1979.

Clearly not . . . but then they may take heart from the Israeli Labour Party.

804. Mitchell, Austin. "Labour's response to Thatcher." *Political Quarterly.* July 1980: 257–73.

805. Mother Jones. "Coal miner's son: an interview with Neil Kinnock, Maggie Thatcher's leading rival." *Mother Jones.* January 1985: 22–26.

"Maggie Thatcher's leading ineffectual rival" may have been a more appropriate description.

806. Pirie, Madsen. "Buying out of socialism: the Thatcher administration has found a sure-fire way to reduce big government: sell it to the people." *Reason.* January 1986: 22–27.

Discusses the positive results of increasing privatisation under Thatcher including the shrinkage of the welfare state and the selling of 13 percent of council houses in Britain.

807. Wilson, Eben. "How far can Thatcher go?" *Reason.* October 1980: 33–36.

Places Thatcher's economic and social policies within the context of undoing decades of British socialism and argues that it will not be easy.

See also: Adams, Jad. *Tony Benn: A Biography.* (no. 487); Crewe, Ivor. "What's left for Labour." (no. 674); Joseph, Keith. *Reversing the Trend.* (no. 504).

Q. Thatcher's Management and Leadership Styles

808. Burch, Martin. "The British Cabinet: a residual executive." *Parliamentary Affairs.* 41(1), 1988: 34–48.

Assesses Thatcher's management style of her Cabinet and concludes that under her leadership the Cabinet has "taken on a more residual role in policy making."

809. Burch, Martin. "Mrs. Thatcher's approach to leadership in government: 1979–June 1983." *Parliamentary Affairs.* Autumn 1983: 399–416.

Argues that Thatcher's initial approach was a response to the problems of policy application rather than policy formation. With the Prime Minister and the Treasury working closely together, the rest of the Cabinet was subject to diminished responsibility.

810. Doherty, Michael. "Prime-Ministerial power and ministerial responsibility in the Thatcher era." *Parliamentary Affairs.* January 1988: 49–67.

Shows a Prime Ministerial Government as distinct from a Cabinet one.

811. Gardyne, Jock Bruce. *Ministers and Mandarins.* London: Sidgwick and Jackson, 1986.

Written from the viewpoint of a Treasury minister.

812. Gergen, David R. and King, Anthony. "Following the leaders: how Ronald Reagan and Margaret Thatcher have changed public opinion." *Public Opinion.* June 1985: 17–19+.

King examines the British public's perception of Thatcher arguing that Britons may have rallied to her after the Falklands War, but not to all of her Conservative policies for a new society.

813. Jenkins, Roy. "Challenging patterns of leadership: from Asquith via Baldwin and Attlee to Mrs. Thatcher." *Contemporary Record*. 2(2), 1988: 20–24.

A comparative look at the four Prime Ministers listed in the title.

814. Jenkins, Simon. "Thatcher style: the trials and triumphs of a party ideologue." *The Economist*. May 21st 1983: 21–22.

815. King, Anthony (editor). *The British Prime Minister*. London: Macmillan, 1985. 275.

Role of the Prime Minister in the postwar British system of government particularly since 1969. The work has some focus on Thatcher's Prime Ministerial style.

816. Minogue, Kenneth and Biddiss, Michael (editors). *Thatcherism: Personality and Politics*. London: Macmillan Press, 1987. 168.

Examines the impact of Thatcherism as an attitude of mind and a style of action on the Conservative Party, Cabinet government, economic and foreign policy and on British society.

817. Prior, James. *A Balance of Power*. London: Hamish Hamilton, 1986.

Ministerial memoirs, by one of Thatcher's wets. Prior was moved out of the way into Northern Ireland and eventually out of the Government.

818. Steele, David R. and Stanyer, Jeffrey. "Administrative developments in 1979: a survey."*Public Administration*. Winter 1980: 387–419.

Discusses the administration of the government with specific reference to comparing declared intentions against implemented proposals.

See also: *The London Times*. "Is Mrs. Thatcher really such a bossy lady?" (no. 185); *The London Times*. "Prior to Northern Ireland in what is seen as last attempt to build Cabinet in tune with her economic aims." (no. 179); *The London Times*. "President and Prime Minister: the contrast in leadership." (no. 163).

R. Thatcherism and Other Ideologies

819. Andrews, Leighton. *Liberalism after Thatcher*. Hebden Royd Publications, 1985.

820. Artley, A. "The power of England's Evita." *Spectator*. June 6th 1987: 9–11.

821. Astley, Neil (editor). *Dear Prime Minister: Open Letters to Margaret Thatcher and Neil Kinnock*. Bloodaxe Books, 1990. 160.

822. Bates, Betty. *Thatcher Payne-In-The-Neck*. New York: Dell Publications, 1987.

823. Beaton, Alistair and Hamilton, Andy. *Thatcher Papers*. Sevenoaks: New English Library, 1980.

824. Benton, S. "Tales of Thatcher." *New Statesman*. April 28th 1989: 8–11.

825. Bevins, Anthony. "How Thatcher became a Thatcherite." *Independent*. May 1st 1989: 6.

826. Biddiss, Michael (editor). *Thatcherism: Personality and Politics*. See Kenneth Minogue, number 816 above.

827. Brittan, S. "Traumatic if not radical."*Financial Times*. March 24th 1987: 16.

828. Blundell, John. "What to make of Margaret Thatcher? In five years as Britain's Prime Minister, she's broken with forty years of British politics." *Reason*. August 1984: 34–39+.

Assesses Thatcher's impact in the context of postwar history.

829. Bonnett, Kevin. "Authoritarian populism, two nations and Thatcherism." See Bob Jessop, number 796 above.

830. Bonnett, Kevin. "Thatcherism and the politics of hegemony: a reply to Stuart Hall." See Bob Jessop, number 797 above.

831. Bradbury, M. and others. "Thatcher's monuments." *Observer Magazine*. April 23rd 1989: 19+.

On the achievements of Thatcher during her first ten years.

832. Brittan, S. ". . . and the same old problems: Thatcherism and beyond." *Encounter*. April 1985: 51–61.

833. Bromley, Simon. "Authoritarian populism, two nations and Thatcherism." See Bob Jessop, number 796 above.

834. Bromley, Simon. "Thatcherism and the politics of hegemony: a reply to Stuart Hall." See Bob Jessop, number 797 above.

835. Bromley, S. *Thatcherism: a Tale of Two Nations.* See B. Jessop, number 589 above.

836. Buiter, Willem H. and Miller, Marcus. "The Thatcher experiment: the first two years." *Brookings Pas Economic Activity.* Number 2, 1981: 315–79.

Comments on, and discussion of, Thatcher's monetary and fiscal policies.

837. Bulpitt, Jim. "The discipline of the new democracy: Mrs. Thatcher's domestic statecraft." *Political Studies.* Number 1, March 1986: 19–39.

Examines the Thatcher Government on the basis of electoral strategy and achieving a necessary degree of governing competence.

838. Burgess, Anthony and Cosgrave, Patrick. "Cette femme Thatcher with eyes like Caligula and the mouth of Marilyn Monroe." *You.* February 10th 1985.

President Mitterand of France was reputed to have told his new European Minister Roland Dumas, "Cette femme Thatcher! Elle a les yeux de Caligule, mais elle a la bouche de Marilyn Monroe." (This woman Thatcher! She has Caligula's eyes, but she has Marilyn Monroe's mouth.")

839. Butt, Ronald. "Thatcherissima: the politics of Thatcherism." *Policy Review.* Autumn 1983. 30–40.

One of three consecutive articles on Thatcherism.

840. Coleman, Terry. *Thatcher's Britain: A Journey through the Promised Lands.* London: Corgi, 1988. 208.

841. Cyr, Arthur. "Britain moves toward 1990." *Current History.* 87(532), 1988: 369–72.

Shows how Thatcher continued her policies helped by a prosperous economy and a very weak opposition.

842. Cyr, Arthur. "Political developments in Britain." *Current History.* 85(514), 1986: 366–68.

Shows how Thatcher's position was being threatened by the new Liberal–Social Democratic Alliance and by a Labour Party that had shifted its position to the right. Even then Thatcher went on to win an overwhelming majority in the 1987 elections.

843. Derbyshire, Ian and Derbyshire, J. Denis. *Politics in Britain: from Callaghan to Thatcher.* Chambers, 1990. 80.

844. Derbyshire, J. Denis. *Politics in Britain: from Callaghan to Thatcher.* See Ian Derbyshire, number 843 above.

845. Duke, Vic. *A Measure of Thatcherism: A Sociology of Britain.* See Stephen Edgell, number 846 below.

846. Edgell, Stephen and Duke, Vic. *A Measure of Thatcherism: A Sociology of Britain.* London: HarperCollins, 1991. 271.

Draws on a wide spectrum of empirical data which are discussed in relation to Thatcherism with specific reference to social issues.

847. Evain, Claude. "L'éxperience Thatcher à mi-parcours." (The Thatcher experience halfway through). *Chrons. Actualité.* Number 4, 1982: 112–18.

848. Faber, Doris. *Margaret Thatcher: Britain's Iron Lady.* London: Viking Women of Our Time Series, 1986.

849. Gamble, Andrew. "Thatcher revisited." *Parliamentary Affairs.* January 1986: 121–23.

850. Gelb, Norman. "Mrs. Thatcher's strategy: Conservative infighting." *New Leader.* October 5th 1981: 11–12.

851. Hall, Stuart and Jacques, Martin (editors). *The Politics of Thatcherism.* London: Lawrence and Wishart, 1983. 344.

852. Harriman, Ed. *Thatcher: A Graphic Guide.* Camden Press, 1986. 170.

853. Haseler, Stephen. *The Battle for Britain: Thatcher and the New Liberals.* London: Tauris, 1989. 195.

Analyses Britain as a nation in transition from paternalism to radical economic policy.

854. Hearn, Michael. "Margaret Thatcher, un portrait politique." (Margaret Thatcher, a political portrait). *Etudes.* 364(1), 1986: 15–25.

On Thatcher's political leadership with emphasis on her achievements in restricting the welfare state, consolidating the EEC as a force for democratic stability and defending the free world.

855. Hindness, Barry (editor). *Reactions to the Right.* London: Routledge, 1990. 193.

Ideological responses of the political left to Thatcherism including market socialism, secondary education, privatisation, the welfare state and racism.

856. Hirst, Paul H. *After Thatcher*. London: Collins, 1989.

857. Hole, Dorothy. *Margaret Thatcher: Britain's Prime Minister*. Enslow Publishers, 1990. 128.

858. Holmes, Martin. *Thatcherism: Scope and Limits, 1983–1987*. London: Macmillan Press, 1989. 184.

859. Howells, P. "Mrs. Thatcher's theory of human nature." *Contemporary Review*. October 1980: 183–90.

860. Hutton, Will. "Thatcher's half-revolution." *Wilson Quarterly*. 9(4), 1987: 123–34.

Shows how privatisation and greater deregulation have caused higher unemployment but have also reduced Britain's budget deficit.

861. Jacques, Martin (editor). *The Politics of Thatcherism*. See Stuart Hall, number 851 above.

862. Jenkins, S. "Fall and rise of Margaret Thatcher." *The Economist*. April 21st 1979: 39–42.

863. Jenkins, S. "I have not finished yet." *The Times*. November 19th 1990: 14.

864. Jenkins, Simon. "Mrs. Thatcher at mid-term: Portrait of a Prime Minister at bay." *The Economist*. October 10th 1981: 19–22.

865. Jessop, Bob and others. "Farewell to Thatcherism? Neo-Liberalism and new times." *New Left Review*. January 1990: 81–102.

Domestic and international dimensions of Thatcher's economic strategy at the beginning of her resignation year.

866. Johnson, C. "Britain: the Thatcher record." *World Today*. May 1987: 77–80.

867. Kavanagh, Dennis. "Thatcher's third term." *Parliamentary Affairs*. 41(1), 1988: 1–12.

Gives a brief history of the Thatcher years with emphasis on the economic conditions that helped her win a third term of office.

868. King, Anthony. "Following the leaders: how Ronald Reagan and Margaret Thatcher have changed public opinion." See David R. Gergen, number 812 above.

869. Krieger, Joel. *Reagan, Thatcher and the Politics of Decline*. Oxford: Oxford University Press, 1986.

870. Larin, Vladimir. "Thatcherism." *Moscow New Times*. Number 10, March 1981: 18–20.

871. Leach, Richard H. "Thatcher's Britain." *Current History*. May 1981: 197–200+.

Examines political conditions in Britain after two years of Thatcherism.

872. LeFournier, Philippe. "Is Britain reviving? The 'Thatcher revolution' impresses." *World Press Review*. Spring 1983: 29–31.

Translated from L'Expansion of Paris (June 16th 1983).

873. Leruex, Jacques (editor). "Le Thatcherisme: doctrine et action." (Thatcherism: doctrine and action). *Notes et Etudes Documentaires*. Number 15, 1984: 1–143.

Collection of articles based partly on a seminar held by the Centre d'études et de recherches internationales of the Fondation nationale des sciences politiques. Includes aspects of economic policy, the civil service, foreign policy and the sale of Government business enterprises.

874. Ling, Tom. "Authoritarian populism, two nations and Thatcherism." See Bob Jessop, number 796 above.

875. Ling, Tom. "Thatcherism and the politics of hegemony: a reply to Stuart Hall." See Bob Jessop, number 797 above.

876. Ling, Tom. *Thatcherism: A Tale of Two Nations*. See Bob Jessop, 589 number above.

877. Little, Graham. *Strong Leadership: Thatcher, Reagan and an Eminent Person*. Oxford: Oxford University Press (Australia), 1989. 289.

878. Madgwick, P. "Mrs. Thatcher and the study of politics." *Parliamentary Affairs*. January 1988: 164–69.

879. Madgwick, Peter and Turner, John. *Ungovernability Revisited*. Glasgow: Studies in Public Policy number 171, 1989. 32.

Regards Thatcherism as a response to the political conditions of the 1970s.

880. Maitland, Olga. *Margaret Thatcher: The First Decade.* London: Sidgwick and Jackson, 1989. 140.

881. *Marsh David and Rhodes, R. A. W. *Implementing Thatcherism: A Policy Perspective.* Colchester: University of Essex Department of Government, Essex Papers in Politics and Government, number 62, 1989. 60.

Focuses on what has changed under Thatcher and why. It concludes that the supposed change under the Thatcher revolution has been surprisingly limited.

882. *Marsh, David and Rhodes, R.A.W. *Implementing Thatcherite Policies: Audit of an Era.* Buckingham: Open University Press, 1992. 212.

Examines the changes that took place under Thatcher without the issues of personalities. Concludes that her failure was due to lack of attention to implementation.

883. *Marsh, David and Tant, Tony. *There Is No Alternative: Mrs. Thatcher and the British Political Tradition.* Colchester: Papers in Politics and Government, 1989. 38.

884. Midland Bank. "Can Mrs. Thatcher do it?" *Midland Bank Review.* Autumn 1980: 9–19.

Looks at the prospects of success for Thatcher's economic policies.

885. Miller, Janet and James, Michael. "Thatcher unveils 'police- state' bill." *Intercontinental Preview.* March 5th 1984: 120–22.

Critical views on some of the provisions of the Police and Criminal Evidence Bill introduced for parliamentary debate in November 1983.

886. Miller, Marcus. "The Thatcher experiment: the first two years." See Willem H. Buiter, number 836 above.

887. Moon, J. "The cult of personality: perspectives on Margaret Thatcher." *Parliamentary Affairs.* Spring 1985: 261–63.

888. Mount, Ferdinand. "Thatcher's decade." *National Interest.* 1988–89: 10–20.

Attributes the Conservative Government's success directly to Margaret Thatcher's personality and style of leadership.

889. Nickell, S. "The Thatcher miracle?" See R. Layard, number 942 below.

890. Norton, Philip. "Thatcher or Thatcherism." *Parliamentary Affairs*. July 1987: 417–22.

891. Nott, John. "Renaissance for Great Britain?" *Enterprise*. May 1980: 5–7.

Shows the effects of some of Thatcher's economic policies.

892. Parkinson, Michael. "The Thatcher Government's urban policy, 1979–1989: a review." *Town Planning Review*. October 1989: 421–40.

Centralisation and privatisation policies in the light of U.S. experience.

893. Pearce, Edward. "The end of Thatcher: transitional thoughts." *Encounter*. 66(4), 1986: 33–35.

Examines Thatcher's position in the light of the Westland affair scandal and Michael Heseltine's resignation.

894. Pearce, Edward. *Looking Down on Mrs. Thatcher*. London: Hamish Hamilton, 1987. 192.

895. Pearce, Edmund. "The noisiest diminuendo in history." *New Statesman*. Volume 4, number 179, November 29th, 1991. 19.

On Margaret Thatcher's performance during a debate on Europe in the House of Commons.

896. Pincher, Chapman. *Truth about Dirty Tricks: From Harold Wilson to Margaret Thatcher*. London: Sidgwick and Jackson, 1990. 300.

897. Prins, G. "Mrs. Thatcher's reward—or punishment." *New Statesman*. March 27th 1987: 10–11.

898. Prosser, Tony (editor). *Waiving the Rules: The Constitution under Thatcherism*. See Cosmo Graham, number 581 above.

899. Rhodes, R. A. W. *Implementing Thatcherite Policies: Audit of an Era*. See David Marsh, number 882 above.

900. Rhodes, R. A. W. *Implementing Thatcherism: A Policy Perspective*. See David Marsh, number 881 above.

901. Riddell, Peter. *Thatcher Decade*. Oxford: Basil Blackwell, 1989. 208.

902. Riddell, Peter. *Thatcher Era*. Second revised edition of *Thatcher Decade*. Oxford: Basil Blackwell, 1991. 224.

903. Riddell, Peter. *The Thatcher Government*. London: Martin Robertson, 1983. 262. Revised edition in 1985 (Oxford: Basil Blackwell).

A book by the political editor of the *Financial Times* which covers the issues of Thatcherism.

904. Robins, Lynton (editor). *Public Policy under Thatcher*. See Stephen P. Savage, number 907 below.

905. Sackett, Victoria. "Thatcherissima: the shape of things to come." *Policy Review*. Autumn 1983. 30–40.

One of three consecutive articles on Thatcherism.

906. Savage, R. "Dix ans de Thatcherisme." (Ten years of Thatcherism). *Bulletin Documentaire*. September 1989: 245–90.

Evaluation of Thatcherism with a discussion of the 1989 budget. Asks if Thatcherism is a renewal or persistent decline of the British economy.

907. Savage, Stephen P. and Robins, Lynton (editors). *Public Policy under Thatcher*. London: Macmillan Education Ltd., 1990. 291.

Concerns itself with the legislative impact and policy initiatives of the Thatcher Government. It covers all aspects of Thatcherism including a readable section on equal opportunities.

908. Seldon, Anthony (editor). *Ruling Performance: British Governments from Attlee to Thatcher*. See Peter Hennessy, number 612 above.

909. Seldon, Anthony (editor). *Thatcher Effect: A Decade of Change*. See Dennis Kavanagh, number 1406 below.

910. Seldon, Arthur. "What is happening to Margaret Thatcher?"*Journal of Contemporary Studies*. Autumn 1981: 25–34.

911. Senker, Peter. "Ten years of Thatcherism: triumph of ideology over economics."*Political Quarterly*. Volume 60, number 2, April 1989: 179.

Evaluates the British economy under Thatcher seen as being either a miracle or a collapse.

912. *Simpson, David. *Understanding Mrs. Thatcher: Conservative Economic Policy, 1979–1987*. David Hume Institute, 1988. 20.

913. Sloman, Anne. *Thatcher Phenomenon*. See Hugo Young, number 928 below.

914. *Smedley, Philip Marsden (editor). *Britain in the Eighties: Spectator View of the Thatcher Decade*. London: Paladin, 1991. 400.

A collection of articles which appeared in *The Spectator* during Thatcher's decade. Very readable because of the immediacy conveyed by contemporary articles covering all aspects of Thatcherism though much of it is tongue in cheek.

915. Smith, Harry. "Thatcherism in practice." *Labour Monthly*. July 1979: 289–98.

An analysis that is critical of Thatcher's economic policies.

916. Solomos, John. "The simmering cities: urban unrest during the Thatcher years." See John Benyon, number 1323 below.

917. Stephenson, Hugh. *Mrs. Thatcher's First Year*. Norman: University of Oklahoma Press, 1980. 128.

918. Szamuely, G. "Tory hallelujah: Margaret Thatcher's decade." *Policy Review*. Summer 1987: 44–48.

919. Tant, Tony. *There Is No Alternative: Mrs. Thatcher and the British Political Tradition*. See David Marsh, number 883 above.

920. Thomson, George Malcolm. *The Prime Ministers, from Robert Walpole to Margaret Thatcher*. New York: William Morrow and Company, 1981. 260.

921. Torre, Paolo Filo Della. *Viva Britannia: Mrs. Thatcher's Britain*. London: Sidgwick and Jackson, 1985. 104.

922. *Turner, Graham. "Missing Margaret." *The Sunday Telegraph Review*. June 28th 1992: IV–V.

Lord Wyatt, Kingsley Amis, Paul Johnson and Bernard Levin used to be regarded as the angry young men of the Left. Amis was a member of the Communist Party, and Johnson once spoke of the Tory Party as "lower than vermin." Turner's article is a result of a lunch meeting during which these men claim that they have seen the Thatcherite light. Forsaking their socialist beliefs, they are now determined that Thatcher's legacy should continue. This article is crucial reading since it shows the ubiquitous power that Thatcher had on intellectuals. More importantly, it illustrates that, although no longer prime minister, Thatcher's influence can still be felt by those whose professional concerns are to shape emerging minds. They see Thatcher as returning as a force to be reckoned with, "Every time she utters a word, they scamper away in terror."

923. Ungar, S. J. "Dateline Britain: Thatcherism." *Foreign Policy*. Number 35, Summer 1979: 180–91.

924. Wickham, Sylvaine. "Thatcher et l'Europe liberale." (Thatcher and liberal Europe). *Chrons Actualité*. December 15th 1990: 424–29.

Evaluation of Thatcher's neo-liberal policies with emphasis on growth of the manufacturing sector and on the budget deficit.

925. Wintour, P. and Rogers, R. "She-bear in her pride." *New Statesman*. April 27th 1979: 578–80.

926. Woddis, R. and Minnion, J. "Mrs. Toad of Toad Hall." *New Statesman*. December 21st 1984: 34–35.

A facetious article on Thatcher.

927. Worcester, Kent. "Ten years of Thatcherism." *World Policy Journal*. Spring 1989: 297–320.

An article which celebrates Thatcher's tenth anniversary as Prime Minister and analyses Conservative trends in British politics.

928. *Young, Hugo and Sloman, Anne. *Thatcher Phenomenon*. London: British Broadcasting Corporation, 1986. 144 (available in hardback and paperback).

Although not a biography, this work is of much personal interest.

See also: Crewe, Ivor. *Thatcherism: Its Origins, Electoral Impact and Implications for Down's Theory of Party Strategy*. (no. 632); *The London Times*. "Edited text of speech to the General Assembly of The Church of Scotland." (no. 251); Thatcher, Margaret. *Let Our Children Grow Tall: Selected Speeches, 1975–1977*. (no. 550).

IX   Economic Affairs

Almost every aspect of British life has changed dramatically because of Thatcher's economic policies. There are attitudes born of the culture enterprise that would have been undreamed of before 1979. Individual acquisitiveness has become part of the new British psyche: creating wealth through hard work and efficiency.

A. Criticism of Economic Policy

Whatever benefit the enterprise culture has brought to Britain, those opposed to Thatcher saw it as pure greed by the strong and endless poverty for the weak.

929.   Bernheim, Roger. "Margaret Thatcher's verblassendes charisma." (Margaret Thatcher's fading charisma). *Schweizer Monatshefte.* 64(9), 1984: 679–87.

Discusses unemployment and inflation since 1983 when Thatcher was elected for her second term of office.

930.   Bonnett, K. *Thatcherism: A Tale of Two Nations.* See B. Jessop, number 589 above.

931.   *Brown, Gordon. *Where There's Greed: Margaret Thatcher and the Betrayal of Britain's Future.* Edinburgh: Mainstream Publishing, 1989. 182 (available in hardback and paperback).

Gordon Brown is a Labour Member of Parliament and a member of the Shadow Cabinet. He argues that the Thatcher economic miracle was not a real legacy. He attacks the effects of Thatcherism including a claim that £120 billion have been wasted, families have been impoverished and divided and that the rhetoric of competition has destroyed Britain's international competitiveness. He also argues that the welfare state has been destroyed through the erosion of health care and infrastructure. Britain, he alleges, is now also lacking the essential ingredients of research and training for the future. He concludes that even ordinary civil liberties have been undermined by Thatcher's Government. A readable, though at times infuriating, book since it only speaks from a rather misguided socialist viewpoint.

932. Buchanan, Keith. "Planned ruination: Thatcher's Britain." *Monthly Review.* 39(9), 1988: 1–9.

Argues that Thatcher's policies have divided Britain into a prosperous south and a poor north and west where unemployment is high and where economic prospects are low.

933. Business. "Regions." *Business.* April 1990: 111–13+.

Analyses the gap between most regions and the prosperous south-east of England. Alleges that the Thatcher years have left the north–south divide wider than it was to start with and suggests that Europe could offer the best hope of closing it.

934. Business Weekly. "Britain: Thatcher may face a winter of discontent." *Business Weekly.* January 11th 1982: 52.

At the time of writing, Thatcher's popularity had plummeted to its lowest ebb. By the end of the winter it seemed that nothing short of a miracle could help her. The Falklands War factor cured this depression.

935. Business Weekly. "What hath Thatcher wrought?" *Business Weekly.* June 6th 1983: 44–48+.

An article arguing that four years of Thatcherism have not cured the sick man of Europe. The boom of the mid-1980s had not yet started at the time of writing.

936. Carter, A. "Masochism for the masses." *New Statesman.* June 3rd 1983: 8–10.

937. Coates, David and Hillard, John. *The Economic Decline of Modern Britain.* Brighton: Wheatsheaf, 1986.

938. Craven, B. M. "The Thatcher years 1985–1990: the failure of ideas." *British Review of Economic Issues.* October 1990: 37–51.

Focuses on privatisation and reform of public utilities, the National Health Service (NHS), local government services. Criticises the supply-side strategies in these areas.

939. Economist. "Strike one for Thatcher." *The Economist.* July 3rd 1982: 13–14.

Argues for ways of fighting against public-sector unions' monopoly power if Britain is to move ahead of its competitors.

940. Eltis, Walter. "Stormy times for Mrs. Thatcher." *Wall Street Journal.* April 4th 1980: 10+.

Discusses hostile reactions to Thatcher's economic policies.

941. Lavalette, Michael and Mooney, Gerry. "The struggle against the poll tax in Scotland." *Critical Social Policy.* Autumn 1989: 82–100.

A discussion of how the south-east has benefited at the expense of the north. The civil disobedience campaign against the poll tax (community charge) in Scotland and its implication for the later introduction in England and Wales. Violent demonstrations in England and Wales spelled the end of the Community Charge and its replacement, under Major, by the Council Tax.

942. Layard, R. and Nickell, S. "The Thatcher miracle?" *American Economic Review.* 79(2), 1989: 215–19.

Compares Britain's economic performance with the rest of Western Europe and concludes that Thatcher's perfomance has not been very inspiring. It argues that Thatcher's economic miracle has not been supported by the facts of the existence of high unemployment.

943. Mooney, Gerry. "The struggle against the poll tax in Scotland." See Michael Lavalette, number 941 above.

944. Ravier, Jean-Pierre (editor). "Crise ou sortie de crise en Grande-Bretagne?" (Crisis or the end of crisis in Great Britain?). *Annuaire Anglais.* Number 9/10, Centre de recherche sur les pays de langue anglaise, 1987. 240.

Deals with the economic and social consequences of the depression. Includes sections devoted to the district of Bradford, the channel tunnel, ethnic minorities and the police, economic policy, the position of the Church of England and employers' associations on the economic crisis, the 1985–86 teachers' strike, industrial relations, the alternative movement, the Social Democratic Party (SDP) and the housing shortage in London.

See also: Keys, David. *Thatcher's Britain: A Guide to the Ruins.* (no. 798); Malpass, Peter. *Reshaping Housing Policy: Subsidies, Rent and Residualisation.* (no. 779); Squires, Peter. *Anti-Social Policy: Welfare, Ideology and the Disciplinary State.* (no. 785).

B. Economic Developments

945. Anderson, Jeffrey J. "When market and territory collide: Thatcherism and the politics of regional decline." *West European Politics.* April 1990: 234–57.

Influence of Government policy in structuring the options for regional groups and mediational role of regional civil service. Responses of interest groups in the North East and the West Midlands in the eighties.

946. Bean, Charles R. "Crecimiento economico y desarrollo del Reino Unido: de la post-guerra al caso de la Senora Thatcher." (Growth, economy and development of the United Kingdom: from post-war to Mrs. Thatcher). *Desarrollo y Soc.* September 1984: 33–57.

Examines the causes of slow economic growth in Britain and the policies adopted to stimulate the economy, especially since 1979. Translated by Montes, Dilia E.

947. Beenstock, Michael and others. *Could Do Better.* Institute of Economic Affairs Occasional Paper Special 62, 1982. 111.

Assesses Thatcher's early performance in terms of economic progress. Contains contrasting views on her performance.

948. Clayton, Dorothy H. and Thompson, Robert J. "Reagan, Thatcher and social welfare: typical and non-typical behaviour for Presidents and Prime Ministers." *Presidential Studies Quarterly.* Summer 1988: 565–81.

Compares the methods used by Reagan and Thatcher to achieve their policy goals for social welfare.

949. Brindley, T. *Remaking Planning: Politics of Urban Change in the Thatcher Years*. London: Unwin Hyman, 1988. 192 (available in hardback and paperback).

950. Budd, Alan. "The Australian economy: Thatcherism after seven years." *Economic Outlook*. October 1983: 26–31.

Comparisons of policies and outcomes in Australia and Britain. The work reflects the extent of Thatcher's influence on policies outside Britain.

951. Coates, David and Hillard, John. *The Economic Revival of Modern Britain: The Debate between Left and Right*. Aldershot: Gower Publishing Company, 1987. 320.

952. Crafts, N. *British Economic Growth before and after 1979*. London: Centre for Economic Policy Research, 1989.

953. Director. "The re-making of Britain." *Director*. Spring 1983: 22–27.

An interview with Thatcher on her economic policies.

954. Jones, Bernard M. *Local Government Finance: Changes in the Thatcher Years*. London: Pavic Publications, 1989.

See also: Jenkins, Peter. *Mrs. Thatcher's Revolution: Ending of the Socialist Era*. (no. 795); *The London Times*. "Reagan reveals that Thatcher admitted to mistake over her economic policies." (no. 173); Thatcher, Margaret. *Small Today—Bigger Tomorrow: Three Speeches from the Small Business Bureau Conference, 1984*. (no. 457).

C. The Economy

955. Aaronovitch, Sam. *The Road from Thatcherism: The Alternative Economic Strategy*. London: Lawrence and Wishart, 1981. 138.

956. Aaronovitch, Sam. "Thatcherism and Britain's decline." *Political Affairs*. September 1982: 34–40.

957. Abromeit, Heidrun. "Thatcherismus, oder: Die Widersprueche der neuen Wirtschaftspolitik in Grossbritannien." (Thatcherism or the contradictions of the new economic policy in Great Britain). *Leviathan*. Number 4, 1982: 463–82.

958. Beliaev, M. "Iaponskii kapital v anglii." (Japanese capital in Great Britain). *Mirovaia Ekonomika i Mezhdunarodnye Otnosheniia*. (7), 1985: 133–37.

Examines Thatcher's importation of foreign business into Britain in order to compete with the Japanese by setting up local industries funded by the Japanese themselves.

959. Butler, Nick (editor). *The Economic Consequences of Mrs. Thatcher.* See Nicholas Kaldor, number 972 below.

960. Coutts, Ken and others. "The economic consequences of Mrs. Thatcher." *Cambridge Journal of Economics.* March 1981: 81–93.

961. Gidts, Ruud Korffde. "The U.K. economy under Mrs. Thatcher." *ABN Economic Review.* February 1984: 7–21.

962. Green, Francis (editor). *The Restructuring of the U.K. Economy.* London: Harvester Press, 1989. 322.

Discusses whether Thatcherism has reestablished the United Kingdom as a stable base for successful capital accumulation in the foreseeable future.

963. Hardy, Peter. *Right Approach to Economics?: Margaret Thatcher's United Kingdom.* Sevenoaks: Hodder and Stoughton, 1991. 204.

964. Hillard, John. *The Economic Revival of Modern Britain: The Debate between Left and Right.* See David Coates, number 951 above.

965. Holz, Jean-Paul. *L'expérience Thatcher: succes et limites de la politique économique britannique.* (The Thatcher experience: the successes and limitations of British economic policies). Paris: Economica, 1985. 197.

Includes discussion of industrial relations, privatisation, fiscal and monetary policies, wages, inflation, employment, public finance and foreign trade.

966. Hoover, Kenneth R. "The rise of Conservative capitalism: ideological tensions within the Reagan and Thatcher Governments." *Comparative Studies in Society and History.* 29(2), 1987: 245–68.

Defines Conservative capitalism as being characterised by a reverse in the growth of taxation, shifting resources away from human services, realigning traditional mores for personal behaviour and advancing the market at the expense of government.

967. International Currency Review. "The British economy." *International Currency Review.* Number 6, 1979: 81–86.

Analyses the economic policy failures of the Thatcher Government.

968. Jenkins, Peter. "Thatcher Cabinet divided: outcome of economic policies in question." *Europe.* July 1981: 3–6.

969. Jessop, B. *Thatcherism: The British Road to Post-Fordism?* Colchester: University of Essex Department of Government paper number 68, 1989. 60.

Analyses the British economy in a Fordist mass production / mass consumption context. Critical of Thatcher's policies which are viewed as neoliberal accumulation strategy.

970. Johnson, Christopher. *Economy under Mrs. Thatcher.* Harmondsworth: Penguin, 1991. 336.

971. Jones, R. J. Barry (editor). *The Worlds of Political Economy.* London: Pinter, 1988. 197.

Amongst other approaches (e.g., liberalism, Marxism, and economic realism), Thatcher and Reagan are compared.

972. *Kaldor, Nicholas and Butler, Nick (editors). *The Economic Consequences of Mrs. Thatcher.* London: Duckworth, 1983. 119.

Speeches on the economics of Thatcherism delivered in the House of Lords between 1979 and 1982.

973. Keegan, William. *Mrs. Thatcher's Economic Experiment.* London: Allen Lane, 1984. 240.

Examines Thatcher's economic policy with emphasis on monetarism and Conservatism.

974. Laffer, Arthur. "Margaret Thatcher's tax increases." *Wall Street Journal.* August 20th 1979: 12.

975. Leys, Colin. "Thatcherism and British manufacturing: a question of hegemony." *New Left Review.* May 1985: 5–25.

A critique of the relationship between Thatcher's policies and British industrial interests, especially the position of British manufacturing. Attributes Thatcher's alleged failure to inadequately organised corporate interests and the lack of participation in international markets.

976. Logan-Turner, R. "Mrs. Thatcher's enterprise culture." *Social Studies Review.* 5(3), 1990.

977. *Maynard, Geoffrey. *The Economy under Mrs. Thatcher*. Oxford: Basil Blackwell, 1988. 185.

Nontechnical assessment of the Government's impact on the economy. Analysis of fiscal, monetary and labour market policies.

978. Meyer, Stephen A. "Margaret Thatcher's economic experiment." *Federal Reserve Philadelphia*. May 1982: 3–13.

Discusses the effects of monetary and fiscal policies and asks whether such policies could be a lesson to the Reagan administration.

979. Mitchell, A. "Political aspects of unemployment: the alternative policy." *Political Quarterly*. January 1981: 38–50.

980. Patten, Chris. "Mrs. Thatcher and the British economy." *Institute of Socioeconomic Studies Journal*. Winter 1981–1982: 34–43.

981. Peden, George C. *British Economic and Social Policy: Lloyd George to Margaret Thatcher*. Oxford: Philip Allan, 1991. 288 (available in hardback and paperback).

David Lloyd George became a Member of Parliament (MP) in 1890. He became President of the Board of Trade joining the Cabinet in 1905, Chancellor of the Exchequer in 1908, Minister of Munition and Secretary of State for War in 1915 eventually becoming Britain's Prime Minister.

982. Pennant-Rea, Rupert. "Britain: the economy; three years' hard Thatcher." *The Economist*. May 1st 1982. 43–44+.

983. Pratten, C. F. "Mrs. Thatcher's economic experiment." *Lloyds Bank Review*. January 1982: 36–51.

984. Roy, Donald. "War Mrs. Thatcher wirklich notwendig?" (Was Mrs. Thatcher really necessary? Economics and Society). *Wirt und Ges*. Number 2, 1988: 227–39.

Deals with British economic orientations in the 1980s. Translated by Ernst Jauernik.

985. Seldon, Arthur. "The British turn to cut taxes: Margaret Thatcher's new economic policy." *Taxing and Spending*. Autumn 1979: 14–24.

986. Smith, David. *From Boom to Bust: Trial and Error in British Economic Policy*. London: Penguin, 1992. 272.

Smith is the *Sunday Times* economic editor. He shows how Thatcher's Government allegedly made serious economic mistakes after the initial successes of the mid-1980s. Thatcher and Lawson's decisions to abandon monetary targets in 1985 is seen purely as Lawson's mistake. Allegedly, Smith claims, Thatcher knew nothing as she was not kept informed—which for a Prime Minister with a notorious eye for detail is extremely difficult to believe.

987. Smith, David. *Mrs. Thatcher's Economics*. London: Heinemann Educational, Studies in the United Kingdom Economy Series, 1988. 92.

988. Stephen, Frank H. "The Thatcher Government's economic ideology: must intervention be precluded?" *Fraser of Allander Institute Quarterly Economic Commentary*. November 1984: 82–84.

989. Thomas, Graham P. *Government and the Economy Today*. Manchester: Manchester University Press, 1992. 312.

Traces the growth of economic management by government from the heyday of Keynes to Thatcher. There is a specific assessment of Thatcher's approach.

990. True, Nicholas. *Giving*. London: Centre for Policy Studies, 1990.

Cutbacks in public spending invariably meant less money on certain aspects of social welfare. This work suggests ways of encouraging charities.

991. Vimont, Claude. "L'évolution de l'emploi en Grande-Bretagne sous le gouvernement de Madame Thatcher." (Employment changes under the Thatcher Government). *Chrons. Actualité*. June 15th 1987: 213–20.

See also: *Economist*. "Britain's economy: Whatever became of the Thatcher miracle?" (no. 138); *Economist*. "Conservative economics." (no. 120); *Economist*. "Money for most: the Thatcher Government believes that economic prosperity is founded on business enterprise." (no. 107); Harris, Ralph. "Thatcherissima: the economics of Thatcherism." (no. 7).

D. Miscellaneous

992. Green, Francis. "Taking care of Business? Reagan and Thatcher compared." *Dollars and Sense*. October 1986: 9–11.

993. Guzzardi, Alter. "Don't sell the great Thatcher experiment short."
      Fortune. May 18th 1981: 38–43.

Argues that with all the Prime Minister's well-reported woes, the
economy shows signs of life.

994. Parkin, Michael. *Economic Policy in the United Kingdom: Pro-
      ceedings of a Conference.* See Thomas J. Sargent, number 998
      below.

995. Presthus, R. "Mrs. Thatcher stalks the quango: a note on patronage
      and justice in Britain." *Public Administration Review.* May 1981:
      312–17.

996. Putka, Gary and Winkler, Matthew. "U.K. comeback: after years
      of crisis, Britain gains footing, and optimism grows; despite a high
      jobless rate, businesses see stability under Thatcher policies." *Wall
      Street Journal.* August 27th 1984: 1+.

997. Robertson, David Brian. "Mrs. Thatcher's employment prescrip-
      tion: an active neo-liberal labour market policy." *Journal of Public
      Policy.* July 1986: 275–96.

A conference paper that, amongst other things, discusses the Thatcher
Government's activism in the expansion of the Manpower Services Commission (MSC), the reduction of impediments to lower wages, the increase
of incentives for individual initiatives and the introduction of new training
schemes.

998. Sargent, Thomas J. and Parkin, Michael. *Economic Policy in the
      United Kingdom: Proceedings of a Conference.* Minneapolis:
      General Mills Foundation, 1981. 52.

Thatcher's management of the economy and stopping moderate inflation.

999. Thornley, Andy. *Urban Planning under Thatcherism: The
      Challenge of the Market.* London: Routledge, 1991. 253.

Analyses legislative and procedural changes in the planning system
since 1979.

1000. *The Times.* Decision to join move towards monetary union reflects
      pressure on her to adopt conciliatory tone. June 24th, 1989: 1.

E. Monetarism

Monetarist policies are the most daring aspect of Thatcherist economic policies. Their implications have often been misunderstood by Thatcher's detractors. Thatcher established that economic policies were essentially nonsense if one does not control the money supply and ensure the most efficient and thrifty use of public spending. Monetarism is no more Thatcher's invention than Keynesianism was any post-war politician's. Thatcher's monetarist antecedents included Sir Keith Joseph, Enoch Powell, and even the Labour government of the late 1970s. Having had her chance of power, Thatcher succeeded—or failed—where others feared to tread.

1001. Chrystal, K. Alec. "Dutch disease or monetarist medicine? The British economy under Mrs. Thatcher." *Federal Reserve St. Louis.* May 1984: 27–37.

1002. Davidson, I. "The political ecology of Britain: monetarism, money and moods." *Encounter.* April 1985: 68 73.

1003. Economist. "Public-spending swap shop." *The Economist.* November 3rd 1979: 16–17.

Argues that the Thatcher Government has not axed public spending but rather that it has "robbed" one budget to boost another

1004. Foster, J. "The political economy of Mrs. Thatcher's monetarism." *Fraser of Allender Institute Quarterly Economic Commentary.* October 1981: 44–60.

1005. Frank, Andre Gunder. "After Reaganomics and Thatcherism, what?" *Contemporary Marxism.* Winter 1981–82: 18–28.

A Marxist analysis of the shift from Keynesian demand management via supply-side economics to corporate state planning.

1006. Frazer, W. "Milton Friedman and Thatcher's monetarist experience." *Journal of Economic Issues.* June 1982: 525–33.

1007. Hoover, Kenneth and Plant, Raymond. *Conservative Capitalism.* London: Routledge, 1989. 341.

1008. Meltzer, Allan H. "Tests of inflation theories from the British laboratory." *Banker.* July 1981: 21–27.

Argues that the first two years of the Thatcher Government have brought neither overwhelming success nor outright failure; and that a more insistent regard for monetary control and a more effective grip on public spending could however yield lasting benefits.

1009. Plant, Raymond. *Conservative Capitalism*. See Kenneth Hoover, number 1007 above.

1010. *Pliatzky, Leo. *The Treasury under Mrs. Thatcher*. Oxford: Basil Blackwell, 1989. 174.

On the evolution of policy from 1979 in the areas of public expenditure management of the civil service, privatisation, monetary policy and budgetary policy.

1011. Redenius, Charles. "The supply-side alternative: Reagan and Thatcher's economic policies." *Journal of Social Political and Economic Studies*. Summer 1983: 189–209.

1012. Revzin, Philip. "Mrs. Thatcher's finance minister." See Peter Truell, number 65 above.

1013. Saldivar, V. Ameirico. "Gran Bretana: la disciplina del monetarismo. Requiem por el estado benefactor." (Great Britain: the discipline of monetarism. Requiem for the welfare state). *Investigacion Economica*. 44(173), 1985: 279–326.

Reviews the causes for the recession of 1975 onward. Evaluates the Thatcher effect including her cuts in welfare spending and her confrontation with the miners' strike.

1014. Shaw, G. K. "Fiscal policy under the first Thatcher administration 1979–1983." *Finanzarchiv*. Number 2, 1983: 312–42.

1015. Shaw, G. K. "Fiscal policy under the second Thatcher administration 1983–87." *Finanzarchiv*. Number 1, 1987: 104–28.

An article, in English, assessing Thatcher's monetarist policies and their impact on inflation and employment.

1016. Shaw, G. K. *Keynesian Economics*. Aldershot: Gower, 1988. 155.

An essay on the nature of the Keynesian revolution and the controversies and reactions arising from it. Includes the Thatcher experiment and Reaganomics.

1017. Smithin, John N. *Macroeconomics after Thatcher and Reagan: The Conservative Revolution in Macroeconomic Policymaking*. London: Elgar Publications, 1990. 208.

1018. Tomlinson, J. *Monetarism: Is There an Alternative?* Oxford: Basil Blackwell, 1986

1019. *Walters, Alan. *Britain's Economic Renaissance: Margaret Thatcher's Reforms, 1979–1984*. Oxford: Oxford University Press, 1986. 206.

Alan Walters was Thatcher's economic adviser. This is his readable and nontechnical book argued in understandable language. Shows how Thatcher moved away from Keynesian economic principles to monetarist policy. Walters argues that with Thatcher's approach the fiscal deficit and monetary aggregates were set to decline. As a result of her policies output grew, productivity advanced and inflation went down to 5 percent. The long-term financial stability increased opportunities, especially when coupled with deregulation and privatisation.

See also: Joseph, Keith. *Monetarim Is Not Enough.* (no. 503).

F. Privatization

With monetarism went privatization, which, among other benefits, increased the efficiency of customer service, leading invariably to Prime Minister John Major's much maligned Citizen's Charter.

1020. Abromeit, Heidrun. "British privatisation policy." *Parliamentary Affairs*. 41(1), 1988: 68–85.

Explains how privatisation included transferring public tasks to the private sector and making public enterprise resemble private firms. This policy, it is argued, may not have met with the expected success but it has achieved an impressive redistribution of ownership between the private and the public sectors.

1021. Alcock, Pete. "A better partnership between state and individual provision." *Journal of Law and Society*. 16(1), 1988: 97–111.

Shows how the largest item of British public spending was social security and how Thatcher has slashed this down through privatisation, administrative reforms and new legislation.

1022. Anderson, D., Lait, J., and Marsland, D. *Breaking the Spell of the Welfare State*. London: Centre for Policy Studies, 1983.

1023. Bagwell, Philip Sidney. *End of the Line? The Fate of Public Transport under Thatcher*. New York: New Left Books, 1984. 208.

A critique of Thatcher's policy on deregulation which led to a small cut in public transport with a dramatic increase in efficiency of service in most areas.

1024. Beaumont, P. B. "Privatisation, contracting-out and public sector industrial relations: the Thatcher years in Britain." *Journal of Collective Negotiations Public Sector.* Number 2, 1991: 89–100.

Particular emphasis on reduction in employment and contracting out in health and local government services.

1025. Bell, Philip and Cloke, Paul. "The changing relationship between the private and public sectors: privatisation and rural Britain." *Journal of Rural Studies.* Number 1, 1989: 1–15.

1026. Brooks, Stephen. "The mixed ownership corporation as an instrument of public policy." *Comparative Politics.* 19(2), 1987: 173–91.

Using Canada, France and Great Britain as examples, the author shows how mixed ownership of corporations has worked and how, even with Thatcher's privatisation programme, mixed ownership continued to be used. Partial state ownership is shown as having no effect on the dynamics of capital accumulation.

1027. Cloke, Paul. "The changing relationship between the private and public sectors: privatisation and rural Britain." See Philip Bell, number 1025 above.

1028. Curry, Lynne. "Britain pushes forward with privatisation: sale of state assets creates a new breed of stockowners." *Europe.* December 1986: 18–19.

This new breed of stock owners contributed substantially to the reelection of Thatcher to a third term of office.

1029. Foreman-Peck, James. "The privatisation of industry in historical perspective." *Journal of Law and Society.* 16(1), 1988: 129–48.

Outlines the history of nationalisation and recent privatisation in Britain. It concludes that neither strategy is without problems.

1030. Gamble, Andrew. "Privatisation, Thatcherism and the British state." *Journal of Law and Society.* (16)1, 1988: 1–20.

Shows that although Thatcher was committed to denationalisation from the very beginning of her Premiership, she did not start laying the real plans for privatisation until 1983 after she won her second term of office. The British electorate needed to go through a learning process before such action could be taken.

1031. Grimstone, Gerry. "Privatisation: the unexpected crusade." *Contemporary Record.* 1(1), 1987: 23–25.

Traces the history of Thatcher's privatisation programme starting in 1979. The article covers the period up to 1987. Beyond that period, and during Thatcher's third term of office, privatisation gathered pace dramatically.

1032. Hanke, Steve H. and Walters, Stephen, J. K. "Privatising waterworks." *Proceedings of the Academy of Political Science.* 36(3), 1987: 104–13.

When water was privatised there was a considerable outcry since many people regarded water (like electricity and gas) as an entitlement which should not be monopolised. This article argues that monopoly dulls the benefits meant to come from privatisation and suggests that a system of franchise bidding would improve the service by creating competition.

1033. Hargrove, Charles. "Denationalisations en Grande-Bretagne." (Denationalisation in Great Britain). *Revue des Deux Mondes.* (10), 1985: 42–48.

Shows the way that Thatcher denationalised much of British state ownership with special reference to British Telecom. It urges the French Government to do the same if it really were eager to dismantle state-owned industries.

1034. *Hastings, Sue and Levie, Hugo (editors). *Privatisation?* Nottingham: Spokesman Books, 1983. 205.

Based on a Trade Union Research Unit seminar to discuss the sale of British Government business enterprises and the use of private contractors in public services. Includes a preface by Rodney Bickerstaffe.

1035. Levie, Hugo (editor). *Privatisation?* See Sue Hastings, number 1034 above.

1036. Morgan, Kenneth O. "Nationalisation and privatisation: history since 1937." *Contemporary Record.* 2(4), 1988: 32–34.

Traces the history of nationalisation from the planning in the 1930s and 1940s to the implementation in the 1950s with a slowdown in the 1960s and 1970s. Thatcher's denationalisation programme is also looked at.

1037. Rose, Richard. "Privatisation as a problem of satisficing and dissatisficing." *American Review of Public Administration.* June 1989: 97–118.

On striking a balance between the public and private sectors in the Thatcher revolution.

1038. Walters, Stephen J. K. "Privatising Waterworks." See Steve H. Hanke, number 1032 above.

See also: Letwin, Oliver. *Privatising the World: A Study of International Privatisation in Theory and Practice.* (no. 509).

X Foreign Affairs

Over the years, Thatcher's handling of foreign affairs made her an international figure: much admired, even when hated.

A. Eire and Northern Ireland

This section has been included here since Thatcher's Anglo-Irish Agreement was reached with the Republic of Ireland. Northern Irish issues relating to the North alone have been included in other relevant sections.

1039. Cox, W. "Managing Northern Ireland Intergovernmentally: an appraisal of the Anglo-Irish Agreement." *Parliamentary Affairs*. Volume 40, 1987.

1040. Fanning, Ronan. "U.K., Ireland sign historic agreement: pact gives Republic of Ireland access to the government process in Northern Ireland." *Europe*. January 1986: 38–39+.

Includes the opposition in Northern Ireland to the Anglo-Irish Agreement (also known as the Hillsborough Agreement) signed by Thatcher and Fitzgerald.

1041. Gaffikin, Frank and Morrissey, Mike. *Northern Ireland: The Thatcher Years*. London: Zed Books, 1990. 238 (available in hardback and paperback).

1042. Magee, E. (editor). *Thatcher Years in Northern Ireland.* London: Longman, 1989. 32.

1043. McDowell, Michael. "A new Ulster initiative: Mrs. Thatcher steps in." *New Leader.* May 5th 1980: 8–9.

1044. Morrissey, Mike. *Northern Ireland: The Thatcher Years.* See Frank Gaffikin, number 1041 above.

1045. O'Leary, B. "The Anglo-Irish agreement: folly or statecraft?" *West European Politics.* Volume 10, number 1, 1987.

1046. Troost, W. "Noord-Ierland en de Engels-Irish betrekkingen." (Northern Ireland and the English-Irish relationship). *Spiegel Historiael.* 18(10), 1983: 490–96.

A history of the Northern Irish conflict since the 1920s with a look at the relationship between Britain and the Republic. Concludes that some meaningful relationship has been established but that Thatcher's intransigence has been a major obstacle to meaningful progress.

See also: *The New York Times.* "On Northern Ireland." (no. 332); *The New York Times.* "On the Republic of Ireland." (no. 316).

B. Europe

Thatcher's antagonism toward European hegemony spanned most of her political career. She has become a much more outspoken anti-European since her resignation in November 1990.

1047. Atlantic Community Quarterly. "Europe: the obligations of liberty." *Atlantic Community Quarterly.* Summer 1980: 131–36.

1048. Butler, Michael. "Simply wrong about Europe." *The Times.* November 26th 1991: 14.

Butler was former ambassador to Europe. Here he gives a critique of Thatcher's views.

1049. Cosgrave, Patrick. "Cette femme Thatcher with eyes like Caligula and the mouth of Marilyn Monroe." See Anthony Burgess, number 838 above.

1050. *Crouch, Colin and Marquand, David (editors). *The New Centralism: Britain out of Step in Europe?* Oxford: Basil Blackwell, 1989. 149.

Analyses and compares central-local government relations in Britain, France, West Germany, Italy and Scandinavia.

1051.   *Delors, Jacques. *Our Europe*. London: Verso, 1992. 166.

A Translation by Brian Pearce of President Delor's *La France par l'Europe*. It argues the case for Europe, a case which Thatcher has spent and still spends much time fighting against with all her might.

1052.   Economist. "Electing realistic Europeans." *The Economist*. March 24th 1979: 13–14.

1053.   Economist. "Mrs. Thatcher's summit view." *The Economist*. June 23rd 1979: 50+.

On the European Community's summit meeting in Strasbourg, France, June 21st and 22nd 1979. Emphasis on the advantages and disadvantages of British membership, both to Britain and to the other members, and on a common oil policy.

1054.   Economist. "The reluctant European: Margaret Thatcher's hostility to much EEC-ery is bad for Britain, bad for Europe, bad for America." *The Economist*. June 10th 1989: 13–14.

1055.   Economist. "She makes her stand." *The Economist*. June 29th 1991: 27.

On Thatcher's speech against European federalism.

1056.   Herbstein, Denis. "European Community: under Thatcher's coat-tails." *Africa Report*. September 1986: 20–23.

Examines Europe's attitude toward South Africa. The European Economic Community (EEC) found it difficult to agree on united measures against South Africa.

1057.   *Heseltine, Michael. *The Challenge of Europe: Can We Win?* London: George Weidenfeld and Nicolson, 1989, Pan Books, 1991. 216.

Heseltine is a committed European. His challenge to Margaret Thatcher brought her down over the issue of Britain's place in Europe. In this book he argues cogently and intelligently for Britain's role in the heart of Europe where Britain's destiny lies.

1058.   Marquand, David (editor). *The New Centralism: Britain out of Step in Europe?* See Colin Crouch, number 1050 above.

1059. Pearce, Edward. "Another afternoon of pure, unadulterated hooey." *New Statesman.* Volume 4, number 182, December 20th 1991: 26.

On the Parliamentary debate on Britain's role in the European Economic Community (EEC).

1060. *The Times.* "EEC budget: Mrs. Thatcher was right to hold out." May 8th 1980: 18.

1061. *The Times.* "Thatcher ready to see European Economic Community go bankrupt." December 4th 1983: 11.

1062. *The Times.* "Firm in rejection of British entry in European Monetary System." June 11th 1986: 1.

1063. *The Times.* "Thatcher gets a lesson on why we must join the European Monetary System." October 5th 1986: 68.

1064. *The Times.* "It's oui, si, yup for the Iron Lady." May 17th 1987: 14.

1065. *The Times.* "Time to scrap the Euro-con." July 5th 1987: 25.

1066. *The Times.* "Mitterrand ready for tough talking." January 29th 1988: 10.

1067. *The Times.* "Scornful Europeans look for signs of Thatcher realism." September 23rd 1988: 7.

1068. *The Times.* "Thatcher's rhetoric masks deep commitment to Europe." October 17th 1988: 10.

1069. *The Times.* "Thatcher rules out British participation in European Monetary System during her Premiership." October 26th 1988: 1.

1070. *The Times.* "The Iron Lady gives ground over Europe." June 25th 1989: A17.

1071. *The Times.* "Thatcher, the European Community realist." July 5th 1989: 16.

See also: *Economist.* "Making a European of Mrs. Thatcher." (no. 121); *The London Times.* "Thatcher criticizes idealistic view of French Revolution on eve of Paris summit." (no. 269); Thatcher, Margaret. *Britain and Europe.* (no. 445).

C. Falklands

Little has been written on pre-1982 Falklands. In fact, the islands were relatively unknown to the majority of Britons before the fateful April morning when the news broke in 1982. Some of the works listed include background history.

1072. Barnett, Anthony. "Iron Britannia: war over the Falklands." *New Left Review*. July 1982: 5–92.

Gives the background of the events during April–June 1982. Heavily critical of Britain's position and of Thatcher.

1073. Bluth, Christoph. "The British resort to force in the Falklands/Malvinas conflict 1982: international law and just war theory." *Journal of Peace Research*. 24(1), 1987: 5–20.

Examines the history of the Falklands in the context of international law. Concludes that Thatcher's actions were motivated by electioneering with little basis in history or in international law.

1074. Bogdanov, M. Iu. "Washington, London i Folklendskaia voina." (Washington, London and the Falklands War). *Novaia i Noveishaia Istoriia*. (3), 1986: 211–15.

Shows how the Argentinians occupied the Falklands on the basis that an ally of the United States, which Argentina was at the time, would get away with it. Argues that pro-British sympathies in the Congress and in the Defence Department meant that Reagan was persuaded to support Britain even if it was somewhat late in the day.

1075. Bogdanov, V. "The meaning of Mrs. Thatcher's victory: in a long perspective." *Encounter*. September, 1983: 14–19.

1076. *Dalyell, Tam. *One Man's Falklands*. London: Cecil Woolf, 1982. 144.

Labour Member of Parliament's crusade against Thatcher's handling of the Falklands War.

1077. *Dalyell, Tam. *Thatcher: Patterns of Deceit*. London: Cecil Woolf, 1986. 64.

Dalyell had a running battle with Thatcher and her Government over many of her policies and actions. This work is the text of a speech due to be delivered in Parliament, but an all-night filibuster ensured that Dalyell could not deliver the speech. The author alleges that Thatcher's deceit ran through all her conduct of affairs. Here he uses the Falklands, the United States bombing of Libya and the Westland affair to prove his thesis.

1078.   *Dalyell, Tam. *Thatcher's Torpedo: Sinking of the* Belgrano. London: Cecil Woolf, 1983. 80.

Dalyell's allegation that Thatcher ordered the sinking of the Argentinian ship the *Belgrano* and tried to cover up her involvement in the incident.

1079.   Dvorak, Johann. "Regierung, parlament und krieg in Groosbritannien: die Falkland-krise 1982." (Government, Parliament and war in Great Britain: the 1982 Falkland crisis). *Zeitgeschichte*. 11(4), 1984: 105–19.

Analyses the roles of both Government and Parliament in the Falklands War. Though Members of Parliament supported the war effort, many resented having a war imposed on the nation for what they perceived to be electoral gains.

1080.   Freedman, L. *Britain and the Falklands War*. Oxford: Basil Blackwell, 1988. 128.

1081.   *Gavshon, Arthur and Rice, Desmond. *The Sinking of the* Belgrano. London: Secker and Warburg, 1984.

Thatcher's go ahead to sink the *Belgrano* and the Government's later claim that the decision was taken by the captain on the ground caused a political furor that lasted for years.

1082.   *Hastings, Max and Jenkins, Simon. *The Battle for the Falklands*. London: Michael Joseph, 1983. 372.

The most readable and definitive book available on the campaign to liberate the Falklands. Max Hastings accompanied the taskforce and was the first to walk into Port Stanley ahead of the British vanguard. Simon Jenkins covered the political scene from London and Washington. The work succeeds in re-creating both events and atmosphere after lucidly setting the historical context to the conflict.

1083.   Jenkins, Simon. *The Battle for the Falklands*. See Max Hastings, number 1082 above.

1084.   Kempe, Frederick. "Thatcher's fate hangs on Falklands." *Wall Street Journal*. May 14th 1982: 29.

A statement that proved true—though very much to Thatcher's benefit since the Falklands factor increased her popularity dramatically and ensured her reelection for a second term of office.

1085. Norpoth, Helmut. "The Falklands War and Government popularity in Britain: rally without consequence or surge without decline?" *Electoral Studies*. April 1987: 3–16.

Shows how the Falklands victory positively influenced the Conservative victory in 1983 general elections.

1086. Quijano, Oswaldo. "Malvinas: un ojo de la cara de Margaret Thatcher." (Falklands: an eye in the face of Margaret Thatcher) *Quetlacer*. Number 30, August 1984: 62–67.

British Falkland Islands policy since the war with emphasis on its roots in, and effects on, domestic politics.

1087. *The Times*. "Thatcher accused of ordering the sinking of the *General Belgrano* as means of stifling Argentine peace overtures." November 26th 1982: 2.

1088. *The Times*. "Thatcher asked to explain apparent inconsistency of Government replies over the sinking of the *General Belgrano*." December 14th 1982: 2.

1089. *The Times*. "Thatcher defends decision to sink the *General Belgrano*." April 25th 1983: 5.

1090. *The Times*. "Details of relevant speeches regarding *Belgrano* between December 1982 and February 1984." February 15th 1985: 2.

See also: *Economist*. "Elizabeth or Boadicea?" (no. 97); Harris, Robert. *Gotcha! The Media, The Government and the Falklands Crisis*. (no. 659); Sanders, D. "Government popularity and the Falklands War: a reassessment." (no. 663).

D. Foreign Policy

Thatcher's foreign policy echoes an American president's most apt and famous dictum, which could be paraphrased as follows: "There is no such thing as friends. There is *British* interest only."

1091. Atlantic Community Quarterly. "Foreign policy: the West in the world today." *Atlantic Community Quarterly*. Spring 1980: 12–19.

1092. Bowring, P. and Lee, M. "Tread softly, Iron Lady." *Far Eastern Economic Review*. September 17th 1982: 23–24.

1093. Buckley, William F. "Notes and asides." *National Review*. Volume 43, number 22, December 1991: 18.

On Thatcher and her image in international affairs.

1094. Byrd, Peter (editor). *British Foreign Policy under Thatcher*. Oxford: Philip Allan, 1988. 192 (available in hardback and paperback).

Analyses the key foreign policy issues confronting Thatcher. Shows foreign policy to be a mixture of new policies with some continuity despite Thatcher's rhetoric. Includes sections on the special relationship between the United States and Britain, the Middle East, the Falklands and general defence policies.

1095. Economist. "Rhodesia memorandum." *The Economist*. April 7th 1979: 20–21.

1096. Economist. "Split by the lady." *The Economist*. November 7th 1987: 46.

On South African blacks.

1097. Edmonds, Martin. "British Foreign Policy." *Current History*. 83(492), 1984: 157–59.

Shows how Thatcher's foreign policy shifted from the pragmatic to the practical to simply reflecting her own personal convictions and governing style.

1098. Egedo, Ihebom. "Nigeria and apartheid: her position in the Commonwealth." *Round Table*. January 1987: 33–39.

Examines, amongst other things, Thatcher's opposition to sanctions against South Africa. This was an area of contention between her and the rest of the Commonwealth.

1099. Ferguson, James and Pearce, Jenny (editors). *The Thatcher Years: Britain and Latin America*. London: Third World Publications, 1988. 87.

Examined are: the Falklands War, Britain's role in the debt crisis of South America, Britain's support for United States policy and arms sales.

1100. Gelb, Norman, "Thatcher takes on the Commonwealth: staving off sanctions." *New Leader*. July 1986: 6–7.

1101. Golubev, A. V. "Sovetsko-Angliiskie otnosheniia na rubezhe 70–80–kh godov." (Soviet–British relations at the turn of the eighties). *Voprosy Istorii.* (7), 1984: 43–58.

Covers the period 1979–83 with emphasis on the heavily anti-Soviet policies and rhetoric of the Thatcher Government.

1102. Kinnock, Neil. "South Africa: measures that matter." *Round Table.* January 1987: 22–32.

Kinnock's views on why the imposition of comprehensive economic sanctions will speed the end of apartheid with the implications for the Thatcher Government.

1103. Nowak, Kazimierz. "Polityka zagraniczna wielkiej Brytanii w okresie rzadow konserwatywnych Margaret Thatcher." (British foreign policy during the Conservative rule of Margaret Thatcher). *Studia Nauk Politycznych.* (5), 1984: 147–66.

Examines trends in Thatcher's foreign policy in her first term. Argues that Thatcher's desire to strengthen Britain's relations with NATO and the United States was done at the expense of relations with the Eastern Bloc. Britain became heavily reliant on the American military–industrial complex.

1104. Pearce, Jenny (editor). *The Thatcher Years: Britain and Latin America.* See James Ferguson, number 1099 above.

1105. Pearce, Edward. "The gathering of the warlords: South African turmoil." *Encounter.* September 1986: 37–38.

1106. Popov, Viktor Ivanovich. "Iz istorii Sovetsko-Britankikh parlamentskikh sviazei." (Contributions to the history of Soviet–British parliamentary relations). *Istoriia SSSR.* (2), 1988: 39– 63.

Soviet contacts with British Members of Parliament in the 1940s were strengthened under Thatcher in the 1980s. After Gorbachev's visit of 1984 new contacts were established that enabled exchange visits and allowed Thatcher to adopt a more conciliatory attitude. There was a revival of scientific, technological and commercial exchange between the two countries. This in turn led to the easing of the arms race and to the relaxation of tensions between the two. The improvement in relations allowed Thatcher to act as a mediator between Reagan and Gorbachev on arms talks between the two super powers.

1107. Sharp, Paul. "Thatcher's wholly British foreign policy." *Orbis*. Volume 35, number 3, Summer 1991: 395.

1108. Smith, M., Smith, S., and White, B. *British Foreign Policy: Traditional Change and Transformation*. London: Unwin Hyman, 1988.

Includes White's analysis of East–West relations under Thatcher.

1109. Smith, S. *British Foreign Policy: Traditional Change and Transformation*. See M. Smith, number 1108 above.

1110. *The Times*. "Cuddling up to the bear." July 26th 1988: 10.

1111. *The Times*. Article questions Thatcher's ability to keep abreast of foreign affairs during next decade. February 18th 1990: C5.

1112. *The Times*. Foreign press is critical of Prime Minister. April 13th 1990: 6.

1113. White, B. *British Foreign Policy: Traditional Change and Transformation*. See M. Smith, number 1108 above.

1114. Ying, Hua. "Mrs. Thatcher sets new record." *Beijing Review*. June 22nd 1987: 13.

1115. Yongxing, Xue. "Thatcher diplomacy and East–West detente." *Beijing Review*. January 18th 1988: 14–16.

See also: Heseltine, Michael. *The Challenge of Europe: Can We Win?* (no. 1057).

E. Foreign Visits

1116. Ali, S. "Iron ladies clash." *Far Eastern Economic Review*. April 24th 1981: 34–35.

On Mrs. Thatcher's visit with Indira Gandhi of India.

1117. Arbatov, G. "Mission to Moscow: Maggie and Mikhail's chemistry in the Kremlin." See M. Jones, number 1122 below.

1118. Beijing Review. "British Prime Minister visits China." *Beijing Review*. October 4th 1982: 9–10.

1119. Beijing Review. "Malvinas [Falklands]: Thatcher's visit criticised." *Beijing Review*. January 24th 1983: 13.

On Thatcher's much talked about visit to the Falklands.

1120. Bowring, P. "Still on borrowed time." *Far Eastern Economic Review*. October 1st 1982: 10–11.

On Thatcher's visit to China during the Hong Kong negotiations.

1121. Economist. "Thatcherite it isn't." *The Economist*. November 5th 1989: 52–53.

On Thatcher's visit to Poland.

1122. Jones, M., Arbatov, G., and Witherow, J. "Mission to Moscow: Maggie and Mikhail's chemistry in the Kremlin." *Sunday Times*. April 5th 1987: 10–12.

1123. Sayle, M. "Story with a moral." *Far Eastern Economic Review*. October 8th 1982: 40–41.

On Thatcher's visit to Japan.

1124. Sheng, Xin. "Differences remain after Moscow talks." *Beijing Review*. April 13th 1987: 11–12.

1125. *The Times*. "Iron Lady set to woo voters from Moscow." March 22nd 1987: 12.

1126. *The Times*. "Mrs. Thatcher's role in Russia." March 27th 1987: 12.

1127. *The Times*. "Oz and her: hang on to your hat, Denis." July 31 1988: 12.

On her visit to Australia.

1128. *The Times*. "It's wizard in Oz (in spite of the natives)." August 7th 1988: B1.

On Thatcher's visit to Australia.

1129. *The Times*. "Thatcher's role in Poland." August 29th 1988: 10.

1130. *The Times*. "Poland: Thatcher's lifeline." November 1st 1988: 16.

1131. *The Times*. "Maggie's Warsaw Pact." November 6th 1988: A16.

1132. *The Times*. "The long road to Moscow." September 24th 1989: A17.

1133. Witherow, J. "Mission to Moscow: Maggie and Mikhail's chemistry in the Kremlin." See M. Jones, number 1122 above.

1134. Yan, Ren. "Thatcher extends 'preachy' hand." *Beijing Review*. November 21st 1988: 16.

On Thatcher's visit to Poland.

See also: *Economist.* "The blue-eyed lady." (no. 114); *Economist.* "A cosy date in Oggersheim." (no. 129).

F. Gorbachev

Thatcher takes considerable credit for her alleged influence on Gorbachev's development and the eventual collapse of "the evil empire." The truth is probably more akin to the fact that Thatcher was astute enough to see where things were heading and to spot Gorbachev's potential. Once the Soviet Union collapsed into a loose and semi-democratic confederation, Thatcher's market economy became an apparently incontrovertible replacement.

1135.   Current Digest of Soviet Press. "Gorbachev pays a visit to Britain." *Current Digest of Soviet Press.* January 16th 1985: 1–7.

Originally published in *Pravda*, this details the meetings of Gorbachev and Thatcher, Gorbachev's meeting with business representatives and his address to Parliament in December 1984.

1136.   Ticktin, Hillel. "Mikhail Gorbachev and Mrs. Thatcher: allies in crisis." *Critique.* (22), 1990: 92–104.

Analyses the way that both Thatcher and Gorbachev presided over the decline of their respective systems whilst giving it a new lease of life despite the decline.

1137.   *The Times.* "How Thatcher could help glasnost along." March 11th 1987: 12.

See also: *The London Times.* "Gorbachev: the Tory gamble that could fail." (no. 222); *The London Times.* "How Thatcher changed her Gorbachev line." (no. 223); Jones, M. and others. "Mission to Moscow." (no. 1122).

G. Hong Kong

1138.   Beijing Review. "China, Britain sign historic Hong Kong pact." *Beijing Review.* December 24th 1984: 6–7.

On the Anglo–Chinese agreement on Hong Kong.

1139.   Beijing Review. "China's solemn stand on Xianggang." *Beijing Review.* October 11th 1982: 10–11.

China's stand on the Hong Kong (Xianggang) issue before the agreement reached with Britain.

1140.   Lau, E. "The world is witness." See D. Lee, number 1141 below.

1141.   Lee, D. and Lau, E. "The world is witness." *Far Eastern Economic Review*. December 27th 1984: 10–11.

On the signing of the joint Chinese–British declaration on Hong Kong.

H. The United States

Most British observers find it very hard to understand the nature of the "special relationship" between Ronald Reagan and Margaret Thatcher. On a political level, the two had the same mission regarding the free market, freedom of choice, monetarism/Reaganomics, and Western supremacy. On a personal level, the relationship is more complex—more difficult to understand. This relationship may be encapsulated in two stories; one real and the other clearly fictional. Apparently every time that Reagan wanted to make a decision he would be reminded that "Margaret Thatcher is going to be on the phone in an instant." The president's response was invariably: "Oh, I don't want that!"

When Thatcher and Reagan died, they faced God. He looked at Reagan and said, "My son, you have done well. You are here in this place. I bless you." God then turned to Thatcher and repeated the same. Thatcher snapped, "I am not Your son, and what's more, this is not Your place. It is my place."

I am indebted to Geoffrey Smith for both stories (see number 1149 below).

1142.   Carter, Jimmy. "Visit of Prime Minister Margaret Thatcher of the United Kingdom." *World Comp. Press Documents*. December 24th 1979: 2264–68.

Exchanges between Carter and Thatcher during the latter's visit of December 17th 1979. Also includes text of a White House statement dated December 18th 1979.

1143.   *Daily Telegraph*. Thatcher defends Government offer of money to Government Communication Headquarters workers in return to giving up union membership and denies U.S. pressure led to decision. January 27th 1984: 1.

1144. Hale, David. "Reagan versus Thatcher." *Policy Review*. Winter 1982: 91–109.

A comparison of Reaganomics and Thatcher's economic policies.

1145. Leruez, Jacques. "La 'relation speciale' Americano–Britannique sous Ronald Reagan et Margaret Thatcher." (The 'special relationship' between the United States and Great Britain under Ronald Reagan and Margaret Thatcher). *Revue Française de Science Politique*. 39(4), 1989: 563–83.

Discusses Thatcher's success in achieving a respectable budget surplus in 1987 and the special relationship between the United States and Britain. Argues that Britain has had to pay a heavy price for this relationship in terms of Grenada, the bombing of Libya and the Campaign for Nuclear Disarmament. Also accepts that there are benefits for Britain from this special relationship. Alleges a strong anti-American feeling in Britain as a result of Thatcher's friendship with Reagan.

1146. Reagan, Ronald. "Visit of Prime Minister Margaret Thatcher of the United Kingdom." *World Comp. Press Documents*. March 2nd 1981: 194–202.

Exchanges between Reagan and Thatcher during the latter's visit of February 26th and 27th 1981.

1147. Reagan, Ronald. *World Comp. Press Documents*. November 21st 1988: 1505–12.

Exchanges between Reagan and Thatcher.

1148. Samuelson, Robert J. "Margaret Thatcher and Ronald Reagan." *National Journal*. July 26th 1980: 1231–33.

Argues that parallels between Britain and the United States are more apparent than real. Great Britain is not the United States and the policies of its Conservative Government are quite different from those of the Republican Party.

1149. *Smith, Geoffrey. *Reagan and Thatcher*. London: Bodley Head, 1990. 288.

Examines the very special relationship between Margaret Thatcher and Ronald Reagan. It includes less-discussed political areas such as Thatcher's support over Irangate, her work on East–West dialogue, their disagreement over nuclear deterrent and Thatcher's style and its effects on the American Republican Party election strategies which brought Reagan to power.

1150. *The Times*. View of the "special relationship" between Britain and the United States. May 1st 1980: 1.

1151. *The Times*. Thatcher speaks of "particularly happy" relationship with Reagan. February 18th 1982: 7.

1152. *The Times*. Thatcher addresses audience at Georgetown University on economic policy and receives honorary doctorate. February 28th 1981: 1.

1153. *The Times*. "How Margaret Thatcher earned an encore at Reagan's White House." March 1st 1981: 8.

1154. *The Times*. Thatcher sends message to Reagan following attempt on his life. March 31st 1981: 1.

1155. *The Times*. Thatcher is praised by President Reagan. May 27th 1983: 5.

1156. *The Times*. Text of speech given at meeting with Reagan. September 30th 1983: 8.

1157. *The Times*. "A-doin' what comes Thatcher-ly." October 2nd 1983: 11.

1158. *The Times*. Thatcher explains her opposition to the United States intervention in Grenada. October 31st 1983: 1.

1159. *The Times*. Thatcher is critical of United States actions in Grenada. January 23rd 1984: 1.

1160. *The Times*. Thatcher promises cooperation with President Reagan. November 8th 1984: 1.

1161. *The Times*. Thatcher stresses support for President Reagan. February 18th 1985: 1.

1162. *The Times*. Main points of speech to joint meeting of Houses of Congress outlined. February 21st 1985: 1.

1163. *The Times*. Thatcher stresses Britain's good relationship with the United States and her own good relations with Reagan. February 21st 1985: 6.

1164. *The Times*. Contents and style of speech to Congress seen as hitting right note. February 22nd 1985: 10.

1165. *The Times*. Reason for Thatcher's popularity in the United States discussed. February 23rd 1985: 8.

1166. *The Times*. United States economic recovery and attitude to work seen as model of plans for the United Kingdom. February 24th 1985: 15.

1167. *The Times*. Nature of special relationship with the United States discussed, implications of Thatcher's speech to Congress and response of Reagan assessed. February 27th 1985: 6.

1168. *The Times*. "How Thatcher got through to Reagan on saving Salt-2." June 23rd 1985: 25.

1169. *The Times*. Thatcher discusses with President Reagan arms control and need to press ahead with Strategic Defence Initiative confirming belief in Reagan's integrity. November 17th 1986: 9.

1170. *The Times*. Success of Thatcher's visit to the United States discussed. November 18th 1986: 7.

1171. *The Times*. "Slim pickings at Camp David." November 21st 1986: 20.

1172. *The Times*. Thatcher pledges support for Reagan over Iran-Contra crisis. December 7th 1986: 1.

1173. *The Times*. Thatcher is reported disturbed by the anti-American feelings in Europe. December 10th 1986: 1.

1174. *The Times*. United States press comments on Thatcher's election campaign. May 17th 1987: 14.

1175. *The Times*. United States view of Thatcher discussed. June 6th 1987: 10.

1176. *The Times*. Thatcher offers congratulations to President-elect Bush and underlines desire to continue "special relationship." She comments on new Administration's need to address budget deficit. November 10th 1988: 7.

1177. *The Times*. Thatcher pays tribute to "special relationship" with the United States. May 2nd 1989: 16.

1178. *The Times*. Details of possible rift with President Bush over projected defence spending cuts. November 20th 1989: 1.

1179. *The Times*. "Can Thatcher sway Bush?" November 23rd 1989: 12.

1180. *The Times*. United States media's coverage of British domestic affairs examined. April 13th 1990: 6.

1181. *The Times*. Mrs. Thatcher's new world relations with United States. August 6th 1990: 8.

1182. Vivekanandan, B. "Whither the Anglo–American Special Relationship?" *Round Table*. October 1990: 370–88.

Focuses on the Reagan–Thatcher relationship in the 1980s.

1183. World Comp. Press Documents. "News Conference of the President and Prime Minister Margaret Thatcher of the United Kingdom in Hamilton, Bermuda, April 13, 1990." *World Comp. Press Documents*. April 23rd 1990: 569–75.

1184. Zeegers, Jacques. "Thatcher–Reagan: faut-il suivre leur exemple en Belgique?" (Thatcher–Reagan: should we follow their example in Belgium?). *Reflets et Perspectives*. Number 6, 1985: 385–402.

Examines British and U.S. economic and monetary policies and their possible applicability to Belgian economic conditions. Also evaluates the Belgian Prime Minister Wilfried Marten's policies.

See also: *The London Times*. "Belief in the American way not shared by majority of Britons." (no. 213); *The London Times*. "Election campaign used as a model by the United States Republican Party." (no. 152); *The New York Times*. "On Grenada." (no. 359); *U.S. News*. "Thatcher's economic woes: a lesson for the U.S.?" (no. 66).

XI   Union Laws

Thatcher succeeded in curbing union powers in a way that ensured her government's ability to carry out its economic policies unhindered by labor relations. These, and accompanying changes, ensured the shift of British party politics further to the right. Consequently the socialism of the Labour Party became unrecognizable as it shifted away from extreme left-wing policies.

A. Industrial Relations

1185. Beaumont, P. B. "Public sector employment, wages and strikes in the U. K.: the Thatcher years (1979–1984)." *Journal of Collective Negotiations Public Sector*. Number 2, 1986: 173–89.

1186. Booth, A. and Pack, M. "Baldwin, Thatcher and the aftermath of industrial disputes." *Political Quarterly*. July 1985: 271–78.

Stanley Baldwin (1867–1947) was Conservative Prime Minister three times between 1923 and 1937. During the 1926 general strike he refused to negotiate with the strikers. A year later he passed the anti-trade union law the Trade Disputes Act. This law and unemployment caused his resignation in 1929. He returned as Prime Minister for the third time refusing to rearm in the face of Hitler's threat but eventually rearming between 1935 and 1937 after the Italian conquest of Ethiopia, the German occupation of the Rhineland and the Spanish Civil War. Thatcher succeeded in her anti-union measures where Baldwin did not.

1187. Burton, John. "Unionism and Thatcherism." *Government Union Review*. Summer 1983: 72–85.

Examines the relations between the Government and the trade unions under Thatcher.

1188. Dickens, Linda. "Learning to live with the law? The legislative attack on the British trade unions since 1979." *New Zealand Journal of Independent Relations*. April 1989: 37–52.

On the move away from collective industrial relations, the restricted terrain for lawful industrial action and legal intervention in internal union affairs.

1189. Dorey, Peter. "Thatcherism's impact on trade unions." *Contemporary Record*. April 1991: 9–11.

Argues that Thatcher had the greatest impact on trade unions above anything else.

1190. Drewry, Gavin. "The GCHQ case: a failure of Government communications." *Parliamentary Affairs*. 38(4), 1985: 371–86.

When Thatcher decided to ban trade union membership to workers at the Government Communications Headquarters as a security measure, there was a great deal of discussion on the issues of freedom of association, national security and the civil service. Eventually the matter was referred to the Court of Appeal and on to the House of Lords where it was adjudicated to be legally acceptable.

1191. Freeman, Richard and Pelletier, Jeffrey. *The Impact of Industrial Relations Legislation on British Union Density*. National Bureau of Economic Research, Working Paper number 3167, 1989. 37.

An essay based on a quantitative analysis of changes in union density between 1945 and 1986. It shows the relation of the Thatcher Government's laws to the sharp drop in density in the 1980s.

1192. Grant, David. "Mrs. Thatcher's own goal: unions and the political funds ballots." *Parliamentary Affairs*. 40(1), 1987: 57–72.

On the passing of the Trade Union Act in 1984 which required union members to decide every ten years if they wished to retain political funds. Argues that although the Conservatives believed that this would weaken the already weakened Labour Party, that this did not happen since union leaders used the opportunity to get in touch with the members and to encourage them to participate more heavily in Labour affairs.

1193. *Hanson, Charles. *Taming the Trade Unions: A Guide to the Thatcher Government's Employment Reforms, 1980–1990*. London: Macmillan Academic and Professional, 1991. 168.

1194. Longstreth, Frank H. "From corporatism to dualism? Thatcherism and the climacteric of British trade unions in the 1980s." *Political Studies*. Spring 1988: 413–32.

Inpact on the British trade unions of the break in relations with the Thatcher Government, the economic recession and Labour market development in the 1980s.

1195. Lublin, Joann S. "Doctor's orders." *Wall Street Journal*. February 24th 1988: 1+.

Trade unionists and Labour Party supporters were outraged by Thatcher's plans to cut health costs by inviting companies to bid for certain hospital services. Under Thatcher's Government and later on Major's Health Minister Kenneth Clarke, hospitals and surgeries were given their local financial management opportunities leading to dramatic changes in health care.

1196. *Marsh, David. *Trade Unions under Mrs. Thatcher: Loss without Limit?* Colchester: Papers in Politics and Government, 1991. 41.

1197. McBride, Stephen. "Mrs. Thatcher and the post-war consensus: the case of trade union policy." *Parliamentary Affairs*. July 1986: 330–40.

Discusses attempts to restructure British working class organisations and the relevant industrial relations system.

1198. Mitchell, Neil J. "Where traditional Tories fear to tread: Mrs. Thatcher's trade union policy." *West European Politics*. January 1987: 33–45.

Analysis of Thatcher's trade union policy concentrating on pressure group theory.

1199. Pack, M. "Baldwin, Thatcher and the aftermath of industrial disputes." See A. Booth, number 1186 above.

1200. Pelletier, Jeffrey. *The Impact of Industrial Relations Legislation on British Union Density*. See Richard Freeman, number 1191 above.

1201. Rainbird, Helen. *Training Matters: Union Perspectives on Industrial Restructuring and Training*. London: Basil Blackwell, 1990. 189.

Examines how trade unions perceive and organise around training policy issues and is critical of Thatcher's policies on technology, labour market deregulation and retraining.

1202.   Shenfield, Arthur. "Thatcher's reform of Britain's labour unions." *Government Union Review.* Winter 1989: 1–13.

An examination of Britain's unions' part in its economic decline. Thatcher reversed this trend by taking charge of the country's economic policy.

1203.   *The Times.* Thatcher establishes two secret committees to study ways of combatting strikes and their effects. January 30th 1980: 4.

1204.   *The Times.* Suggestion that striking teachers be locked out of schools without pay condemned by all sides. December 23rd 1985: 1.

1205.   Towers, Brian. "Running the gauntlet: British trade unions under Thatcher, 1979–1988." *Industrial and Labour Relations Review.* January 1989: 163–88.

Concentrates on the significance of the decline in membership, changes in the economy and government intervention.

1206.   Wedderburn, B. "Thatcher's threat to workers." *New Statesman.* January 26th 1979: 101.

See also: *Daily Telegraph.* "Meeting with Trade Union Congress discussed in leading article." (no. 148); *Daily Telegraph.* "Outlines and some details of Conservative proposals to curb union powers." (no. 141).

B. The Miners' Strike

1207.   *Adeney, Martin and Lloyd, John. *The Miners' Strike, 1984–1985: Loss without Limit.* London: Routledge and Kegan Paul, 1986. 319.

1208.   Beynon, Huw. "The miners' strike in Easington." *New Left Review.* (148), 1984: 104–15.

Keith Patterson's exhibition at the Side Gallery is described. Narrates the miners' strike and chronicles Thatcher's policies.

1209.   Bielstein, Klaus. *Gewerkschaften, neo-Konservatismus und oekonomischer strukturwandel: zur Strategie und Taktik der Gewerkschaften in Grossbritannien.* (Trade unions, neo-Conservatism and economic structural change: on the strategies and tactics of trade unions in Great Britain). *Arbeitskreis Dt.* England-Forsch. Brockmeyer, 1988. 553.

Covers the period 1979 to 1986 and includes discussion of Thatcher's economic and social policies, industrial development and trade union membership and strategies.

1210. Burgi, Noelle and Leruez, Jacques. "La grève des mineurs britanniques—mars 1984–mars 1985." (The British miners' strike—March 1984–March 1985). *Revue Française de Science Politique.* 36(50, 1986: 646–71.

A detailed study of the strike showing why both sides were unable to step down and to negotiate. Argues that Arthur Scargill's failure has not given Thatcher the benefits that she had expected.

1211. *Coulter, J., Miller, S. and Walker, M. *State of Siege. Miners' Strike 1984. Politics and Policing in the Coalfields.* London: Canary Press, 1984.

The policing of the miners' strike became a major issue with considerable violence being shown on television every night.

1212. Crick, Michael. *Scargill and the Miners.* Harmondsworth: Penguin, 1985.

A study of Scargill's leadership of the miners during the mid-1980s strike.

1213. Durr, Karlheinz. "Der bergarbeiterstreik in Grossbritannien 1984–85." (The coal miners' strike in Great Britain, 1984–85). *Politische Vierteljahresschrift.* 26(4), 1985: 400–422.

Argues how deindustrialisation introduced conflict which ultimately helped to cause and to defeat the miners' strike. Thatcher's success ensured that the two party system in Britain became even weaker through the weakening of labour unions and consequently the Labour Party.

1214. *Green, Penny. *The Enemy Without: Policing and Class Consciousness in the Miners' Strike.* Milton Keynes: Open University Press, 1990. 235.

Given from the point of view of the unions and their families. Shows how the policing tactics, the Government, the media, the welfare agencies and others changed the political consciousness of the striking community.

1215. Leruez, Jacques. "La grève des mineurs britanniques: mars 1984–mars 1985." (The British miners' strike: March 1984–March 1985). See Noelle Burgi, number 1210 above.

1216. Lloyd, John. *The Miners' Strike, 1984–1985*. See Martin Adeney, number 1207 above.

1217. Miller, S. *State of Siege. Miners' Strike 1984. Politics and Policing in the Coalfields*. See J. Coulter, number 1211 above.

1218. *The Times*. Interview with Thatcher during the miners' strike. June 14th 1984: 2.

1219. Walker, M. *State of Siege. Miners' Strike 1984. Politics and Policing in the Coalfields*. See J. Coulter, number 1211 above.

1220. *Wilsher, Peter and others. *Strike: Thatcher, Scargill and the Miners*. London: Andre Deutsch, 1985. 284.

Based on reports for the *Sunday Times* and investigations carried out after the strike of 1984–85.

See also: *The London Times*. "Draws parallel between miners' strike and the Falklands War attacking tactics of miners' leaders and praising the courage of those going to work." (no. 193); *The London Times*. "Thatcher says Government would welcome take over of individual pits by miners' cooperatives." (no. 206).

XII Education

Thatcher's educational reforms have been devised as part and parcel of her overall policy of changing the face of Britain. The new graduates of the new educational system may be truly dubbed "Thatcher's children."

A. Educational Policies

1221. Ambler, John S. "Constraints on policy innovation in education: Thatcher's Britain and Mitterrand's France." *Comparative Politics*. October 1987: 85–105.

1222. Chitty, C. *Towards a New Education System: The Victory on the New Right?* London: The Falmer Press, 1987.

Thatcher overhauled the British education system, much to the delight of rightwingers.

1223. Cini, Michelle. "The redirection of science and technology policy under the Thatcher Governments." See Stephen Wilks, number 755 above.

1224. Critical Social Policy. "Special issue: education in the 1990s." *Critical Social Policy*. Winter 1989–1990: 4–124.

Analyses Thatcher's education policies with reference to the City Technology Colleges (CTCs), race and gender in the making of the

National Curriculum, educational law, parent power and translating race equality policies into practice.

1225. Hargreaves, Andy and Reynolds, David (editors). *Education Policies: Controversies and Critiques*. London: The Falmer Press, 1989. 234.

Covers many areas of the Thatcher Government's educational reforms including the General Certificate of Secondary Education (GCSE) examination, the Certificate of Prevocational Education (CPVE) assessment and the Technical and Vocational Education Initiative (TVEI).

1226. Harvey, A. D. "The Thatcher revolution in academe: the first twelve years." *Contemporary Review*. Volume 258, number 1505, June 1991: 297.

1227. Johnson, Richard. "Thatcherism and English education: breaking the mould, or confirming the pattern?" *History of Education*. 18(2), 1989: 91–121.

Claims that Thatcher's educational reforms have failed because of a confused and reactionary new right which has failed to understand the contradictions within a capitalist society and the consequences of their policies on social relations.

1228. Menter, Ian. "Lessons of Thatcherism: education policy in England and Wales 1979–1988." See Geoff Whitty, number 1239 below.

1229. Morris, Marian and others. *TVEI and the Management of Change: An Overview*. London: National Foundation for Educational Research, 1990. 141.

The Technical and Vocational Education Initiative was supposedly a major curriculum initiative sponsored by the Department of Employment. When launched in 1983 its focus was intended to be the provision of young people "with the learning opportunities which [would] equip them for the demands of working life in a rapidly changing society." From 1987 the Extension of TVEI was to all students between 14 and 18. This book is the result of an evaluation project undertaken by the NFER between 1989 and 1990.

1230. OECD. *Alternatives to Universities*. Paris: Organisation for Economic Co-operation and Development (OECD), 1991. 85.

Analyses the recent development of the non-university sector of higher education showing an enhancement of this sector's public image. Soon after its publication, John Major announced that British polytechnics would become fully fledged universities.

1231. Regan, David. *City Technology Colleges.* London: Centre for Policy Studies, 1990.

City Technology Colleges (CTCs) were created as examples of excellent educational practice.

1232. Reynolds, David (editor). *Education Policies: Controversies and Critiques.* See Andy Hargreaves, number 1225 above.

1233. Salter, Brian and Tapper, E. R. "The politics of reversing the ratchet in secondary education: 1969–1986." *Journal of Educational Administration and History.* 20(2), 1988: 57–70.

Alleges unconvincingly that the Conservatives lacked a coherent political philosophy which in fact forced them to make concessions to leftist intellectual primacy. Apparently this led Thatcher to implement programmes and initiatives that challenged leftist ideas in the secondary school system. It is more likely to argue that the Conservative educational philosophy was a daring response to the bankrupt intellectual influences of the mid-1960s and related left wing thought.

1234. Searle, Chris. "From Forster to Baker: the new Victorianism and the struggle for education." *Race and Class.* 30(4), 1989: 31–50.

Forster introduced the 1870 Education Act which was the first really dramatic move towards universal education. This article discusses this act and Thatcher's new educational programmes.

1235. Tapper, E. R. "The politics of reversing the ratchet in secondary education: 1969–1986." See Brian Salter, number 1233 above.

1236. *The Times.* Thatcher's keenness to create a system of direct grant schools confirmed. February 25th 1986: 1.

1237. *The Times.* Thatcher's remarks suggesting that schools might be allowed to introduce selection and charge fees under new plans at odds with those of her Education Secretary. May 23rd 1987: 1.

1238. *The Times.* Thatcher gives clear indication of hope that scheme allowing schools to opt out of local education authority control will lead to more grammar schools. May 25th 1987: 1.

1239. Whitty, Geoff and Menter, Ian. "Lessons of Thatcherism: education policy in England and Wales: 1979–88." *Journal of Law and Society.* 16(1), 1988: 42–64.

Shows how Thatcher's reforms are meant to exercise more control over teachers, to change the curriculum and to legislate a clearly Conservative agenda.

1240. *Wragg, E. C. *Wragged Edge: Education in Thatcher's Britain.* London: Trentham Books, 1988. 150.

Ted Wragg fought a lost crusade on behalf of progressive education and against Thatcher's educational reforms. His beliefs in progressive education are probably shared by a very large number of teachers and other practitioners. They relate largely to child centred education with a considerable modicum of what Conservative thinkers would regard as the wishy washy progressive methodologies of the defunct 1960s.

See also: *Education Reform Act, 1988.* (no. 1241); Maclure, Stuart. *Education Re-formed.* (no. 1243); Wilks, Stephen. "The redirection of science and technology policy under the Thatcher Government." (no. 755).

B. Education Reform Act

1241. *Education Reform Act, 1988.* London: Her Majesty's Stationery Office, 1988. 284.

The most far-reaching and radical education reform produced since 1944. It introduced, amongst other reforms, the National Curriculum, a broadly Christian act of collective worship, compulsory religious education, standing advisory councils on religious education (SACRE), assessment councils, local management scheme (LMS), grant-maintained status for schools (GMS), city technology colleges (CTCs), reorganisation of provision and funding for higher education, the abolition of the inner London education authority (ILEA) and the establishment of University Commissions. The Act has changed the face of British education over the last four years. Much wasteful use of scarce resources has been stamped out. Power to make decisions on education within the legal framework set have been given to the schools and their governors. The changes, though daunting in their radicalism, have been generally perceived to have improved educational provision dramatically. In the summer of 1992 the Conservative Government published its White Paper on the future of education and on the progress of grant maintained status. Also a new requirement was established in 1992 for the rigorous inspection of schools.

1242. *Leonard, Martin. *The 1988 Education Act: A Tactical Guide to Schools*. Oxford: Blackwell Education, 1988. 230.

Describes the provision of the Act showing how the changes affect different schools. It also offers practical advice on how to manage schools under the new rules.

1243. *Maclure, Stuart. *Education Re-formed: A Guide to the Education Reform Act 1988*. Sevenoaks: Hodder and Stoughton, 1988.

1244. Mikdadi, Faysal. "To everyone according to his work." *The Times Educational Supplement*. January 8th 1988: 2.

The *1988 Education Reform Act* caused a sensation in the world of education. One of its proposals was for schools to opt out of local education authority (LEA) control. This article defends opting out as of benefit to schools, parents and children.

1245. Morris, Robert. *Central and Local Control of Education after the Education Reform Act 1988*. Harlow: Longman Group, 1990. 150.

As assessment of the changes caused by the *1988 Education Reform Act* with specific reference to the legislative background, the curriculum, parent power, religious education and the general shift of power from local education authorities (LEAs) to schools.

See also: Morris, Robert G. *Education Policy and Legislation: A Critical Examination of the Arguments for a New Major Education Act to Replace That of 1944*. (no. 1451).

C. General Certificate of Secondary Education

1246. Bates, Stephen. "GCSE 'fixing' probe." *Daily Mail*. August 29th 1988: 15.

Article detailing allegations by Mikdadi and other examiners that the new General Certificate of Secondary Education (GCSE) French and English examinations were "fixed" in order to ensure the public success of the new examinations.

1247. Bates, Stephen. "GCSE passes the test." *Daily Mail*. August 25th 1988: 17.

An analysis of the first GCSE results introduced by the Conservatives in September 1986.

1248. Edwards, Peter. "Meaning and message vital in French oral exams." *The Times Educational Supplement.* September 30th 1988: 25.

An attack on Mikdadi's claim that the new General Certificate of Secondary Education (GCSE) examination was easier than its predecessor.

1249. Mikdadi, Faysal. "Critical not jaundiced." *The Times Educational Supplement.* September 16th 1988: 22.

An article detailing the problems arising during the first two years of Kenneth Baker's (Minister for Education) new examination leading to the General Certificate of Secondary Education (GCSE).

1250. Mikdadi, Faysal. "Doublespeak of educationalists." *East Anglian Daily Times.* June 9th 1988: 12.

A short piece that attempts to explain that the drop in examination results is due to incompetent management and to a plethora of new initiatives. Teachers are shown as struggling on despite the odds.

1251. Mikdadi, Faysal. "Righting wrongs." *The Times Educational Supplement.* October 14th 1988: 18.

Many claims were made for the success of the newly introduced General Certificate of Secondary Education (GCSE) examinations at sixteen. Many made claims that standards had been dramatically dropped in order to achieve this success. This is a short response to an accusation by an examination association officer that critics had exaggerated their experiences as examiners of French.

1252. Park, B. "In a word." *The Times Educational Supplement.* September 30th 1988: 25.

B. Park, Joint Secretary to the Northern Examining Association Examinations Committee, claims inaccuracies in Mikdadi's allegation that the new General Certificate of Secondary Education (GCSE) examination was easier than its predecessors.

See also: HMSO. *Better Schools.* (no. 1256).

D. Government Acts and Reports

1253. *Education Act, 1944*. London: Her Majesty's Stationery Office, 1944. 109.

This major act was the basis of British education until the *Education Reform Act* of 1988.

1254. *Education Act, 1980*. London: Her Majesty's Stationery Office, 1980. 48.

The Act in which the new concept of parental preference in their choice of school was first introduced.

1255. Elton, Lord Rodney. *Discipline in Schools*. Her Majesty's Stationery Office, 1989. 292.

Lord Elton's report commissioned by Secretary of State for Education Kenneth Baker to look into discipline in schools.

1256. HMSO. *Better Schools*. London: Her Majesty's Stationery Office, 1985. 94.

A report presented to Parliament leading to the establishment of the General Certificate of Secondary Education (GCSE) with a clear hint on the radical reforms to come in the late 1980s.

1257. Kingman, Sir John. *Report of the Committee of Inquiry into the Teaching of English Language*. London: Her Majesty's Stationery Office, 1988. 99.

A report on the teaching of English advocating the teaching of "standard English" and the effective training of teachers. *The Kingman Report* was seen in 1988 as a foundation on which the new National Curriculum would be based.

1258. Mikdadi, Faysal. "Converting language report into action." *East Anglian Daily Times*. May 5th 1988: 12.

Article explaining the practical implications of the *Kingman Report* for the teaching of English. Also published in the Ipswich *Evening Star* of the same date.

1259. Mikdadi, Faysal. "Meaning of school discipline." *East Anglian Daily Times*. July 12th 1988: 17.

Evidence submitted to the Committee of Enquiry on discipline in schools. The enquiry, chaired by Lord Elton, was published in 1989.

1260. *Swann, Lord Michael. *Education for All: The Report of the Committee of Enquiry into the Education of Children from Ethnic Minority Groups.* London: Her Majesty's Stationery Office, 1985. 807.

Arguably the most comprehensive report on access to equalising opportunity in education. Its findings have led to a few minor changes in achieving racial equity in schools. However, many of its recommendations went largely ignored as schools set up cosmetic attempts at multiculturalism.

E. The National Curriculum

1261. *Emerson, Chris and Goddard, Ivor. *All about the National Curriculum.* Oxford: Heinemann Educational, 1989. 129.

Charts the history of the educational reform underpinning the National Curriculum, discusses the implications of these reforms and includes sections on assessment, in-service training for teachers and subject requirements (for mathematics, science, English and design and technology only).

1262. Goddard, Ivor. *All about the National Curriculum.* See Chris Emerson, number 1261 above.

1263. Lawlor, Sheila. *Correct Core.* London: Centre for Policy Studies, 1988.

Gives simple curricula for English, mathematics and science. Argues a back-to-basics approach.

1264. Lawton, Denis. *Education, Culture and the National Curriculum.* London: Hodder and Stoughton, 1989. 104.

Covers changes in education with particular reference to the *1988 Education Reform Act* (ERA). ERA is discussed in the context of educational theories and social change and in the context of its implications for teachers.

1265. *Lawton, D. and Chitty, C. *The National Curriculum.* London: Bedford Way Series Paper 33, Institute of Education, University of London, 1988.

1266. Moon, Bob (editor). *New Curriculum—National Curriculum.* Milton Keynes: The Open University, 1991. 184.

1267. *Moon, Bob. *A Guide to the National Curriculum.* Oxford: Oxford University Press, 1991. 114.

A guide intended for parents, teachers and school governors on all aspects of the National Curriculum.

1268.   National Curriculum Council (NCC). London: Her Majesty's Stationery Office.

The NCC published folders on the statutory requirements and nonstatutory guidance for each subject in the National Curriculum. These folders may be bought from Her Majesty's Stationery Office, P.O. Box 276, London SW8 5DT or from the National Curriculum Council, Albion Wharf, 25 Skeldergate, York YO1 2XL.

See also: Chitty, C. *Towards a New Education System: The Victory of the New Right?* (no. 1222); Wheatcraft, Geoffrey. "That woman versus the chattering classes." (no. 624).

F. Policy Impact

1269.   Beck, Antony. "The impact of Thatcherism on the Arts Council." *Parliamentary Affairs*. July 1989: 363–79.

On issues of commercialization and accessibility of the arts, incentives reducing the dependence of the arts on public finance.

1270.   Hasler, A. "Reagan, Thatcher and the intellectuals." *Public Opinion*. September 1988: 8–10.

Thatcher was regarded as essentially antiintellectual.

1271.   *Lawlor, Sheila. *Away with LEAs: ILEA Abolition as a Pilot*. London: Centre for Policy Studies, 1988.

The Inner London Education Authority (ILEA) was abolished by the Thatcher Government. Lawlor argues for the abolition of all local education authorities (LEAs).

See also: *The London Times*. "Oxford dons vote against award of honorary degree." (no. 199); Wragg, E. C. *Wragged Edge: Education in Thatcher's Britain*. (no. 1240); Young, Hugo. "Thatcher v. the intellectuals." (no. 73).

G. Schools

1272.   CERI. *One School, Many Cultures*. Paris: Centre for Educational Research and Innovations (CERI), 1989. 79.

Examines education in European countries with specific reference to the multicultural, multiethnic and multilingual nature of contemporary society.

1273.   *Lawlor, Sheila. *Opting Out*. London: Centre for Policy Studies, 1987.

Suggesting that a more efficient education service would be provided if schools were to opt out of local education authority control. All funds would be delegated to schools to manage as they see fit.

1274.   Letwin, Oliver. *Aims of Schooling*. London: Centre for Policy Studies, 1988.

Argues the importance of good, sound grounding in education.

See also: HMSO. *Better Schools*. (no. 1256); *The New York Times*. "Education and schools." (no. 394).

H. Teachers and Teaching

1275.   Beswick, Francis. "Case study on cognitive versus unconscious bias: a comment." *The College of Preceptors Newsletter*. October 1986: 10–12.

An article critical of Mikdadi's "Case study on cognitive versus unconscious bias: the Arab–Israeli conflict" published in *The College of Preceptors Newsletter* (see number 1281).

1276.   Department of Education and Science (now the Department for Education). *School Teacher Appraisal: A National Framework*. London: Her Majesty's Stationery Office, 1989. 80.

Report of the National Steering Group on the School Teacher Appraisal Pilot Study.

1277.   Graham, Duncan G. *Those Having Torches*. Ipswich: Suffolk Education Department, 1985. 149.

Teacher appraisal was one of the most controversial reforms under Thatcher. This is the pilot study that set appraisal in motion in the mid-1980s.

1278.   Graham, Duncan G. *In the Light of Torches: Teacher Appraisal—A Further Study*. London: The Industrial Society, 1987. 124.

Teacher appraisal was a much contested issue in the 1980s. This is a follow-up of *Those Having Torches* (see number 1277 above).

1279. Honeyford, Ray. "Whose bias?" *The College of Preceptors Newsletter*. February 1987: 15–16.

A forcible attack on Mikdadi's "Case study on cognitive versus unconscious bias: the Arab–Israeli conflict" published in *The College of Preceptors Newsletter* (see number 1281 below).

1280. *Lawlor, Sheila. *Teachers Mistaught: Training in Theories or Education in Subjects?* London: Centre for Policy Studies, 1990. 46.

Arguing that teacher training concerned itself mainly with theories, Lawlor suggests that teachers should be trained in schools and in the classroom. She also suggests that teacher trainers at colleges and universities should return to the classroom. John Major's Government has decided that teacher training should involve much more classroom practice.

1281. Mikdadi, Faysal. "Case study on cognitive versus unconscious bias: the Arab–Israeli conflict (Schools Council History 13–16 Project)." *The College of Preceptors Newsletter*. August 1986: 19–23.

An article arguing that the history project is essentially biased reflecting the state of education in Britain in the 1980s.

1282. Mikdadi, Faysal. "Culture and language in teaching and learning." *Multicultural Teaching*. Volume 1, number 2, Spring 1983: 28–31.

An attempt to understand the place of culture and language in the child's school life.

1283. Mikdadi, Faysal. "Response." *The College of Preceptors Newsletter*. February 1987: 16–19.

Response to two articles attacking Mikdadi's views on history teaching (see numbers 1275, 1279 and 1281 above).

1284. Mikdadi, Faysal. "Speaking up." *The Times Educational Supplement*. February 28th 1986.

A short piece on a teacher's right to speak up during the teachers' industrial action and during a cause célèbre over multiculturalism in schools.

1285. *The Times*. Thatcher hints that schools might be able to pay over the odds to attract best teachers under new reform plans. May 26th 1987: 4.

XIII   Equal Opportunities

This is probably the most contentious section of this bibliography, just as it was the most contentious part of Thatcher's Premiership. The vast majority of Thatcher observers feel that she did nothing for equal opportunities. Indeed, they feel that her premiership caused positive harm to women and to minority groups. A minority of observers believe that Thatcher's policies themselves allowed her successor, John Major, to promise "a classless society." Thatcher's own messianic insistence on personal freedom, initiative, hard work, wealth creation, and acquisitiveness can be said to have aided this process. Her own personal attitude to equal opportunities as political issues was that of exasperation and contempt.

A. Equality and Citizenship

1286.   Aughey, A. "The politics of equal citizenship." *Talking Politics.* 2(1), Autumn 1989.

1287.   Beetham, David. "Civil liberties, Thatcherism and Charter '88." *Political Quarterly.* Volume 60, number 3, July 1989: 273.

1288.   BOZO. "Big stick: being an account of the contempt shown for our way of life by Mrs. Thatcher and most politicians—concluding with an impassioned plea for its defence in these islands instead of its travesty on some remote rocks inhabited by hermits, sheep and penguins." *BOZO*, 1982. 60.

A *cri de coeur* against Thatcher's Falklands policy.

1289.   Browne-Wilkinson, N. "The U.K.'s Alice-in-Wonderland position on human rights." *Independent.* April 27th 1989.

1290.   Gelb, Norman. "Britain's new ruling class: easing out the aristocrats." *New Leader.* June 27th 1983: 8–9.

Thatcher filled the highest ranks of the Conservative Party and the Government with persons (mainly men) from outside the traditional ruling classes.

1291.   Gorz, Andre. *Farewell to the Working Class.* London: Pluto Press, 1982.

During the Thatcher years there was a shift in working class positioning. As people bought their own council houses, shares from privatised companies and other acquisitions the working class voting pattern shifted to the Conservative.

1292.   Phillips, Joan. *Policing the Family: Social Control in Thatcher's Britain.* Junius Publications, 1988. 112.

The role of the Conservative Party in promoting traditional forms of morality in the context of capitalist decline. The work illustrates the state regulation of sexuality and women's rights under Thatcher.

1293.   Plant, Raymond. *Citizenship and Rights in Thatcher's Britain: Two Views.* See Norman P. Barry, number 559 above.

See also: Barry, Norman. *Citizenship and Rights in Thatcher's Britain: Two Views.* (no. 559); Ewing, K. D. *Freedom under Thatcher: Civil Liberties in Modern Britain.* (no. 571); *The New York Times.* "On citizenship." (no. 337); Thornton, P. *Decade of Decline: Civil Liberties in the Thatcher Years.* (no. 596).

B. Gender

1294.   Baxter, Sarah. "Sympathy not sorrow: Tory women aren't mourning Thatcher's departure." *New Statesman.* Volume 4, number 158, July 5th 1991: 8.

1295.   Brunt, Ros. "Thatcher uses her woman's touch." *Marxism Today.* June 1987: 22–24.

1296. *Campbell, Beatrix. *The Iron Ladies: Why Do Women Vote Tory?* London: Virago Press, 1987.

A feminist Marxist analysis of Thatcher the woman with emphasis on gender versus sexuality where a denial of sexuality allegedly becomes a violation of the truth. One can not help but wonder whether such sexist analysis would ever be written about a male Prime Minister.

1297. Campbell, Beatrix. "Model female, or female role model?" *The Times.* November 23rd 1990: 20.

Feminist Marxist analysis of Thatcher.

1298. Carr, Winifred. "After Margaret Thatcher, can anyone deny it: middle aged women beat men for stamina?" *Daily Telegraph.* Febraury 13th 1975.

1299. Coyle, A. "The limits of change: local government and local equal opportunities for women." *Public Administration.* Number 67, 1989: 50+.

1300. Itzin, Catherine. "Margaret Thatcher is my sister, counselling on divisions between women." *Women's Studies International Forum.* Volume 8, 1985: 75–83.

1301. Marshal, Kate. *Moral Panics and Victorian Values: Women and the Family in Thatcher's Britain.* Junius Publications, 1986. 57.

1302. Mooney, Bel. "Votes and seats for women." *Sunday Times.* June 5th 1983.

1303. Mount, Ferdinand. "A woman's right to be left to her own devices." *Daily Telegraph.* March 12th 1984.

1304. Rose, J. "Getting away with murder." *New Statesman.* July 22nd 1988: 34–37.

A look at Thatcher's attitude to women with psychological aspects of feminine stereotypes.

1305. *The Times.* Many women feel that Thatcher has not improved image of women. March 11th 1986: 3.

1306. *The Times.* Thatcher is believed to have actively assisted high-flying women to get top jobs. September 25th 1987: 2.

1307. *The Times.* Thatcher's personal support for the ordination of women priests. July 31st 1988: A1. August 1st 1988: 1.

1308. Warner, Marina. *Monuments and Maidens: The Allegory of the Female Form.* London: Picador Books. 424.

Argues Thatcher's de-eroticisation from a feminist point of view. Thatcher the sexual venus has been replaced by the matron or governess. Lacks subtlety with a sexist one-sidedness.

1309. *Webster, Wendy. *Not a Man to Match Her: The Marketing of a Prime Minister.* London: The Women's Press, 1990. 199.

A readable feminist analysis of Thatcher. Webster's thesis is that Thatcher has been a product of marketing strategies which present her as tough and triumphant amongst men. Thatcher, she argues, has sublimated her sexuality in order to join a macho world. Thatcher is also presented as having done much damage to women by consigning them to the home, and is seen as progressing through several roles each according to the necessities of her political life at the time. She is, in other words, a travesty of feminist truths. Such analysis would have delighted Thatcher whose strong views against feminism are widely known.

See also: *Daily Telegraph.* "Swedish women politicians criticise radio reporter's coverage of campaign as sexist." (no. 145); *The London Times.* "Labour Member of Parliament deplores sexist slogans applied to Thatcher." (no. 165); *The London Times.* "Leading women comment on Thatcher." (no. 246).

C. The Law

1310. Atkins, S. "The Sex Discrimination Act of 1975: The End of a Decade." *Feminist Review.* Number 24, 1986: 57–70.

Feminists argue that Thatcher did a great deal of damage to the women's cause.

1311. *Benyon, John (editor). *Scarman and after: Essays Reflecting on Lord Scarman's Report, the Riots and Their Aftermath.* Oxford: Pergamon Press, 1984. 270.

Lord Scarman reported on the causes/reasons behind the inner-city race riots in Brixton. His report's recommendations were selectively implemented.

1312. Pannick, D. *Sex Discrimination Law.* Oxford: Oxford University Press. 1986. 358.

1313. *Scarman, Lord. *The Brixton Disorders, 10–12 April 1981: Report of an Inquiry by the Rt. Hon. Lord Scarman.* London: Her Majesty's Stationery Office, 1981. 46.

Lord Scarman has much to say on policing strategies, community policing, community relations, racism and other causes of the Brixton riots. Thatcher saw the riots as being questions of law and order. Apart from policing the report's recommendations went unheeded.

See also: Chesshyre, Robert. *The Force Inside the Police.* (no. 706).

D. The Media

1314. Baxter, Sarah. "Thatcher and the media." *Women: A Cultural Review.* Spring 1991: 71–73.

On Thatcher's personal crusade against the media.

1315. Murray, Nancy and Searle, Chris. *Racism and the Press in Thatcher's Britain.* London: Institute of Race Relations, 1989. 48.

Produced by one of those institutions despised by Thatcher. Her Government was constantly accused of doing little or nothing for race relations.

See also: Ponting, Clive. *The Right to Know: The Inside Story of the Belgrano.* (no. 662); Walters, Peter. "The crisis of 'responsible' broadcasting: Mrs. Thatcher and the BBC." (no. 597).

E. Poverty

1316. Andrews, Kay and Jacobs, John. *Punishing the Poor: Poverty under Thatcher.* London: Macmillan, 1990. 352.

Thatcher was blamed for an increase in the number of the poor and a worsening of their conditions. During her Premiership as many did well as those who did badly.

1317. Armstrong, Isobel. "Women and children last? Women under Thatcherism." *Women: A Cultural Review.* Spring 1991: 74–77.

Alleges that the Thatcher Governments failed to address women's issues.

1318. Blake, R. "Suffering by suppression." *Spectator.* November 10th 1990: 10–11.

1319.   Field, Frank. *Losing out: The Emergence of Britain's Underclass.*
        Oxford: Basil Blackwell, 1989. 199.

Shows the pattern of class inequalities during the post-war period and
how class differences under Thatcher are widening for the first time
because of forces that fix the underclass in place. Proposes recommendations for policy reforms.

1320.   Jacobs, John. *Punishing the Poor: Poverty under Thatcher.* See
        Kay Andrews, number 1316 above.

1321.   *The Times.* Thatcher claims unemployment and poor housing
        could not justify Brixton riots. April 14th 1981: 1.

1322.   *The Times.* Thatcher accepts that unemployment may well be a
        factor contributing to the Toxteth riots. July 8th 1981: 1.

See also: Jessop, B. *Thatcherism: A Tale of Two Nations.* (no. 589);
Loney, Martin. *The Politics of Greed: The New Right and the Welfare State.*
(no. 593); McGlone, Francis. "Away from the dependency culture? Social
security policy." (no. 742); Scanlon, Joan. *Surviving the Blues: Growing
up in the Thatcher Decade.* (no. 620).

F. Race

1323.   Benyon, John and Solomos, John. "The simmering cities: urban
        unrest during the Thatcher years." *Parliamentary Affairs.* 41(3),
        1988: 402–22.

Argues that riots have been caused by racism, discrimination, unemployment, political exclusion and Thatcher's failure to maintain order.

1324.   *Bryan, B., Dadzie, S. and Scafa, S. *The Heart of the Race: Black
        Women's Lives in Britain.* London: Virago Press, 1985.

Along with feminists accusing Thatcher of sexism, the race relations
lobby charged her with racism. All in all black women allegedly received
a very bad deal from the Thatcher Government.

1325.   CRE. *Review of the Race Relations Act 1976: Proposals for
        Change.* London: Commission for Racial Equality (CRE), 1985.

This is the first review of the Act. The Commission Chair expressed his
disappointment that "there was no formal response from the Government"
under Thatcher in his foreword to the second review in 1991. See number
1326 below.

1326. *CRE. Second Review of the Race Relations Act 1976: A Consultative Paper.* London: Commission for Racial Equality, 1991. 71.

Britain is the only country in Europe with a Race Relations Act. The Act has had its successes but generally speaking minority ethnic groups have regarded it as somewhat weak. Some Conservatives saw it as yet another example of unhealthy government paternalism. This review tries to contextualise all these—and other—issues. The final recommendations were presented to the Secretary of State in 1992.

1327. Dadzie, S. *The Heart of the Race: Black Women's Lives in Britain.* See B. Bryan, number 1324 above.

1328. *Daily Telegraph.* Thatcher's angry response to BBC television Panorama programme linking party with racist elements. February 3rd 1984: 1.

1329. Economist. "Disarranging Marriages." *The Economist.* December 8th 1979: 12+.

Argues that most of Thatcher's ministers are embarrassed at their mean little antiimmigration policy and urges that they keep on being embarrassed.

1330. *Figueroa, Peter. *Education and the Social Construction of 'Race'.* London: Routledge, 1991. 216.

A very readable critique of the *Swann Report*, set within Figueroa's own experiences of racism in areas of housing and education. Included are carefully researched and dynamic discussions of the philosophy and sociology of multiculturalism and antiracism. Education is seen as reinforcing racism and thus in need of reconstruction.

1331. Gordon, P. *Citizenship for Some: Race and Government Policy 1979–1989.* London: Runnymede Trust, 1989.

1332. *Jenkins, R. and Solomos, J. (editors). *Racism and Equal Opportunity Policies in the 1980s.* Cambridge: Cambridge University Press, 1987.

Includes Jenkins's "Equal Opportunities in the Private Sector: The Limits of Voluntarism."

1333. Mikdadi, Faysal. "Action research into multicultural education." *Education Today.* Volume 36, number 1, 1986: 54–61.

Research findings on multicultural teaching in the wake of the *Swann Report* (see number 1260 above). Also published in Nixon, Jon and Watts, Mike. *Whole School Approaches to Multicultural Education*. London Macmillan, 1989: 72–76.

1334. Mikdadi, Faysal. "Culture and religion in a multi-cultural society: a dilemma for everybody." *Education Today*. Volume 37, number 1, 1987: 80–82.

An article that attempts to explain the position of British Moslems with particular reference to their schooling, way of life and adaptation. Also published in Nixon, Jon and Watts, Mike. *Whole School Approaches to Multicultural Education*. London: Macmillan, 1989: 77–78.

1335. Mikdadi, Faysal. "Misguided rights." *The Times Educational Supplement*. December 23rd 1988: 12.

An article arguing for freedom of choice within a multicultural society.

1336. Mikdadi, Faysal. "Right to choose." *The Times Educational Supplement*. May 17th 1985.

A piece on a citizen's right to choose his/her culture regardless of their ethnicity.

1337. Scafa, S. *The Heart of the Race: Black Women's Lives in Britain*. See B. Bryan, number 1324 above.

1338. Searle, Chris. *Racism and the Press in Thatcher's Britain*. See Nancy Murray, number 1315 above.

1339. Solomos, J. (editor). *Racism and Equal Opportunity Policies in the 1980s*. See R. Jenkins, number 1332 above.

1340. Solomos, J. *Race and Racism in Contemporary Britain*. London: Macmillan, 1989. 224.

1341. Stamp, Gavin. "Princes of their own times." *The Spectator*. January 18th 1986.

Comparing Prince Edward (later King Edward VIII) and Prince Charles as two princes of their time: modern, efficient and unstuffy. Ends with a feeling of optimism that the Thatcher 1980s "are not half so bad as the 1930s" with their "enterprise culture" taking the edge over "employee mentality."

1342. Troyna, Barry (editor). *Racial Inequality in Education*. London: Tavistock Publications, 1987. 211.

Argues that the British education system in the 1980s systematically generates and maintains racial inequality.

See also: *The London Times*. "Greater London Council leader accuses Thatcher of dragging nation into a mire of racism." (no. 176); Swann, Lord Michael. *Education for All*. (no. 1260).

G. Thatcher's Image and Attitude

1343. Anderson, Bruce. "The ordinariness of the long-distance Prime Minister." *Sunday Telegraph*. January 3rd 1988.

1344. Bowman, Marion. "How to handle a woman." *Guardian*. November 14th 1991: 38.

Differences in approaches to women by Thatcher and Major.

1345. Broder, D. S. "Queen Maggie I. Is Thatcher destroying British democracy?" *Washington Post*. July 23rd 1989.

As the years went by Thatcher's style of government came under increasing attack as autocratic and undemocratic.

1346. Edmunds, Lynne. "Debate—It's all part of family life for Mrs. Thatcher." *Daily Telegraph*. December 11th 1974.

1347. Greig, Gordon. "The Prime Minister's punishing programme." *Daily Mail*. November 28th 1987.

1348. Grice, Elizabeth. "The steel that makes supermag a winner." *Daily Express*. March 31st 1987.

1349. Malcolm, N. "Margaret Thatcher, housewife superstar." *Spectator*. February 25th 1989: 8–10.

1350. Maxwell, Sharon. "Is there a woman inside Maggie?" *Cosmopolitan*. December 1986.

1351. O'Brien, Conor Cruise. "Mrs. Thatcher's dual monarchy." *Observer*. June 5th 1983.

Thatcher came in for a great deal of criticism over her increasingly Presidential style. In the Falklands victory thanksgiving parade she took the part traditionally taken by the Head of State. Her use of the royal "we" culminated in her announcement when her grandchild was born, "We are a grandmother."

1352.   Warden, John. "Maggie, a Churchill in carmen rollers." *Daily Express*. January 12th 1983.

See also: Atkinson, Max. *Our Masters' Voices: Language and Body Langauge of Politics*. (no. 701); Rook, Jean. "The best MAN in England? Maggie's a female task force." (no. 51).

XIV Removal from Power

A. The Aftermath

1353. Castro, Janice. "Grapevine." *Time*. Volume 139, number 2, January 13th 1992: 9.

Anecdotes about executives' fears of fired employees with Thatcher making trouble for Major.

1354. Cole, John. "Friends make bad enemies." *New Statesman*. Volume 4, number 179, November 29th 1991: 9.

On supporters of Thatcher during her last and lost fight for the Conservative leadership.

1355. Coward, Mat. "The new year's dishonours list 1992." *New Statesman*. Volume 4, number 182, December 20th 1991: 61.

1356. Grice, Andrew, Hughes, David and Cassidy, John. "The Tory family at war." *Sunday Times*. Section 1, June 23rd 1991: 10–11.

1357. Guardian. "Vanity at the Thatcher court." *The Guardian*. May 9th 1991: 19.

Cites Thatcher interview in *Vanity Fair* on her shattered political career.

1358. Hilton, Isabel. "Breaking up is hard to do." *Independent*. May 11th 1991: 27.

Psychological analysis of Margaret Thatcher's style of leadership and the transfer of power to Prime Minister Major.

1359.   Lewis, Peter. "Invitation to a true blue murder party." *Sunday Times*. Section 5, September 8th 1991: 4–5.

About the making of television drama documentary entitled, *Thatcher: The Final Days*.

1360.   Malcolm, Noel. "Margaret Thatcher: the silent years." *Spectator*. February 16th 1991: 8–10.

Examines Thatcher's plans for the future.

1361.   New Statesman. "End of an error: Thatcherism, if it ever existed, has ended with the departure of Thatcher." *New Statesman*. Volume 4, number 158, July 5th 1991: 4.

1362.   Pedersen, Daniel. "The schoolmarm and the pupil: has Mrs. Thatcher started to turn on John Major?" *Newsweek*. Volume 117, number 25, June 24th 1991: 36.

1363.   Phillips, Andrew. "Thatcher's dark shadow: a former leader divides the governing Tories." *Maclean's*. Volume 104, number 27, July 8th 1991: 33.

Includes aspects of Thatcher's emotional reaction to her defeat.

1364.   *Publishers Weekly*. "ICM to represent Thatcher." Volume 238, number 28, June 28th 1991: 10.

ICM is International Creative Management which is acting as Thatcher's literary agent.

1365.   Raphael, R. "After the fall." *Observer*. December 2nd 1990: 17–21.

1366.   *The Times*. "Defiant Prime Minister stands by her record." November 23rd 1990: 7.

1367.   Time. "Turning a lady into a Lord." *Time*. Volume 138, number 1, July 8th 1991: 41.

On Thatcher's move to the House of Lords.

1368.   Wapshott, Nicholas. "Maggie goes to war." *Observer*. November 24th 1991: 25.

Examines the impact of Thatcher's intervention on Europe.

1369. Wapshott, Nicholas. "Thatcher's long shadow." *Observer*. June 23rd 1991: 19.

Thatcher's continuing impact on the Conservative Party after her resignation.

1370. Waterhouse, Rosie. "Thatcher's world tour strikes a rich seam." *Independent*. November 11th 1991: 3.

Reports on fund raising for the newly formed Thatcher Foundation.

See also: Turner, Graham. "Missing Margaret." (no. 922).

B. The Challenge

1371. *Anderson, Bruce. *John Major: The Making of the Prime Minister*. London: Fourth Estate, 1991. 324.

Although somewhat hastily produced, this book gives an insight into Conservative politics and, more importantly, into Thatcher's years as Prime Minister overseeing, in her tenth year, Major's meteoric rise to power.

1372. Barnes, Julian. "Letter from London." *New Yorker*. Volume 67, number 49, January 6th 1992: 69.

1373. Baxter, Sarah. "Heseltine swings back into the driving seat." *New Statesman*. Volume 120, number 4060, November 22nd 1991: 32.

On Michael Heseltine and the abolition of Thatcher's Community Charge (Poll Tax) and its replacement with Council Tax.

1374. Melcher, Richard A. and Meremont, Mark. "Working-class meteor." *Business Weekly*. December 10th 1990: 24–25.

Written soon after Thatcher's resignation. Reports that John Major promises a kinder, gentler Thatcherism.

1375. Meremont, Mark. "Working-class meteor." See Richard A. Melcher, number 1374 above.

1376. *The Times*. "Will Europe write the final chapter for Thatcherism." November 5th 1989: B3.

1377. *The Times*. Poll of Conservative Members of Parliament reveals desire for new Party leader. March 11th 1990: A1.

1378. *The Times.* Heseltine watches and waits for the kill. April 1st 1990: C2.

1379. *The Times.* Speculation that Prime Minister may face leadership challenge soon. October 29th 1990: 1.

See also: *The London Times.* "Article discusses whether the time is ripe for Prime Minister to resign leadership." (no. 279); *New Statesman.* "Vale of cheers? on the tenth anniversary of her regime, Mrs. Thatcher's power may be on the wane." (no. 36).

C. The Fall

1380. Alderman, R. K. and Carter, Neil. "A very Tory coup: the ousting of Mrs. Thatcher." *Parliamentary Affairs.* April 1991: 125–39.

A discussion of the political events that led to Thatcher's downfall including procedures, campaign errors and the perceived need to avoid a Heseltine leadership.

1381. Barder, Christopher. "The fall of Mrs. Thatcher." *Politics Review.* September 1991: 31–33.

Asks whether the Conservative Party will regret the loss of Thatcher.

1382. Benyon, John. "The fall of a Prime Minister." *Social Studies Review.* January 1991: 102–07.

Reasons for Thatcher's removal with a description of events leading to her resignation.

1383. Carter, Neil. "A very Tory coup: the ousting of Mrs. Thatcher." See R. K. Alderman, number 1380 above.

1384. Economist. "Was it, or was it not, a plot?" *The Economist.* March 9th 1991: 21–24.

The story leading to Thatcher's fall.

1385. Garland, N. "Fall of an icon." *Independent Magazine.* December 29th 1990: 36–39.

1386. Hughes, C. "The Thatcher resignation." *Independent.* November 23rd 1990: 3–6.

1387. Jenkins, Simon. "My dash for freedom." *The Times.* June 29th 1991: 12.

Interview with Thatcher on her announcement of her retirement from the House of Commons.

1388. Stephens, P. "The Thatcher resignation." *Financial Times.* November 23rd 1990: 15–22.

1389. *The Times.* Leading articles: "Why this obsession with political hara-kiri." March 13th 1990: 14.

On Thatcher's insistence on staying on despite Member of Parliaments' desire to see her go.

1390. Wapshott, N. "The fall of Thatcher." *The Observer.* November 25th 1990: 78.

1391. Wapshott, N. and Keegan, W. "Now the Tories start to panic." *The Observer.* March 4th 1990: 21.

1392. *Watkins, Alan. *Conservative Coup: Fall of Mrs. Thatcher.* London: Duckworth, 1991. 256.

Analyses the lead up to Thatcher's resignation in terms of a Conservative Party coup.

1393. *Young, Hugo. "The fall of Thatcher." *The Guardian.* November 6th 1991: 19.

One of two extracts from Young's updated *One of Us.* The lead up to Geoffrey Howe's resignation over Europe is recounted. The extract ends with Kenneth Baker (Chairman of the Conservative Party) playing down the resignation as that of "mood and style and tone." (See number 1394 below for the second extract. Also see number 486 above).

1394. Young, Hugo. "The fall of Thatcher." *The Guardian.* November 7th 1991: 21.

The second of two extracts from Young's updated *One of Us.* It recounts the story of Geoffrey Howe's decisive speech in the House, Heseltine's subsequent challenge to Thatcher, Thatcher's downfall and John Major's election as Prime Minister. (See numbers 1393 and 486).

XV   General Place in History

It is too early to place Thatcher in a historical perspective. This section should be consulted along with many of the other references cited in this bibliography.

1395.   Castle, Stephen. "Still mourning glory." *Independent on Sunday.* November 17th 1991: 25.

A profile of Thatcher's first year out of office.

1396.   Castro, Janice. "Kissinger associates can sleep soundly." *Time.* Volume 139, number 2, January 13th 1992: 9.

On Thatcher's plans to start a global advice think tank with Ronald Reagan and Mikhail Gorbachev.

1397.   *Clarke, Peter. *A Question of Leadership: Gladstone to Thatcher.* London: Hamish Hamilton, 1991.

An excellent book that attempts to put Thatcher in a proper historical perspective. In his last chapter, Clarke compares Gladstone and Thatcher and her remaking of the Conservative Party.

1398.   Economist. "Her bid for posterity: Margaret Thatcher's reshuffle could keep Thatcherism going long after she has retired." *The Economist.* July 29th 1989: 14–15.

1399.   Cole, John. "Housing hits where it hurts." *New Statesman.* Volume 4, number 182, December 20th 1991: 9.

On mortgages and housing policy as a result of Thatcher's years.

1400.   Cole, John. "Not Mrs. Thatcher; ex-MPs are among John Major's biggest problems." *New Statesman.* Volume 4, number 157, June 28th 1991: 7.

1401.   *Cole, John. *Thatcher Years: A Decade of Revolution in British Politics.* London: British Broadcasting Corporation, 1987. 216 (available in hardback and paperback).

John Cole is political affairs correspondent for the BBC. His is an interesting insight into the British political scene.

1402.   Economist. "Lost and soon forgotten." *The Economist.* Volume 322, number 7740, January 1992: 14.

1403.   Economist. "Mrs. Thatcher's place in history." *The Economist.* April 29th 1989: 58–59.

1404.   Gamble, Andrew. "The end of Thatcherism?" *Social Studies Review.* January 1991: 86–91.

Radical thrust of Thatcherism unlikely to be renewed under John Major.

1405.   Johnson, R. W. "The human time bomb. Is the former Prime Minister going off her rocker?" *New Statesman.* March 22nd 1991: 10.

Examines Thatcher's inability to adjust to powerlessness.

1406.   *Kavanagh, Dennis and Seldon, Anthony (editors). *Thatcher Effect: A Decade of Change.* Oxford: Oxford University Press, 1989. 355.

Essays on the effects of Thatcherism on trade unions, the civil service, education, local government, the cabinet and other areas. Powell's "The Conservative Party" is worth reading in order to understand the antecedents of Thatcherism.

1407.   Rogaly, Joe. "Fading of a megastart." *Financial Times.* June 29th 1991: 8.

An assessment of Thatcher's career, her legacy to the Party and the country. The legacy is seen as ambiguous.

1408.   *The Times.* "Thatcher: history's verdict." December 4th 1983: 15.

1409.   *The Times.* "The mantle of de Gaulle." September 25th 1988: B2.

1410. Vilella, Giancarlo. "Mutamenti e problemi dell'amministrazione britannica nee'epoca del Thatcherismo, 1979–1989." (Changes and problems of the British government in the time of Thatcher, 1979–1989). *Econ. Pubblica.* March 1990: 123–41.

Changes in the role, structure and influence of the British civil service after Thatcher's reforms.

1411. Wyatt, Petronella. "Thatcher cuts first disc on the freedom label." *Sunday Telegraph.* June 28th 1992: 3.

An interview with Thatcher after she recorded Lincoln's Gettysburg Address for EMI Classics. Thatcher speaks of her responsibilities in teaching the difference between right and wrong, to inculcate "feelings like determination. . . . Young people are searching for ideals." Wyatt writes that Thatcher wishes "to become a Messiah to the younger generation."

1412. *Young, Hugo. "Thatcher: the first verdict of history." *Guardian.* June 20th 1991: 21–22.

Results of a survey of fifty top historians assessing Thatcher's policies and her place among post-war Prime Ministers.

See also: *New Statesman.* "Victorian values: historians take issue with Mrs. Thatcher." (no. 37); Turner, Graham. "Missing Margaret." (no. 922).

XVI   Theses, Bibliographies, and Reviews

A. Biographical Entries and Records

1413. *Chambers Biographical Dictionary.* Edited by Thorne, J. O. and Collocott, T. C. Edinburgh: W. and R. Chambers Ltd., 1984. 1313–14.

1414. Ellwein, Thomas and others (editors). *Jahrbuch zur staats und verwaltungswissen schaft* (Yearbook of political and administrative science). Bonn: Nomos, 1988. 494.

A collection of essays (including two in English), research reports and bibliographic essays. Essays included are on administrative reforms of the Reagan administration and Thatcher's civil service.

1415. *The International Who's Who 1991–1992.* London: Europa Publications Limited, 1991. 1602.

1416. *Keesing's U.K. Record.* Cambridge and Harlow: Longman Group U.K. Ltd.

Published every two months with a chronology of events, legislative summary, sections on government, politics, foreign affairs, defence, local government, economic affairs, social affairs, an economic survey and obituaries.

1417. Low, Robert (editor). *The Observer Book of Profiles.* London: W. H. Allen, 1991. 375.

A readable collection of profiles including many associated with Thatcher such as Enoch Powell, Michael Heseltine, Norman Tebbit, Edwina Currie and Neil Kinnock. There is a short profile of Denis Thatcher that concludes: "Ferocious reactionary he may be, but in person he is—they say—not a bad bloke: funny, brave, loyal, however unthinkingly. In her choice of partner for life, as in many things, Mrs. Thatcher has been rather lucky."

1418. *Who's Who 1992: An Annual Biographical Dictionary.* London: A. and C. Black, 1992.

These entries are usually written by the subject himself/herself. Much has been said of Thatcher not including her mother's name in this—or any other—entry.

B. Reviews

1419. Bassett, K. "Urban planning under Thatcherism: the challenge of the market." *Environmental and Planning.* Volume 23, number 10, October 1991: 1526.

1420. Bulpitt, Jim. "Local government and Thatcherism." *Public Administration.* Volume 69, number 2, Summer 1991: 270.

1421. Clawson, Patrick. "Policies of Thatcherism." *Orbis.* Volume 36, number 1, Winter 1992: 143.

1422. Coomber, Ross. "The free economy and the strong state: the politics of Thatcherism." *Sociological Review.* Volume 37, number 3, August 1989: 566.

1423. Coomber, Ross. "The hard road to renewal: Thatcherism and the crisis of the left." *Sociological Review.* Volume 37, number 4, November 1989: 838.

1424. Durham, Martin. "Mrs. Thatcher's political experiment." *Parliamentary Affairs.* 43(1), 1990: 119–22.

1425. Economist. "Books about Mrs. Thatcher." *The Economist.* August 24th 1985: 83.

1426. Eltis, Walter. "Can there be a British economic renaissance?: Alan Walters' progress." *Encounter.* 67(3), 1986: 70–73.

A review of Alan Walters' work *Britain's Economic Renaissance: Margaret Thatcher's Reforms, 1979–1984.* See number 1019 above.

1427. Gamble, Andrew. "The end of the socialist era?" *Parliamentary Affairs.* 41(3), 1988: 430–33.

Reviews seven books that consider the decline of British socialism and the Labour Party.

1428. Gamble, Andrew. "The Tory tradition and the Tory hope." *Parliamentary Affairs.* 31(3), 1978: 334–36.

1429. Harden, Ian. "Waiving the rules: the constitution under Thatcherism." *British Journal of Political Science.* Volume 21, number 4, October 1991: 489.

1430. Harrington, Michael. "One of Us: A Biography of Margaret Thatcher." *The Times Literary Supplement.* Number 4626, November 29th 1991: 14.

A review of Hugo Young's excellent biography. See number 486 above.

1431. Jackson, Peter M. "The changing balance of public and private power." *Parliamentary Affairs.* 42(3), 1989: 433–43.

Reviews books on Thatcher's privatisation programme.

1432. Johnson, Norman. "Beyond Thatcherism: social policy, politics and society." *British Journal of Sociology.* Volume 42, number 2, June 1991: 307.

1433. Jones, G. W. "Conservative characters." *Parliamentary Affairs.* 43(2), 1990: 230–36.

Reviews twenty books on contemporary British Conservative politicians including Thatcher.

1434. Parker, M. St. John. "Analysts or polemicists?" *Parliamentary Affairs.* 43(3), 1990: 388–92.

Reviews books that have a strong polemical commentary and claims that the ability to write in a dispassionate way has disappeared since Thatcherism.

1435. Riddell, Peter. "A Conservative coup: the fall of Margaret Thatcher." *The Times Literary Supplement.* Number 4626, November 29th 1991: 14.

1436. Satre, Lowell J. "The Iron Lady: a biography of Margaret Thatcher." *Presidential Studies Quarterly.* Volume 21, number 3, Summer 1991: 624.

1437. Saunders, Peter. "Beyond Thatcherism: social policy, politics and society." *Sociology*. Volume 23, number 4, November 1989: 655.

1438. Madgwick, Peter. "The free economy and the strong state: the politics of Thatcherism." *Parliamentary Affairs*. Volume 42, number 2, April 1989: 269.

1439. Tuckman, Alan. "The free economy and the strong state: the politics of Thatcherism." *Sociology*. Volume 23, number 3, August 1989: 443.

1440. Tuckman, Alan. "The hard road to renewals: Thatcherism and the crisis of the left." *Sociology*. Volume 23, number 3, August 1989: 443.

1441. Tuckman, Alan. "Thatcherism: a tale of two nations." *Sociology*. Volume 23, number 3, August 1989: 443.

1442. Weyl, Nathaniel. "A labyrinth of treason." *Midstream*. 31(6), 1985: 54–57.

A review of Pincher's *Too Secret Too Long*. It is a rebuttal of Thatcher's denial that her Government was guilty of negligence and betrayal in their handling of Soviet penetration of British intelligence.

C. Theses

1443. *Bunetta, Teresa Hicks. *Margaret Thatcher, Britain's Spokesman for a New Conservatism: A Rhetorical Analysis of the Party Conference Speeches (1975–1978)*. Ph.D. The Louisiana State University, 1979. 257. (Volume 40/10-A of *Dissertation Abstracts International*, page 5246).

Analysis of Thatcher's speeches as the opposition party leader before becoming Prime Minister in 1979.

1444. Daykin, Norma. *Unhealthy Transitions: Young Women, Health and Work in the 1980s*. Ph.D. University of Bristol, 1989. 315. (Volume 51/03-A of *Dissertation Abstracts International*, page 1017).

Having shown that young women at work suffer specifically from marginalisation, sexism and inadequate survival strategies; Daykin shows that such disadvantages have deteriorated even more under Thatcher.

1445. Fallon, Janet Laurentia. *A Burkeian Analysis of the Rhetoric of Margaret Thatcher*. Ph.D. The Ohio State University, 1981. 209.

(Volume 42/07-A of *Dissertation Abstracts International*, page 2931).

An in-depth analysis of Thatcher's campaign strategies and rhetorical efforts during the late 1970s. The work shows how Thatcher was able to effect political and social change on a major scale.

1446. Al-Fayad, Saud Fayad M. *The Impact of International and National Political and Strategic Determinations on French and British Arms Sales to the Arab World, 1945–1983.* Ph.D. University of Denver, 1987. 341. (Volume 49/04-A of *Dissertation Abstracts International*, page 942).

Amongst other things, the work shows how arms sales to the Arab world increased during Thatcher's early years. Economic necessities began to replace historical alliances and friendships as Thatcher searched for trade outlets.

1447. Higgs, Paul. *Privatisation and the Politics of Hegemony: A Study of the Attitudes of Striking NHS Ancillary Workers Towards Privatisation, 1984–1985.* Ph.D. University of Kent at Canterbury, 1987. 240. (Volume 49/04-A of *Dissertation Abstracts International*, page 938).

A Marxist examination of trade union opposition to the privatisation of the National Health Service (NHS). The term "privatisation" is a misnomer since the creation of hospital trusts leads to more efficient use of resources rather than to privatisation.

1448. Knoles, Barbara Ann. *"Orphans of the Storm": The Integration of Women in Parliament, 1918–1988.* Ph.D. Northern Arizona University, 1988. 309. (Volume 50/02-A of *Dissertation Abstracts International*, page 526).

Looking at the progressive accomplishments of women Members of Parliament (MPs) since 1918 and up to Thatcher's Premiership, Knoles concludes that women have achieved equal opportunity and consideration in Parliament. This may be true of what women MPs do. It is probably still untrue of their ability to get to Parliament in order to achieve parity once in the House.

1449. Marsh, Malcolm Ian. *Policy Making in the Post-Collectivist State: Party Government, Parliament and Interest Groups.* Ph.D. Harvard University, 1985. 369. (Volume 46/07-A of *Dissertation Abstracts International*, page 2061).

Mrs. Thatcher established departmental select committees fairly early on in her leadership. This work examines and assesses the performance of these committees concluding positively on the new possibilities for the enhancement of political authority.

1450. Mccormick, John Spencer. *Consensus or Conviction: Thatcherism and the British Environmental Lobby.* Ph.D. Indiana University, 1991. 281. (Volume 52/02-A of *Dissertation Abstracts International*, page 666).

A detailed study, based on documentary evidence and on interviews, of the way in which Britain's environmental lobby repositioned itself within the change from consensus politics to Thatcher's conviction politics.

1451. Morris, Robert G. *Education Policy and Legislation: A Critical Examination of the Arguments for a New Major Education Act to Replace That of 1944.* Ph.D. University of Reading, 1988. 405. (Volume 49/05-A of *Dissertation Abstracts International*, page 1022).

The 1988 Education Reform Act (ERA) was arguably to be Thatcher's most long lasting legacy. It revolutionised the management of schools and the content of the curriculum. This thesis argues that there is no need for Thatcher's radical, right-wing populist education policies since the 1944 Education Act was appropriate within the culture of the service.

1452. Nelsen, Brent Franklin. *The State Offshore: Petroleum, Politics and State Intervention on the British and Norwegian Continental Shelves.* Ph.D. The University of Wisconsin, 1989. 664. (Volume 50/11-A of *Dissertation Abstracts International*, page 3725).

One of the questions most frequently asked by detractors of Thatcherism was, "Where is all that oil money?" Through nonintervention and privatisation under Thatcher, the question becomes a non-sequitur left over from the 1970s Labour government. This thesis explains the shift in state intervention in the oil business over three decades.

1453. Pardey, Kenneth. *The Welfare of the Visually Handicapped in the United Kingdom.* Ph.D. University of Stirling, 1986. 915. (Volume 49/03-A of *Dissertation Abstracts International*, page 634).

After detailing the long-standing British tradition of caring for the blind, Pardey concludes that the Thatcher Government's social security reforms will not help the blind.

1454. Pierson, Paul Douglas. *Cutting against the Grain: Reagan, Thatcher and the Politics of Welfare State Retrenchment.* Ph.D. Yale University, 1989. 440. (Volume 50/12-A of *Dissertation Abstracts International*, page 4084).

A detailed analysis of the consequences of public spending cuts on the welfare state. The work argues that the retrenchment of the welfare state went beyond simple cutbacks in public spending with specific emphases on old age pensions, housing and income support.

1455. Wooding, John Charles. *Dire States: Workplace Health and Safety Regulation in the Reagan/Thatcher Era.* Ph.D. Brandeis University, 1990. 366. (Volume 51/03-A of *Dissertation Abstracts International*, page 993).

A study showing that the incidence of workplace accidents and disease increased under Thatcher and Reagan. The increase in Britain was more elevated. This increase is seen as a reflection of the complexity of the structure/agency relationship within the nature of the capitalist state.

Serial Publications Cited

This is an alphabetical list of all serial publications that appear in the bibliography, including periodicals and newspapers. Numbers refer to entries, not pages.

ABN Economic Review, 961
Across the Board, 583
Africa Report, 1056
Albion, 494
American Economic Review, 942
American Enterprise Institute Economist, 60
American Journal of Comparative Law, 714
American Political Science Review, 661
American Review of Public Administration, 1037
Annuaire anglais, 944
Arbeitstreis Dt., 1209
Arms Control, 665
Atlantic, 624
Atlantic Community Quarterly, 1047, 1091
Australian Outlook, 573

Banker, 1008

Beijing Review, 24, 1114, 1115, 1118, 1119, 1124, 1134, 1138, 1139
BOZO, 1288
British Journal of Political Science, 663, 1429
British Journal of Sociology, 1432
British Review of Economic Issues, 938
Brookings Pas Economic Activity, 836
Bulletin documentaire, 906
Business, 933
Business Weekly, 934, 935, 1374

Cambridge Journal of Economics, 960
Canadian Dimension, 588
Chat, 446
Chrons. actualité, 847, 924, 991
College of Preceptors Newsletter, The, 1275, 1279, 1281, 1283

Author Index

Numbers refer to entries, not pages.

Subject Index

Numbers refer to pages, not entries.

About the Author

FAYSAL MIKDADI is an educational inspector with the Wiltshire Inspection Services in England and a freelance writer. He is the author of *Gamal Abdel Nasser: A Bibliography* (Greenwood, 1991).